Visible Hands

A growing number of states regulate the corporate social responsibility (CSR) of their home country's multinational corporations. These multinationals have subsequently had to change corporate practices in their overseas subsidiaries or suppliers. In this book, Jette Steen Knudsen and Jeremy Moon offer a new framework for analysing government and CSR relations. Arguing that existing research on CSR regulation fails to address the growing role of the state in initiating changes in the international practices of multinational corporations, Knudsen and Moon provide insights into the CSR issues addressed by policies and regulation. They use case studies to analyse three key CSR issue areas: non-financial reporting, ethical trade, and transparency of payments in the extractive industries. In doing so, they propose a new research agenda of government and CSR for scholars and graduate students in CSR, sustainability, political economy, and economic sociology, and for policymakers and consultants in international development and trade.

JETTE STEEN KNUDSEN is Associate Professor of International Business and the Shelby Cullom Davis Chair in International Business at the Fletcher School, Tufts University. She previously worked as Professor of Political Science at Copenhagen University and at Copenhagen Business School, and headed a government think tank, the Copenhagen Centre for CSR. She has published in journals such as *Comparative Political Studies*, *Journal of Business Ethics*, *Policy and Politics*, and *Regulation and Governance*.

JEREMY MOON is Velux Professor of Corporate Sustainability at Copenhagen Business School. He has published extensively on corporate social responsibility, including co-editing the book *Corporate Social Responsibility: Strategy, Communication and Governance* (2017, also with Cambridge University Press). He was the founding director of the International Centre for Corporate Social Responsibility, University of Nottingham.

Business, Value Creation, and Society

SERIES EDITORS:

R. Edward Freeman, *University of Virginia*
Jeremy Moon, *Copenhagen Business School*
Mette Moring, *Copenhagen Business School*

The purpose of this innovative series is to examine, from an international standpoint, the interaction of business and capitalism with society. In the twenty-first century it is more important than ever that business and capitalism come to be seen as social institutions that have a great impact on the welfare of human society around the world. Issues such as globalization, environmentalism, information technology, the triumph of liberalism, corporate governance, and business ethics all have the potential to have major effects on our current models of the corporation and the methods by which value is created, distributed and sustained among all stakeholder—customers, suppliers, employees, communities, and financiers.

PUBLISHED TITLES:

Fort *Business, Integrity, and Peace: Beyond Geopolitical and Disciplinary Boundaries*
Gomez and Korine *Entrepreneurs and Democracy: A Political Theory of Corporate Governance*
Crane, Matten, and Moon *Corporations and Citizenship*
Painter-Morland *Business Ethics as Practice: Ethics as the Everyday Business of Business*
Yaziji and Doh *NGOs and Corporations: Conflict and Collaboration*
Rivera *Business and Public Policy: Responses to Environmental and Social Protection Processes*
Sachs and Rühli *Stakeholders Matter: A New Paradigm for Strategy in Society*
Mansell *Capitalism, Corporations, and the Social Contract: A Critique of Stakeholder Theory*
Hemingway *Corporate Social Entrepreneurship: Integrity Within*
Hartman *Virtue in Business: Conversations with Aristotle*
de Bruin *Ethics and the Global Financial Crisis: Why Incompetence is Worse than Greed*
Griffin *Managing Corporate Impacts: Co-Creating Value*
Burg *Business Ethics for a Material World: An Ecological Approach to Object Stewardship*

FORTHCOMING TITLES:

Slager *Responsible Investment: Institutional Investors and Corporate Social Responsibility*
de Bakker, den Hond *Organizing for Corporate Social Responsibility: The Role of Activist Groups*

Visible Hands

Government Regulation and International Business Responsibility

JETTE STEEN KNUDSEN

Fletcher School of Law and Diplomacy, Tufts University

JEREMY MOON

Copenhagen Business School

CAMBRIDGE
UNIVERSITY PRESS

CAMBRIDGE
UNIVERSITY PRESS

University Printing House, Cambridge CB2 8BS, United Kingdom

One Liberty Plaza, 20th Floor, New York, NY 10006, USA

477 Williamstown Road, Port Melbourne, VIC 3207, Australia

314-321, 3rd Floor, Plot 3, Splendor Forum, Jasola District Centre, New Delhi - 110025, India

79 Anson Road, #06-04/06, Singapore 079906

Cambridge University Press is part of the University of Cambridge.

It furthers the University's mission by disseminating knowledge in the pursuit of education, learning and research at the highest international levels of excellence.

www.cambridge.org
Information on this title: www.cambridge.org/9781107512122
DOI: 10.1017/ 9781316224908

© Cambridge University Press 2017

First published 2017
First paperback edition 2019

A catalogue record for this publication is available from the British Library

Library of Congress Cataloging in Publication data
Names: Knudsen, Jette Steen, author. | Moon, Jeremy, 1955– author.
Title: Visible hands : government regulation and international business responsibility / Jette Steen Knudsen, Fletcher School of Law and Diplomacy, Tufts University, Jeremy Moon, Copenhagen Business School.
Description: Cambridge, United Kingdom; New York, NY: Cambridge University Press, 2017. | Series: Business, value creation, and society |
Includes bibliographical references and index.
Identifiers: LCCN 2017034298 | ISBN 9781107104907 (hardback) |
ISBN 9781107512122 (pbk.)
Subjects: LCSH: Social responsibility of business – Government policy. |
International business enterprises – Government policy. |
Trade regulation – Moral and ethical aspects. | Corporate governance.
Classification: LCC HD60.K623 2017 | DDC 174/.4–dc23
LC record available at https://lccn.loc.gov/2017034298

ISBN 978-1-107-10490-7 Hardback
ISBN 978-1-107-51212-2 Paperback

To my mother Else Veller Knudsen,
January 19, 1940–July 14, 2015.
                    – Jette

To Marjahan and Lily.
            – Jeremy

Contents

Figures

Tables

Preface

This book started out as a series of conversations between us about what we saw as the 'missing' role of government in corporate social responsibility (CSR). We are both trained as political scientists so our emphasis on government is not surprising. Moreover, our formative experiences of CSR involved government.

Jette worked as director of the Copenhagen Centre for Corporate Social Responsibility, a government-sponsored think tank for CSR, from 2003 to 2007. She then spent six months working for the CEO of Maersk, a large shipping, terminals, and oil conglomerate, identifying CSR challenges and opportunities across the various business units.

Jeremy encountered CSR in the context of a research project with Jeremy Richardson examining UK government policy responses to unemployment in the early 1980s, which included policies to encourage and even shape CSR to address mass unemployment and urban decay. He researched the way in which Australian governments encouraged CSR in the 1990s, also initially in the context of an economic downturn.

Since CSR is often (still) defined as voluntary social and environmental initiatives by companies that go beyond legal requirements, most of the work on CSR has been conducted in business schools by management scholars. Many of these share neither our antennae for things governmental nor our experiences of CSR as partly, at least, a creature of government, and would regard government policy for CSR as a contradiction in terms. So we saw a need to probe more in depth the role of government as a driver of CSR in corporations.

Our curiosity and motivation were re-doubled when we both encountered ways in which governments even go so far as to make policy for CSR abroad – in other words, outside the territories in

which national governments possess legitimate policymaking authority. And here we have another contradiction in terms –national governments making policies encouraging companies to be responsible
internationally.

So two contradictions in terms about subjects so close to our
hearts (i.e. government and CSR, national government and international company behaviour) seemed like an irresistible challenge for a
book-length study.

Acknowledgements

We thank our Cambridge editors Paula M. Parish and Valerie Appleby as well as our Business, Value Creation, and Society editors, Ed Freeman and Mette Morsing.

We presented earlier versions of this work at the Copenhagen Business School Governing Responsible Business workshop, the Copenhagen Business School Tax workshop, the EGOS Conference 2016, the Fletcher School of Law and Diplomacy at Tufts University, MIT's Institute for Work and Employment Research, the University of Connecticut, the University of Nottingham Business School, Rutgers University, and the SASE Conference 2015.

We received very helpful comments from Karin Buhmann, Ben Cashore, George Frynas, Philipp Genschel, Erin Leitheiser, Cathie Jo Martin, Louisa Murphy, Esben Rahbek Gjerdrum Pedersen, Rune Gottlieb Skovgaard, Kathleen Thelen, Steen Vallentin, Sandra Waddock, and Karen Woody.

Jette Steen Knudsen is grateful for a grant from the Danish Social Science Research Council 2013–14 titled 'Visible Hands: Government Regulation of CSR in Denmark and the UK' that enabled her to pursue some of these ideas. Part of the research on Bangladesh was funded from Tufts University's 'Tufts Collaborates' research programme and from the Carlsberg Foundation. She also received a travel grant from the Dean for Social Sciences at Copenhagen University.

MIT's Department of Political Science provided a stimulating environment during a sabbatical from 2013 to 2014. She is also grateful to her colleagues at the Fletcher School for providing an excellent working environment. Finally, MIT's Sloan School provided a supportive home during the final writing stage in the fall of 2016.

Jeremy Moon is grateful for the support of the International Centre for Corporate Social Responsibility, Nottingham University Business School, where he was working when this project was hatched. He has subsequently moved to Copenhagen Business School (CBS) and is particularly grateful for the support of the CBS CSR Centre and the VELUX Chair of Corporate Sustainability to which he has been appointed.

Chapter 3 is the fruit of various collaborations, first in the European Union–funded research project FP7 CSR IMPACT study in which we collaborated with Christoph Bruun, Peter Hardi, and Rieneke Slager on an initial report (Moon, J., Slager, R., Brunn, C., Hardi, P., and Knudsen, J. S., 2012. 'Analysis of the National and EU Policies Supporting Corporate Social Responsibility and Impact, IMPACT Working Paper 2, "IMPACT Project", European Commission (Framework 7 Program)'). We subsequently collaborated with Rieneke Slager in a paper titled: 'Government Policies for Corporate Social Responsibility in Europe: Institutionalisation and Structured Convergence?' *Policy and Politics* 2015, 43(1): 81–99. We acknowledge that this chapter draws substantially on this paper and thank *Policy and Politics* (Wiley Publishers) for permission to re-produce Tables 3.2 and 3.3.

For excellent research assistance we thank Josefin Dahlen, Katherine Hallaran, Lisa Holub, Samira Manzur, Andrew Nassar, Mariann Markseth Omholt, and Franziska Wiebke.

Abbreviations

AIP	Apparel Industry Partnership
BBE	Federal Civil Participation Network
BGMEA	Bangladesh Garment Manufacturers and Exporters Association
BKMEA	Bangladesh Knitwear Manufacturers and Exporters Association
CAFOD	Catholic Agency for Overseas Development
CERES	Coalition for Environmentally Responsible Economies
CSR	Corporate Social Responsibility
DANIDA	Danish International Development Agency
DfID	Department for International Development UK
DIEH	Dansk Initiativ for Etisk Handel (Ethical Trading Initiative Denmark)
EITI	Extractive Industries Transparency Initiative
ETI	Ethical Trading Initiative
EU	European Union
FDI	Foreign Direct Investment
FLA	Fair Labor Association
GATJ	Global Alliance for Tax Justice
GDP	Gross Domestic Product
GRI	Global Reporting Initiative
GSP	Generalized System of Preferences
HMG	Her Majesty's Government
IEH	Initiativ for Etisk Handel (Ethical Trading Initiative Norway)
IGO	International Governmental Organization
ILAB	Bureau of International Labor Affairs
ILO	International Labour Organization
IMF	International Monetary Fund
ISO	International Organization for Standardization
MFA	Multi Fibre Agreement

MGI	Mediation and Grievance Institution
MNC	Multinational Corporation
MoLE	Ministry of Labour and Employment (Bangladesh)
MSI	Multi-stakeholder Initiative
NCCWE	National Coordination for Workers' Education
NGO	Non-governmental Organization
NNPC	Nigerian National Petroleum Corporation
NTAP	National Tripartite Action Plan
OECD	Organisation for Economic Co-operation and Development
PCSR	Political Corporate Social Responsibility
PRI	Principles for Responsible Investing
PWYP	Publish What You Pay
RMG	Ready Made Garments
SA 8000	Social Accountability 8000
SAI	Social Accountability International
SEBI	Securities and Exchange Board of India
SME	Small and Medium Sized Enterprise
SRI	Socially Responsible Investing
TI	Transparency International
TUC	Trade Union Congress
UN	United Nations
UNEP	United Nations Environment Program
UNGC	United Nations Global Compact
UNITE	Union of Needletrades, Industrial and Textile Employees
USAID	United States Agency for International Development
WRC	Workers' Rights Consortium
WTO	World Trade Organization

1 | Government and Corporate Social Responsibility: Hands Visible and Invisible

In 1601 the English Parliament passed the Charitable Uses Act, which offered exemptions from taxation obligations to those providing specified categories of charity. The Act was duly adopted or emulated in Britain's American and other colonies. On this basis, charitable giving by individuals, foundations, and business organizations was established, continued, and developed in the UK; in many of its, now independent, colonies; and in many other countries. In 1977 the French government introduced legislation for the *bilan social* [social report]. This reporting requirement for companies covered 134 items and indicators relating to employment, salaries, health and safety, training, working conditions, and labour relations. In the early 1980s, the UK Thatcher government introduced public policies to encourage companies to take more responsibility for some of the challenges emerging from mass unemployment and urban decay – policies echoed by the Danish government in the 1990s. In 1999 President Clinton created a task force in response to child labour and sweat shop scandals. This in turn developed into the Fair Labor Association (FLA), a corporate social responsibility (CSR)-oriented multi-stakeholder initiative (MSI).

All these are examples of governments engaging in and encouraging CSR in the form of philanthropy; transparency over domestic labour issues; social cohesion and economic development; and international supply chain labour issues. Yet the relationship between government and CSR, although now receiving more scholarly attention, has been the subject of disagreement and confusion on normative, definitional, and conceptual grounds.

This book investigates the regulation by national governments of international CSR. Our aim is to further an understanding of CSR; of government and CSR; and particularly of the role of national governments in the regulation of international CSR. Our book is therefore

intended as a contribution to the literature on CSR. Some of this literature we see as under-estimating the significance of government policy
for CSR whether conceptually (e.g. McWilliams and Siegel, 2001),
domestically (e.g. Margolis and Walsh, 2003), or in global governance
(Scherer and Palazzo, 2011). In so doing, our analysis also offers a
corrective to the literature on CSR and domestic governance which,
while providing an important context for government policy for CSR
domestically, tends both to overlook the capacity of governments to
exercise their authority in the form of mandate and to omit attention
to the relationships between policy for domestic and for international
issues. Our study also addresses the literature on CSR and global governance, which provides an important context for the new governing
roles of multinational corporations (MNCs) in international CSR but
also, we argue, underestimates the power of national governments to
effect business responsibility beyond their borders (Bansal and Roth,
2000; Brammer et al., 2012; Kostova and Zaheer, 1999; Muller and
Kolk, 2009).

Our central thesis is that national governments make significant
policies for CSR, including international CSR, and we therefore challenge the argument that government is irrelevant for CSR (which we
call the 'dichotomous' perspective – to be explained in Chapter 2). We
argue for the 'related' perspective in which governments make policy
for CSR in two main ways. First, cumulatively, governments structure the opportunities for CSR by embedding certain regulations (be
they rules, conventions, or norms) in national business systems over
the long run (Matten and Moon, 2008). Second, individually governments act as agents to encourage and exploit CSR for public policy
purposes (Gond et al., 2011) by directing public policies to support
CSR organizations and other initiatives. Moreover, we argue that they
make such policies to support CSR through direct and indirect means.
Our analysis is conducted in the light of three key developments. First,
there is the sheer growth of national government policies to support
CSR *directly* in their own countries. Second, there is the emergence of
some of these government policies for CSR, which either have international consequences, or are expressly designed to address international
CSR issues. Third, there is the interaction of these policies for CSR
directly with other public policies which support CSR *indirectly*, by
shaping the regulatory environment for CSR, including in the international sphere.

In our analysis of policies to support CSR *directly*, we investigate: *how* governments deploy different types of policy (i.e. endorsement, facilitation, partnership, or mandate); *what role* these have in CSR initiatives, in terms of whether governments are involved in the inception of CSR initiatives or the support of their operationalization; and *why* they do so, in terms of the governments' own pressures and agendas. We do this, first, through an analysis of aggregate data of European government policies for CSR overall. Second, we do this through case analysis of government and CSR in the specific areas of: non-financial reporting in Denmark; ethical trade, including European and US responses to the Rana Plaza disaster; and transparency of payments in the extractive industries, including European and US regulation on the issue mediated and unmediated by CSR.

In our analysis of policies to support CSR *indirectly*, we investigate: *how* governments do so, in terms of the types of policy they deploy (as above); *why* they do so, in terms of the governments' own pressures and agendas; and *what* are the interactions between policies to support CSR indirectly and related CSR initiatives, particularly those that governments support directly. Here we examine policies in the areas of ethical trade and of transparency of payments in the extractive industries.

We argue that the distinction between government policies that support CSR directly and indirectly, and their relationships to each other, is a major issue that has been overlooked in the literature. Direct policies for CSR, i.e. those that are designed to expressly create, support, and supplement specific CSR initiatives are quite well understood, even though such an analysis has rarely been extended to the international sphere.

However, the literature on government and CSR has paid little attention to government policies for CSR indirectly, i.e. those which target a problem that is also being tackled by a CSR initiative, but are adopted independently of this initiative. For example, governments sometimes use trade policy as a way to promote international labour standards by linking trade access to demands that the exporting country improves labour standards (Brown, 2012; Duina, 2015). Trade policy initiatives can address the same social problem – improving labour standards – as CSR initiatives such as the Ethical Trading Initiative (ETI) or the UN Global Compact (UNGC). Trade policy initiatives that highlight labour standards may be intentionally connected to specific CSR policy programmes. Trade policy initiatives thus can end up supporting CSR indirectly. Alternatively they may be disconnected from CSR programmes even though such government trade policies and CSR programmes may serve the same goal. We focus on public policies that address CSR indirectly but that are adopted in cognizance of public policies that address CSR directly. In other words, our focus is not on policies that just happen to support CSR (and there may be many of these) but rather those which are drawn up purposefully to advance or complement CSR policies.

The role of government in the regulation of international business responsibility is an important topic for several reasons. With globalization, companies increasingly operate overseas and outside the jurisdiction of their home governments, and outside the range of many of the elements of social control which had formed their domestic responsibilities historically (Boswell, 1983). Given the power of MNCs and the impact of their value chains, the responsibility of their operations can have vital social, political, economic, and environmental consequences for populations in host countries. Moreover, the international impacts of companies can also be crucial for the reputations of the companies themselves at home and abroad, impacting upon their attractiveness to investors, customers, employees, and suppliers. Some government representatives have also suggested that the reputations of their own countries as a place to do business rest, in part, on the responsibility of their companies at home and abroad, as well as on their ability to be profitable by serving customers and to create employment.

Thus we see national governments and CSR as mutually engaged in global as well as national governance. Hence we not only examine government policies to support CSR either directly or indirectly, but also the interactions of these different public policy approaches to solving international problems.

Although much of our attention is upon government, what it does, how, and why, our underlying motivation is to contribute to an understanding of CSR, its dynamics and relationships to societal governance. To adopt a thespian metaphor, while our attention is upon a single actor – national government – our interest is in the implications of that one part for the whole play – international CSR – in which there are many additional actors, notably companies and their core stakeholders as well as civil society, and associations, partnerships and MSIs, and, of course, national governments.

Corporate Social Responsibility

The origins of the modern corporation as a legal person separate from its owners emerged in ancient Roman times, was consolidated in medieval Europe, and adopted in the Anglo-American common law in the nineteenth century (Avi-Yonah, 2005). In medieval Europe, corporations were bodies expressly created to perform specified public tasks (to build roads, bridges, canals) and accordingly given powers needed to that end (e.g. to acquire land, to impose tolls). In the late sixteenth and early seventeenth centuries, corporations were established with more commercial objectives (e.g. to trade with the East Indies) but significantly the government controlled their operations and rights.

During the nineteenth and early twentieth centuries, a number of landmark legislative and judicial decisions were made, which have led to the emergence of the modern corporation, which is managed by managers not owners and many of whose shares are publicly traded. These modern corporations tend to be very large and occupy critical positions in many industries and supply chains. They have been justified in terms of their economic, organizational, and technological capacity to bring private and public benefits. Nevertheless, their role has been controversial, particularly regarding the balance of the private and public benefits that they bring. Indeed, it is perhaps cases of corporate malfeasance that have done most to fuel the energy for CSR inside and outside corporations, as well as to encourage the critics of corporations (Vogel, 2005).

At the heart of the ethos of CSR is that corporations not only have social responsibilities, but that they should also be responsive to society. This relationship was nicely captured in Boswell's (1983) analysis of the informal social control of business in Britain (1880–1939). He presented this control as so effective that responsible business behaviour reflected the 'institutional influences' of the society (Boswell, 1983: 239). Boswell saw business social responsibility as both 'personally derived' and structurally built, including by 'social monitors' and informal channels for 'business cooperation with the state' (Boswell, 1983: 243). The period he was concerned with was characterized not only by regulation and litigation concerning the rights and roles of the corporate form, but also with a great deal of regulation designed to ensure business responsibility for the terms and conditions of employment, and the qualities of their products and services, for example. So

Boswell's socially embedded account of the social regulation of business also included a governmental dimension, which is instructive in anticipation of our analysis.

Although much of the thinking behind CSR consists of ethical assumptions about business in general, it is clearly the rise of the corporation that has raised the most acute responsibility issues, particularly arising from the separation of ownership and control, and the immense size and power that corporations possess and can deploy (Berle and Means, 1932; Clarke, 1916). The challenge of wanting to utilize such organizations for public purposes while wanting to contain their activities to those deemed socially acceptable has long preoccupied lawmakers and commentators in Europe and in the United States (Aguilera and Jackson, 2003; Campbell, 2007; Knudsen, 2017; Knudsen et al., 2015; Matten and Moon, 2008; Polanyi, 1944).

In many countries during the twentieth century, particularly in Western Europe, business responsibility became so closely entailed in a fabric of regulation and business-wide norms that the notion of individual CSR became rather muted. This is in large part because the mechanisms of democracy and 'collectivism' (Beer, 1965) or 'neo-corporatism' (Schmitter and Lehmbruch, 1979) enabled business associations to be fully represented participants in the making of policy in the form of primary legislation or regulation in the tri-sector agreements emanating from government-led processes in which organized labour and business were fully engaged. This is what Matten and Moon (2008) described as 'implicit' CSR because the responsibilities of individual corporations are 'implied' in their membership of the respective national business systems such as in the UK or Scandinavia. They contrasted this with 'explicit' CSR, which is characteristic of the North American business system, where regulation tends to be more in the form of primary legislation. In this context, individual corporations take 'explicit' social responsibility initiatives and build these into their company organization and communication. Although there are clearly elements of the implicit and explicit CSR in all business systems, we will see in our later analysis that these different national relationships between business and government have implications for government and international CSR relationships.

Bowen, often regarded as the academic father of modern CSR, defined it as 'the obligations of businessmen to pursue those policies, to make those decisions, or to follow those lines of action which are desirable in terms of the objectives and values of our society' (1953: 6). This is important as it implies that social responsibility is not confined to certain activities *in addition to* the business, but rather that the responsibility should *permeate* the business. In contrast, many definitions in the succeeding decades have narrowed the definition, such that the focus was upon philanthropic acts alone. This narrowing may paradoxically have resulted from certain CSR scholars wanting to be sure that the responsibilities of business were understood to extend beyond running the business well in economic terms. Thus, McGuire suggests, for example, that: 'The idea of social responsibilities supposes that the corporation has not only economic and legal obligations but also certain responsibilities to society which extend beyond these obligations' (1963: 144). The viewpoint that the corporation's responsibility extends beyond legal compliance is a substantial one. Davis also defined CSR as 'the firm's consideration of, and response to, issues *beyond* the narrow economic, technical, and *legal* requirements of the firm' (1973: 313). Carroll wanted both to distinguish different types of responsibility and yet to see them as integrated. He conveyed this in his CSR pyramid with which he defined CSR as the 'the economic, legal, ethical and discretionary expectations that society has of organizations' (1979: 500). More recently, Matten and Moon (2008) echoed Bowen's (1953) integrated definition by offering that CSR was the 'policies and practices of corporations that reflect business responsibility for some of the wider societal good' (2008: 405).

What Bowen did not anticipate is the internationalization of CSR, both in the sense that US and other Western corporations, and more latterly corporations worldwide, have extended their responsibilities across borders, and that the concept of CSR has also internationalized. In some parts of the world, particularly Asia, this development has combined engaging with international systems and organization for CSR with the legacies of the inheritance of ancient ethical frameworks as well as their more modern national frameworks for CSR (Kim and Moon, 2015). Thus these corporations have had to encounter circumstances where the framing and understandings of CSR abroad are rather different from their home countries and where, moreover, the regulation of business responsibilities by government is often lacking or poorly administered. Hence there are incentives and opportunities for irresponsible business abroad (Strike et al., 2006). These developments amply illustrate the significance of the *international* CSR.

So at its broadest, CSR refers to the nature of business and society relationships, but is more usually taken to refer to the specific contributions of business to society. These responsibilities generally include the mitigation of companies' own negative impacts on society, their welfare-enhancing activities, and the responsible/ethical/sustainability attributes of their products and services. Our book analyses how governments contribute to CSR generally (Chapter 3) and, more specifically, in the context of some of the core issues in business – society relationships, namely non-financial reporting, ethical trade, and transparency in financial payments in the international extractives industry (Chapters 4, 5, and 6).

Hands, Invisible and Visible

Students of Adam Smith will have recognized the significance of the title of the book before even opening it. We invoke the much-cited reference of Smith to the facility of those operating in markets to operate for social benefits by simply pursuing their own interests, often oblivious of the public good that this yields, specifically by supporting the domestic economy. It is worth quoting Smith at length here.

As every individual, (therefore,) endeavors as much as he can both to employ his capital in the support of domestic industry, and so to direct that industry that its produce may be of the greatest value, every individual necessarily labours to render the annual revenue of the society as great as he can. He generally, indeed, neither intends to promote the public interest, nor knows how much he is promoting it. By preferring the support of domestic to that of foreign industry, he intends only his own security; and by directing that industry in such a manner as its produce may be of the greatest value, he intends only his own gain, and he is in this, as in many other cases, led by an *invisible hand* to promote an end which was no part of his intention. Nor is it always the worse for the society that it was not part of it. By pursuing his own interest he frequently promotes that of the society more effectually than when he really intends to promote it. I have never known much good done by those who affected to trade for the public good. It is an affectation, indeed, not very common among merchants, and very few words need be employed in dissuading them from it. (Adam Smith Book IV, Chapter II, paragraph IX of *The Wealth of Nations*, emphasis added)

Thus, Smith's application of the term 'invisible hands' is a very particular one. It concerns the benefits to the society as well as to the capital owner arising from decisions of the latter to support the domestic
economy. However, Smith does note, more generally, that the intention
to 'promote the public interest' or to 'trade for the public' good is usually a futile or even counter-productive endeavour.

Subsequently, the term 'invisible hands' has been employed by those
who extend the basic point about the superiority of uncoordinated
actions intended for private benefit as a means of maximizing the
public benefit over the main method of market coordination, by government. Thus, Milton Friedman refers to the invisible hand as the
possibility of cooperation without coercion (1958) in the context of
his arguments against government policies designed to improve welfare which thereby impose regulatory constraints on those very actors
that can create wealth, i.e. market players or businesses. For Friedman
then, the 'invisible hands' contrast with what would be the visible
hands of government and excessive law.

However, there is another side to Adam Smith. While he praised
markets and legitimized capitalism and the idea that private interest could lead to a larger benefit for society as a whole, Adam Smith
also saw a moral role for government to protect workers and citizens
against the interests of the rich and powerful. Smith was sometimes
tolerant of government intervention, especially when the goal was to
reduce poverty and protect the weak. Thus, in the *Wealth of Nations*
(Book 1, Chapter 11) he wrote that 'When the regulation, therefore,
is in support of the workman it is always just and equitable'. Also,
according to Adam Smith the invisible hand needs to be embedded
in some form of regulation which can control the personal interest
of the rich and powerful 'who do not always have the public interest
at heart and seek instead laws and policies that favor themselves and
hold back progress' (Montgomery and Chirot, 2015: 43). In short, the
role of the government is not only to enforce the rule of law but also
to prevent abuses and to ensure a certain level of social welfare for all.
A society with great inequality of wealth and a large segment of the
population toiling in poverty is a moral problem as well as a sign of
a malfunctioning economy (Montgomery and Chirot, 2015). Adam
Smith wrote: 'no society can surely be flourishing and happy, of which
the far greater part of the members are poor and miserable. It is but
equity, besides, that they who feed, clothe and lodge the whole body

of the people, should be themselves ... tolerably well fed, clothed and lodged' ([1776] 1965: 78). While Smith came to be used in support of laissez-faire, he also prefigured many of the nineteenth-century attacks on the dehumanization of industrial mass production.

In short, while Smith famously coined the term 'invisible hand', he also recognized that government regulation could be required to protect citizens from harm due to market excesses. We are inspired by both sides of Adam Smith: on the one hand, with globalization corporations have come to operate abroad including in the Global South where government regulation is 'invisible' in some respects; yet, at the same time, in order to deal with the challenges of poor social and environmental standards in those regions, governments (and here we are thinking in particular on advanced industrialized countries – the Global North) increasingly have become more 'visible' undertaking regulation of international CSR. By invoking the term 'visible hands' we therefore point to the ways in which CSR, a concept based on corporate discretion of market actors, paradoxically perhaps, can be encouraged, strengthened, and complemented by national governments. In so doing we also contend that national governments are not bereft of policymaking capacity in a globalizing world.

Outline of the Book

In Chapter 2 we address the theme of national governments and international CSR as we frame our overall approach. We first present a brief discussion of the literature on CSR and government. We then indicate how the context for government has changed with key regulatory shifts and the emergence of new governance practices nationally, which are consistent with our argument about the ways in which governments regulate CSR. In this light we consider the argument that globalization has diminished policymaking capacity and the implications for international governance and CSR. We flesh out our argument and locate it in the wider literatures on CSR and social science. Our analytical framework is presented in anticipation of the empirical Chapters 4–6. We explain our framework of direct and indirect interactions between government and CSR initiatives, and outline our research questions concerning how, when, and why governments make policy for CSR, and how the direct and indirect policies interact.

In Chapter 3 we contextualize our argument about national government and international CSR by means of an aggregate analysis of the forms of regulation that governments in European countries adopt regarding CSR, and the issue areas to which these regulations are addressed. We find a range of forms of regulation deployed for CSR, from endorsement, through facilitation and partnership, to mandate, though we also find that the full range tends to be used by a sub-set of the European national governments. Another key finding here is the range of policy areas to which government CSR policies have been directed. The most conspicuous, from the perspective of our study, is the emergence of government policies for international CSR.

Whereas Chapter 3 presents a panorama of government policies for CSR in Europe, Chapter 4 presents a case study of the *government non-financial reporting requirements in Denmark* introduced in 2008 within the Danish new Action Plan for Corporate Social Responsibility but subsequently expanded. This Act now 'mandates' CSR by requiring large firms to report on their CSR policies, actions, and impacts, and if the company has not formulated any social responsibility policies, this must also be reported. The purpose of this case study is threefold. First it illustrates the development of public policies for CSR and their design and reach. The second is to explore the relationship between national and international CSR: the government specified as motivation for the new Act, the UNGC (an international CSR MSI), and the Act, ostensibly domestic, also regulates the reporting of Danish companies' international responsibilities. Third, we use this case to explore the relationship between the government and business and other CSR actors, which underpin the regulation.

Chapter 4 therefore sets the stage for our investigation of government regulation in two distinct international CSR issue areas in the two following chapters. In Chapters 5 and 6, we examine how governments shape international CSR initiatives directly and review how these initiatives are connected to public policies aimed at addressing the same social problem albeit indirectly. For each of these cases we compare how public policies for CSR directly interact with other government policies that support CSR indirectly.

Chapter 5 considers public policy in the key CSR area of *ethical trade*. This has been the subject of a great deal of private regulation, often in collaboration with the trade union movement or the International Labor Organization (e.g. UNGC principles 3–6; Social

Accountability 8000) or with civil society (e.g. the fair trade movement). It looks particularly at the role of the UK government in initiating the Ethical Trading Initiative (ETI), launched by Clare Short, secretary of state for international development, in 2002. More than seventy major companies have since joined the ETI, as have trade unions and non-government organizations (NGOs). Member companies are governed by adopting and being accountable for the ETI Base Code covering their international supply chains, particularly concerning workers' rights and working conditions. Also, the chapter focuses upon responses to the 2013 Rana Plaza tragedy, 'the deadliest disaster in the history of the garment industry worldwide' (Institute for Global Labor and Human Rights, n.d.). Here we investigate the ways in which some European governments have entailed their own responses within CSR initiatives directly, through endorsement, facilitation, and partnership, whereas the US government has tended to stand back from such private initiatives and instead is more likely to use its mandatory power to support CSR indirectly. As a result, the US government has made policies to shape the regulatory context in which the more specific CSR initiatives play out.

In Chapter 6 we consider another key CSR issue, *tax transparency in the extractives sector*. This has been a key issue because the resources sector has had a prominent role in many developing economies but the extractives, MNCs' taxation, and other payments to governments have been shrouded in secrecy, prompting doubts about the probity of the arrangements themselves and about the destination of the moneys paid. Our analysis focuses initially on the Extractive Industries Transparency Initiative (EITI) designed to improve transparency of payments made by extractive industry companies (oil, gas, metals, and minerals) to host country governments. It investigates the role of the UK government in initiating the EITI and the UK and subsequently the Norwegian governments in supporting its operations. It considers the intensification of its regulatory effects. It also analyses public policy support for CSR indirectly through more mandatory-based government initiatives to address the problem of inadequate transparency in such payments in the shape of the US Dodd–Frank Act Section 1504 and the EU Accounting Directive Chapter 10. Again, we show how these different forms of regulation are related to and feed off one another in the development of a regulatory complex for payments in the extractive industries.

Chapter 7 brings together our findings, and our discussion extends the debate about international CSR and government more broadly and considers the implications of our findings for conceptualizations of CSR. It opens with a summary of our answers to the research questions raised in the three empirical case study chapters (4, 5, and 6), thus focusing particularly upon how governments make policy for CSR (i.e. which forms of public policy are deployed); what roles these policies have in CSR initiatives (i.e. whether these are at their inception or in support of the continuing operations); why governments make policies for CSR (i.e. their motivations); and what are the interactions between domestic and international, and direct and indirect, policies. On this basis, the chapter returns to three more general related questions raised in Chapter 2 about CSR and government; CSR and domestic governance; and CSR and global governance. In this light, we reflect on the significance and limitations of our findings for conceptualizing CSR and for wider theories about business, government, and governance. We highlight our four main contributions: first concerning the ways in which government and CSR are related both through the embeddedness of inherited policies and through the role of government agency in the context of present challenges. Second, we demonstrate how governments use different forms of public policy and how these develop from one another. Third, we highlight the relationships between government policies for domestic and international CSR. Fourth, we indicate how policies for CSR directly and indirectly interact with one another. More generally we discuss the governance implications of the government–CSR relations we have depicted. We conclude by offering some thoughts on further avenues for research in the light of our analysis.

2 | National Government and International Corporate Social Responsibility

This chapter first locates our contribution in the wider and related literatures pertaining to our core interest, national government, and international Corporate Social Responsibility (CSR). These are 'government and CSR', 'domestic governance and CSR', and 'global governance and CSR'. The significance of the government and CSR literature is self-evident, but it bears recalling that the place of government in conceptualizations of CSR has remained rather tenuous and thus worthy of attention in its own right. The domestic governance literature has opened up ways for conceptualizing the contributions of CSR to domestic governance, particularly by virtue of its emphases on non-coercive government policies that stress facilitation of governance and on different sorts of public–private relationships. The limitations of this literature from our perspective are that there has been little attention to the way domestic government policies for CSR can extend into international ones, and that the capacity of government to use the power of mandate along with other forms of public policy has for CSR issues been rather underestimated. The literature on global governance, like that on domestic governance, has provided conceptual space for CSR, enabling arguments about MNCs having the transnational power to become key governance players, along with international governing organizations and international civil society actors. A key weakness from our perspective is that the global governance literature, including that on CSR and global governance, underestimates the contribution of national governments. A shared weakness of all three views is not only that governments are poorly specified and analysed as CSR actors but also that none addresses the different ways in which governments support CSR, directly and indirectly. In each literature we identify the ways in which the capacity of government to enact effective public policies to regulate international business is conceptualized and understood and, specifically, how that capacity relates to government and CSR.

This chapter also presents the analytical framework that we deploy in the empirical chapters (3–6). In particular our framework highlights a distinction between those public policies that support CSR *directly*, and those that do so *indirectly*. The chapter describes and justifies our analytical approach and selection of case studies. It sets out our key research questions concerning: *how* government policies support CSR; *what roles* these policies play in CSR initiatives; *why* governments choose to make such policies; and *what are the interactions* between different sorts of government policies for CSR.

Government and CSR

The purpose of this section is to present contrasting views on the relationship between government and CSR. This is important, as there are some different assumptions and contentions about this issue among scholars and policy-makers. Our claim, that government is a key actor in driving international CSR, is at odds with the view that CSR is solely a matter of private initiatives adopted by firms that go beyond the legal requirements imposed upon them. However, we also emphasize that the government relationship to CSR is not only one of inheritance of the accumulation of relevant public policies. We distinguish two perspectives in the extant literature on government and CSR, each of which sub-divide into two further views. The two broad perspectives are that (1) government has no role in CSR, which we refer to as the 'dichotomous perspective'; and (2) that government has a role in shaping CSR, which we refer to as the 'related perspective'. The dichotomous perspective divides into two: (1) the overt or 'the express' view, and (2) the tacit or 'implied' view. The 'related perspective' divides into two: (1) the 'embedded' view and (2) the 'agential' view.

A number of scholars take the 'dichotomous' perspective of government and CSR as described by Moon and Vogel (2008). These scholars contend that CSR is by definition that which is not required by government or by the law. The express dichotomous view that CSR is precisely behaviour that is independent of government and the law is illustrated by McGuire (1963) who distinguishes a business's social responsibilities from its legal (and economic) ones. Carroll (1979) developed an influential way of thinking about CSR in terms of four layers of responsibility aligned on a 'CSR pyramid'. The second layer of the pyramid (above that of the primary level, economic responsibility) was the assumption that responsible companies will comply with the law, though Carroll is quiet on government per se. His third and fourth layers were respectively 'ethical' and 'philanthropic' responsibility. Jones stressed that 'behaviour coerced by forces of the law ... is not voluntary' (1980: 59) and for his purposes these behaviours were excluded from CSR. McWilliams and Siegel's (2001) influential theory of the firm analysis defines CSR as 'actions that appear to further some social good beyond the interests of the firm and that which is required by law' (117). Again, there is no mention of government, and the inference one draws from this quote is that they would view government policies for CSR as a contradiction in terms.

There are also implied dichotomous views of government–CSR relations in which conceptualizations or representations of CSR make little or no mention of government or the law. For example, in a seminal article Margolis and Walsh's (2003) concern with CSR and the public interest largely by-passes government as a source of regulation for CSR, other than noting in their introduction that all three branches of the US government have encouraged forms of business social responsibility (269–70). Also, Aguinis and Glavas's (2012) influential review of and research agenda for CSR makes no mention of government.

This implied dichotomous perspective that CSR excludes government regulation is also consistent with early assumptions of the Commission of the European Union (the EU), which originally defined CSR as 'a concept, whereby companies integrate social and environmental concerns in their business operations and in their interaction with their stakeholders on a *voluntary* basis' (European Commission, 2001, emphasis added). Here, and more generally, the idea that CSR is voluntary has been used to signal that it is apart from, or beyond, the reach of the law and other government policy. Significantly, ten years later the European Commission has changed its definition of CSR to 'the responsibility of enterprises for their impacts on society' (European Commission, 2011), which by implication admits behaviour regulated by government.

It follows from this dichotomous perspective that if government regulates social activities by business such as initiatives to improve labour standards or human rights, then consequent business behaviour is simply conformance with that regulation. And the corollary is that CSR operates in 'unregulated spheres'. Our study is in contention with this view in that we do not see government regulation and CSR as dichotomous but, rather, as relational.

More recently, this theme of scepticism about government in CSR has been reflected in an influential literature that argues that companies and civil society actors have taken on new roles in global governance in the name of CSR, known as 'Political CSR' (Scherer and Palazzo, 2011). The Political CSR concept is premised on the view that due to the incapacity of national governments in global governance, corporations effectively assume political responsibilities. So, if not a completely dichotomous view of government and CSR, Scherer and Palazzo's is at least a view of an inverse relationship between the two. In a later article, Scherer et al. (2016: 277) define Political CSR as 'those responsible business activities that turn corporations into political actors, by engaging in public deliberations, collective decisions, and the provision of public goods or the restriction of public bads in cases where public authorities are unable or unwilling to fulfil this role'. A key axiom in this literature is that companies (Scherer and Palazzo, 2007, 2008, 2011; Scherer et al., 2016) and civil society actors (Kaplan, 2015; Sabel et al., 2000) take on roles that have traditionally been seen as the responsibility of the state. We will return to this important theme of Political CSR in further sections.

Our purpose is not to deny that corporations and civil society have taken on new roles in the regulation of global business. It is very clear that this is the case (Locke, 2013; Spar and LaMure, 2003; Yaziji and Doh, 2009). Rather, our purpose is to contend that the corollary that national governments have never featured or have somehow disappeared with this development is, at best, partial.

This brings us to the second, the 'related', perspective of government and CSR. The first version of this is that CSR is 'embedded in' (Moon and Vogel, 2008) or structured by (Matten and Moon, 2008), the institutions, including laws, which governments have created and legitimated (on the embeddedness of institutions see more broadly Dahl and Lindblom, 1992 [1953]; Granovetter, 1985; Hollingsworth and Boyer, 1997). Early proponents of this view were Preston and Post (1975), who offer theoretical support for business involvement in, and accountability for, public policy. They saw the significance of CSR's relationship to government and governmental processes, and thus coined the term 'public responsibility' to distinguish this from 'ad hoc managerial policies and practices' (9). This is reflective of the broader insight that government actions are to a large extent structured by the accumulated policies and institutions that they inherit on taking office (Rose, 1990; see also Drezner, 2001).

Such a view that business responsibility is entailed in public policies has become a feature of more recent scholarship on CSR. Campbell, for example, argues that CSR is best understood as a function of the institutions in companies' respective home countries (Campbell, 2007). Matten and Moon (2008) argue that there are historic patterns of CSR, which reflect national institutions, but that these have become overlain with sector and company-level factors, which transcend national patterns (Garcia-Johnson, 2000).

This embedded view is akin to Matten and Moon's (2008) concept of 'implicit CSR' in which the accumulative effect of government policies, along with deeply institutionalized social norms, shape understandings of how companies should behave, and thus no explicit assumption of responsibility at a company level is expected. However, the embedded view is also consistent with the 'explicit CSR' of individual corporations whereby they take distinctive social responsibilities. Thus, the fact that American corporations, for example, claim responsibility for their employees' health and retirement insurance is a reflection of a 'welfare economy' (Rein, 1982) in which those corporations receive tax exemptions from the government for providing such benefits. Thus, in the 'embedded view', CSR actions are often considered to be entailed in or supported by government regulation, rather than just alternatives to it.

Yet others argue that CSR is in part a function of the national business systems along with such other factors as corporate governance and organizational justice (e.g. Aguilera et al., 2007). These authors assume that CSR is in large part explained by the legal and governmental context in which the respective corporations are embedded (e.g. Albareda et al., 2008; Knudsen, 2017; Midttun et al., 2015). Research in political economy has shown that it is possible to establish consistent patterns between the structures of the economy, economic policies, employment policies, skill formation schemes, and social protection systems (Thelen, 2014). This is particularly true for research in the Varieties of Capitalism approach (Hall and Soskice, 2001); the French School tradition of regulation (Aglietta, 1980; Boyer, 2004), the National Business Systems literature (Whitley, 1999), and the Welfare Capitalism literature (Esping-Andersen, 1990). These approaches identify types or regimes but they are often too static and too abstract to explain recent developments of economic restructuring that are required when national political economies encounter globalization pressures. The Varieties of Capitalism literature, for example, is heavily employer focused and assigns only a limited role to government actions per se.

Globalized trade and capital, outsourcing, and supply chains driven by technological advances such as easier and cheaper communication and transportation, trade liberalization, and deregulation of financial markets allow for the increasing shifting of production of goods and services to less developed countries in order to take advantage of their cheaper wages. As a result governments in advanced industrialized countries are increasingly struggling to maintain welfare states and labour market arrangements such as collective bargaining that have traditionally offered protection to weaker segments of the labour force (Hassel et al., 2016; Martin and Swank, 2012; Thelen, 2014; Trampush, 2009). As borders become more porous the ability of governments to regulate the social performance of their business activities such as wages and working conditions – at home as well as abroad – is then seen as weakened (Risse-Kappen, 1995, 2004). Although the Varieties of Capitalism literature, National Business Systems, and the Welfare Capitalism literatures do not address CSR per se, as we shall see these literatures have been deployed in the CSR literature (e.g. Jackson and Apostolakou, 2010; Kang and Moon, 2012) and they highlight the domestic political and economic contexts in which companies undertake social initiatives including CSR.

A second view in this related perspective is one of agency. Rather than stressing the governmental impact on CSR as a legacy effect, the agential view instead focuses on the way governments regulate to deploy CSR's resources for their current policy agendas (Bartley, 2007; Gond et al., 2011; Knudsen et al., 2015; Lim and Tsutsui, 2012; Steurer, 2010; Vogel, 2008). In this view the government–CSR relationship is not only about an 'inheritance principle' of public policy whereby the vast majority of regulation with which governments govern was enacted by their predecessors (Rose, 1990), but it is also about government choices in the here and now. In short, we identify ways in which governments regulate CSR in part to pursue their own contemporary governance goals. Crucially, whereas the embedded view of CSR and government most obviously applies in the relationship

Table 2.1 *The Literature on Government and CSR*

Government and CSR: dichotomous perspective		Government and CSR: related perspective	
Express dichotomous view	Implied dichotomous view	Embedded related view	Agential related view
CSR is defined as excluding the role of government	CSR is treated as if government has no role	Gives emphasis to the structural effects of inherited government policies	Gives emphasis to the agential effects of government policies

between national governments and domestic CSR, the agential one is more relevant for a consideration of the effect of national government regulation for international CSR, which is not embedded by the accretion of decades or even centuries of domestic institutional development. In the 'agential' view of government and CSR, governments purposively interact with non-government actors to develop CSR policies. This agential view shares with the embedded view the assumption of government as an important actor in the development of CSR, but stresses government agency rather more than structure. In keeping with this view we demonstrate that CSR is not just embedded in governmental institutions, but also that governments use CSR for policy innovation and change, whether to justify deregulation or to consolidate standards. Agency is evident in various types of interactions in response both to business and society initiatives. We present a summary of the perspectives on government and CSR in Table 2.1.

Our focus is on the related perspective of government and CSR. Thus, our selection of cases (Chapters 4–6) reflects our findings on countries where government policies for CSR are most embedded (Chapter 3), but our analysis of these cases focuses on government agency, albeit as structured by the ways in which government and CSR are institutionalized in these countries. This approach parallels political economy scholarship and in particular in the historical institutionalist tradition (Iversen and Soskice, 2006; Mares, 2003; Martin and Swank, 2012; Palier and Thelen, 2010). Recent work in this research tradition has developed a more dynamic approach to exploring the relationships between domestic political and economic institutions and social welfare outcomes. Thelen (2014) argues, for example, that policies adopted by governments to achieve economic growth and employment, while not structurally predetermined, are nonetheless mediated by institutional features of the political economies that are not fully amenable to manipulation by governments, even if they are sometimes sustained by public policies (see also Mahoney and Thelen, 2009. Thelen (2014), for example, shows how countries such as Sweden, Germany, and the Netherlands have responded to shared globalization pressures by selecting distinct growth and employment strategies that reflect differences in the structure of organized interests.

In relation to these perspectives, our argument is that whilst corporations are the key actors in CSR, their behaviour reflects long-term institutional settings of their respective national, international, and sectoral business systems, and moreover that governments are agential in regulating CSR. Thus we contribute to the literature on government and CSR by exploring the ways in which national governments shape CSR through the interactions with business and civil society organizations.

We now turn to the context in which these government–CSR relationships have become more significant. Thus, to contextualize our analysis we introduce two key literatures: one on domestic governance and CSR, the other, on global governance and CSR. We highlight particular strengths and weaknesses of each literature and then seek to pull them together to develop a new framework for analysing the role of government in influencing CSR.

Domestic Governance and Corporate Social Responsibility

The domestic governance literature that we examine contextualizes both the recent rise of CSR and the changing roles of government in their own countries. Following Mayntz (2004; see also Börzel et al., 2011; Héritier and Eckert, 2008; Pierre, 2000) we define governance as:

the entirety of co-existing forms of collective regulation of societal issues: ranging from the institutionalized self-organization of civil society and the different forms of cooperation between public and private actors to the sovereign acts of states. (Mayntz, 2004: 6)

Or to put it more simply, governance is 'the system that provides direction to society' (Peters, 1996 – for a critical discussion of the governance concept see Offe, 2009). The literature here is vast and we focus on two particular themes of analysis. The first concerns the ways in which governments have complemented their means of governing through mandate, premised on their unique resource of authority. This is relevant to us because in our analysis (Chapters 3–6) we explore the different forms of policy that governments deploy for CSR. The second literature focuses particularly on the interplay of public and private initiatives in domestic governance. This is important for us because the CSR initiatives that feature in our analysis are known as 'private initiatives' and our analysis (particularly in the case studies in Chapters 4–6) focuses on different forms of interaction with them by government (which we term 'direct' and 'indirect' – see further sections in the pages that follow).

The literature covering domestic governance and its relationship with CSR was inspired by what was known as the 'new' governance literature of the late 1980s and 1990s (e.g. Moon, 2002). Whilst this literature is also very broad, containing internal debates about the causes of new governance and its effects, there are some key common features that we see as critical to the development of CSR over the past couple of decades. Primarily, this literature suggests that the capacity of government to govern on the basis of its exclusive authority to mandate behaviour alone is exhausted or that governments face new challenges which they cannot address using this traditional mode of governing by mandate. The significance of the use of the term (new) 'governance' is therefore associated with the relative decline in the roles of government as a public goods provider and as a 'command and control' regulator. It is also associated with the adoption of market and network modes by government to complement their conventional authority (Osborne, 2010; Peters, 1996; Pierre, 2000; Rhodes, 1996). This contrasts most obviously with modes of governance, which were synonymous with state authority, which, whilst tempered by legislative oversight and judicial review, reflected governments' possession of the monopoly of legitimate force within national boundaries (Weber, 1949 [1919]).

In part, the new domestic governance literature notes limits to the capacity of governments to govern (Rhodes, 1997) as well as recognizing ideologically and efficiency-driven policies to withdraw the state from some responsibilities (Domberger, 1999; OECD, 2005; Parker, 2009; Savas, 2000; Self, 1993). Governments have been more active in bringing new actors into governance, particularly business and civil society organizations (Bartley, 2007). Rhodes (1997) points to the growing importance of self-governing networks and public–private partnerships, and Kooiman (2000) points to the growth of self-governance and co-governance, including through: 'networks, public–private partnerships, communicative governing, and respon-sive regulation' (2000: 150–51). New domestic governance is not sim-ply a reflection of new (i.e. non-governmental) actors but also of new modes of (non-coercive) governing (see also de Búrca et al., 2014). For example, Rosenau (2005) stresses the themes of participation, learn-ing, and consensus about appropriate standards of business behaviour, which are mainly policed by reputation concerns.

In this context new domestic governance roles for CSR have emerged reflecting different relationships with government. This trend of CSR featuring in domestic governance at the behest of governments has been evidenced in a variety of settings. In a number of countries, economic downturns motivated companies to become active in local economic partnerships to re-invigorate depressed areas and to create employment in the UK (Moore et al., 1985), in Australia (Moon and Willoughby, 1990), and in Denmark (Morsing, 2005). In many coun-tries there was a great increase in CSR applied to a wider range of com-munity roles, often in collaboration with the charity sector (Muthuri et al., 2009). In yet other countries the focus of CSR was upon sustain-ability issues more broadly in, for example, Austria (Strigl, 2005) and Spain (Fernandez and Melé, 2005).

Notwithstanding the increase in CSR in domestic governance, we argue that rumours of the death of the state should not be exagger-ated. In this respect, our argument echoes that of Pierre (2000), who highlights the re-constitution of state authority reflected in the growth of sub-national regional and city governments, and the allocation of ministerial authority to executive agencies. This anticipates our theme, that governments are able to re-invent themselves in domestic gov-ernance, specifically to regulate international CSR. Despite the dimi-nution of its capacity to mandate behaviour through command and control, the state is still alive and kicking using other forms of policy, including less coercive rules that are usually associated with initiatives such as networks and partnerships.

This view is not only associated with political science approaches to CSR, but also by those of socio-legal scholars, notably McBarnet in the context of her work on CSR 'beyond the law', 'through the law', and 'for the law', which she calls the 'new corporate accountability' (2007). She argues that although the UK governments have formally maintained a view that CSR should be voluntary, they have nonetheless both encouraged CSR and regulated it. She illustrates this with reference to reporting requirements placed, first, upon pension funds in 2000, and subsequently on stock-exchange-listed companies under the 'operating and financial review' in 2006 (2007: 32–37). Second, she illustrates this capacity to regulate CSR with reference to public purchasing requirements for environmentally friendly goods and services (2007: 42–43). One example is the adoption by many European governments of public procurement standards precisely to integrate CSR into public policy (McCrudden, 2009). Public procurement is used to address social conditions in other countries including fair trade and the reduction of child labour. Companies are required to conform only if they wish to sell to the respective government agencies. According to McCrudden (2009: 118), legal regulation 'enables the relationship between CSR and public procurement to flourish, for example by explicitly setting out a common standard of what public bodies may do in the use of procurement for achieving CSR goals, but not requiring it, and in reducing legal uncertainties that might lead to unwillingness to use public procurement for CSR purposes'.

We will demonstrate how new forms of domestic governance feature in national policies for international CSR, as well as how these also interact with traditional uses of mandate by national governments aimed at solving the same social problems as are the CSR initiatives they also support.

Whilst governments are one of several actor types in domestic governance and CSR (others being notably business and civil society), we also argue that they bring distinctive regulatory resources to these networks and partnerships and thus they should not be accorded the status of just another actor in a standard or a partnership, or just another stakeholder of a company (Freeman, 1984). Even if the power of governments to use their exclusive mode of 'authority' (Moon, 2002) to command and control has been weakened in some respects by new regulatory shifts, it is important not to lose sight of their distinctive combination of resources. These can be conceptualized in a number of ways. Rose (1984) argued that governments possessed unrivalled powers to mobilize laws, money, and employees to produce public programmes. Hood (1986) distinguished the tools of government by which he referred to 'advice, information, persuasion'; ' "treasure" and cheque-book government', 'tokens of authority' that arise from its unique legal status, 'organization', and the capacity for 'direct action' and 'treatment' of a range of individual, group, and mass issues; and tools of detection. Whilst corporations, particularly, may collectively have grown in respect of some of these powers (Rose, 1984) and tools (Hood, 1986), they cannot rival governments' combination of these domestic resources.

An important and growing literature exists that highlights the important role of government for shaping the way that private CSR programs and initiatives develop. Scholars interested in political economy (with backgrounds in economics, political science, or sociology) have, for example, explored the interplay between domestic political and economic institutions and private CSR initiatives. Focusing on enforcement, scholars find, for example, that private compliance initiatives can interact with public regulation to shape improved labour standards in the Brazilian sugar sector (Coslovsky and Locke, 2013; see also Ronconi, 2010). Other studies show how different labour market models such as in the Latin world and in the United States led to different company approaches to enforcing labour standards (Piore and Shrank, 2008). Börzel et al. (2012) argue that in certain areas of limited statehood, private regulation still depends on some state intervention to be effective – in particular when firms are immune to reputational concerns that require the involvement of several actors in the provision of collective goods.

These examples of research scholarship illustrate that a vibrant and sophisticated research tradition exists that examines the interplay between government institutions and public policy on the one hand and private CSR initiatives on the other. In short, government has agency in shaping CSR.

Domestic Governance and CSR – Summary

We see government policy for CSR as a feature of domestic governance as governments are ready to exploit the ability of corporations, often in partnerships with other businesses and civil society organizations, to fulfil a variety of public policy agendas as we demonstrate in Chapters 3 and 4. Thus we contribute to debates about CSR and domestic governance by indicating the forms of policy that governments bring to CSR and their relationships with private initiatives designed to advance CSR and, in so doing, we explore how domestic CSR can have international implications. Table 2.2 summarizes the positions that we would expect the government to take in the light of the literature on domestic governance and CSR. It presents these positions in the context of the research questions on government and CSR on which we will base our analysis. We elaborate more on our choice of research questions when we explain our analytical approach.

In order to explore the development of international CSR we now turn to debates about CSR and state capacity in the sphere of international business arising from globalization and in the context of global governance.

Global Governance and CSR

Globalization presents a threshold parameter change in that the territories in which governance is enacted are no longer those for which national governments have exclusive legal sovereignty (Scholte, 2005). Globalization has been seen as a main driver of the rise of CSR because, with the outsourcing of production from the 'Global North' to the 'Global South', government regulation to ensure environmental and social protection has been seen as insufficient, and companies and civil society actors have turned to private CSR initiatives to fill the governance gap (Vogel, 2008). The literature on globalization, governance, and CSR extends the logic in the domestic governance literature, highlighting how governments have become less able to regulate as business activities increasingly transcend national borders. The argument is that the weakening of the regulatory capacity of governments results in the rise of private regulation (O'Rourke, 2006; Rasche, 2012; Scherer and Palazzo, 2007, 2011; Scherer et al., 2016). Numerous implications of globalization for government and governance have been identified (Kooiman, 2000). Perhaps the most obvious implication is the growth of international organizations and the creation of new rules (Börzel and Risse, 2010; Knudsen, 2011; Ostry, 1999) addressing such cross-border problems as environmental pollution, currency crises, and AIDS (Rosenau, 2000). These in turn

Table 2.2 Conceptualizations of CSR and Government in the Domestic Governance Literature: Expected Perspectives on Our Research Questions

Research questions	Government and CSR: dichotomous perspective		Government and CSR: related perspective	
	Express dichotomous view	Implied dichotomous view	Embedded related view	Agential related view
1. How do government policies support CSR?	CSR is defined as excluding the role of government	CSR is treated as if government has no role	CSR is embedded in domestic political and economic governance	Gives emphasis to the agential effects of government policies
2. What roles do government policies play in supporting CSR?	Government role is not the focus		System centred	Problem/issue centred
3. Why do governments make policies for CSR?	Government role is not the focus		Motivation as per agential view: Legacy effect on CSR by structured actors' governance responsibilities	Changing societal expectations about the role of business in domestic society. Government views CSR as a means to achieve public policy goals

(continued)

Table 2.2 (*cont.*)

Research questions	Government and CSR: dichotomous perspective		Government and CSR: related perspective	
	Express dichotomous view	Implied dichotomous view	Embedded related view	Agential related view
4. What are the interactions between different sorts government policies for CSR? a. Between domestic and international policies for CSR? b. Between direct and indirect policies for CSR	Government role is not the focus		1. Focus is on public policies for CSR intended for home country firm's domestic activities (BUT not international activities) 2. Focus is on direct CSR public policy only (BUT not indirect CSR public policy)	

generate diverse accountability mechanisms (Fransen and Burgoon, 2012; Keohane, 1984; Krasner, 1983; Risse, 2002; Ruggie, 2004), and the new roles for NGOs (Haufler, 2001) and other non-state actors (e.g. Clapham, 2006; Risse-Kappen, 1995; 2004) in shaping global governance systems. Second, with globalization, companies increasingly operate overseas and outside the immediate jurisdiction of their home governments. Given the power of MNCs and the impact of their value chains, their operations can have vital social, political, economic, and environmental consequences for populations in host countries and in particular in the Global South (Rodrik, 2001; Stiglitz, 2002; Vogel, 2008). These developments are often associated with the view that, axiomatically, these companies can operate internationally beyond the reach of their national governments, a view our book challenges.

The role of business in global governance is a particular focus of interest in debates about the nature and extent of corporate power in this new governance context. A key point in the business in society literature is that the regulatory capacity of the state is inefficient when it comes to dealing with new social and environmental concerns that arise with globalization (de Bakker and den Hond, 2008; Rasche, 2012; Scherer and Palazzo, 2007, 2011). As a result, business engages in self-regulation through soft law in those instances where state agencies are unable or unwilling to regulate (Matten and Crane, 2005).

In this context O'Rourke contends that:

The most dynamic experiments in global governance are not about national regulatory policies, international trade agreements, or even international agency initiatives. Rather, a new class of governance initiatives has emerged that involve private and non-governmental stakeholders in negotiating labour, health and safety, and environmental standards, monitoring compliance with the standards, and establishing mechanisms of certification and labelling that provide incentives for firms to meet these standards. These non-governmental systems of regulation are expanding extremely rapidly across industries and regulatory areas. (O'Rourke, 2006: 899)

Globalization is therefore widely regarded as having a profound effect on CSR. Indeed many commentators and scholars would conclude that the CSR movement of the past fifteen years or so has primarily been driven by globalization (Fransen and Burgoon, 2014; Vogel, 2008). While the economic influence of MNCs is growing in the Global South, paradoxically perhaps, corporations are also simultaneously finding that a wide range of stakeholders in the global sphere increasingly scrutinizes their international business activities. This increased public scrutiny of corporate behaviour is associated with the rise in new technology including internet usage, smart phones, and new social media such as Facebook and Twitter (Castello et al., 2016; Vogel 2008). Thanks to this combination of social media and civil society attention to business, the international social and environmental impacts of companies can be crucial for corporate reputations at home and abroad, with implications for their attractiveness to investors, customers, employees, and suppliers (e.g. Gjølberg, 2009; Hodge, 2006).

It is in this context that several authors have identified new global governance roles for CSR. A major contribution that bridges the literature on international organizations with CSR is Scherer and Palazzo's 'The New Political Role of Business in a Globalized World' (2011). Although they include the state as a main political actor with civil society and corporations, Scherer and Palazzo emphasize global and multi-level governance as the core locus (2011). They argue that we are witnessing an emerging global institutional context for CSR that has shifted from national to global governance in which firms contribute to global regulation and provide public goods (Scherer and Palazzo, 2011; see also Matten and Crane, 2005). Key themes here are the ways in which CSR is regulated 'mutually' (e.g. through business associations for CSR like the World Business Council for Sustainable Development); by and with civil society (e.g. through international multi-actor organizations and standards including the Marine Stewardship Council, the Forest Stewardship Council, and the Global Reporting Initiative); and by and with international government organizations (e.g. the United Nations (UN), the Organization for Economic Cooperation and Development (OECD), the World Bank, and the International Standards Organization) (Prakash and Potoski, 2007). It should not be overlooked, of course, that sometimes these new regulatory mechanisms are also in conflict with one another, as illustrated in the differences in approaches to forestry standards pursued by the more business-oriented World Business Council for Sustainable Development and the more conventional tripartite Forest Stewardship Council (Cashore et al., 2004).

So the starting point for much of this CSR literature on globalization is a weakening of the nation state system (Rasche, 2012; Scherer and Palazzo, 2007, 2011). These arguments about the weakening of the state's regulatory capacity often reflect several overlapping themes, which should be differentiated. First, it is argued or implied that national government capacity has somehow been reduced in absolute terms. In other words some of the conclusions about the domestic role of the state noted in the previous discussion about privatization, liberalization, and new governance get transferred to the international sphere. Second, it is argued or implied that, by dint of globalization, Western governments lose control over a wider range of home country MNCs' operations in other jurisdictions. Third, it is argued or implied that developing country governments are relatively weaker than their Western counterparts, and thus MNCs find themselves in relatively under-regulated business systems as they travel 'East' or 'South'.

In general terms, however, it is characteristically argued that:

the Westphalian nation state system is losing some of its regulatory power because many social and economic interactions are expanding beyond the reach of territorially bound national jurisdiction and enforcement to off-shore locations (Doh, 2005; Palan, 2003) or to oppressive or even failed states (Fukuyama, 2004) where there is no rule of law, no democratic institutions, and no adequate government and regulation. (Scherer and Palazzo, 2011: 902)

Scholars have pointed out that nation states, whose jurisdiction is largely territorially bound, are unable to address these governance voids and that inter-governmental organizations, which to a large extent rely on states for implementation, cannot fill these voids either (Rasche, 2012; Vogel 2008). In this light, Scherer and Palazzo (2011) have proposed a significant theoretical contribution to the literature on CSR and global governance, which they refer to as Political CSR premised on the assumption that government regulation has become weakened. Scherer and Palazzo (2011: 909) sum up their claim that the regulatory power of the state has been eroded in the following manner:

In a globalized world, as we have argued, the capacity of the state to regulate economic behaviour and to set the restrictions for market exchange is in decline. As a political reaction to the widening regulatory gap, governance initiatives have been launched on the global, national, and local level that try to compensate for the lack of governmental power. Unlike the hierarchy of nation-state governance, these new initiatives often rely on heterarchic or network-like relationships. (Detomasi, 2007) These new forms of regulation are more network-oriented in nature in contrast to the traditional command and control nature of government regulation. Furthermore, non-state actors seek to re-establish the political order and in doing so to promote new forms of democratic control.

Scherer and Palazzo argue that:

In fact, with the intensified engagement of private actors, social movements, and the growing activities of international institutions a new form of trans-national regulation is emerging: global governance, the definition and implementation of standards of behaviour with global reach. (2011: 909)

In a recent article Scherer and Palazzo writing with Rasche and Spicer (Scherer et al., 2016) take stock of the Political CSR literature and suggest new directions for what they refer to as 'Political CSR 2.0'. They argue that 'the debate on PCSR might have been too sceptical with regards to governmental regulation both on a national and international level and too much focused on soft-law initiatives and the significance of private authority' (2016: 284). They highlight attempts of government to control the activities of multinational corporations both on a national and international level of rule-making and make references to the UK Bribery Act, the US Foreign Corrupt Practices Act, and the Dodd–Frank Act's focus on protecting human rights in conflict minerals (also known as Section 1502). Second, they state that the pressure of intergovernmental organizations on corporations has increased as well (Scherer et al., 2016: 284). As examples of intergovernmental organizations Scherer et al. (2016) point to the EU, the UN, and the OECD. However, although Political CSR 2.0 is more willing to acknowledge the role of government than its previous version it does not have much to say about how governments can shape CSR. For example, it does not explore the political processes that lead to government initiatives to control the activities of multinational corporations nor how governments can influence intergovernmental organizations and their CSR programs or multi-stakeholder initiatives that focus on CSR issues. Neither does Political CSR 2.0 examine how government involvement in traditional 'hard' law forms of regulation interact with 'softer' forms of CSR programs. This book aims to address this gap in the Political CSR 2.0 literature and develops an argument about the role of government in shaping international CSR and how different forms of government policies interact with CSR.

To sum up, according to the Political CSR literature, many of today's social and environmental problems reflect transnational governance challenges that arise because there is an imbalance between the increasingly international operations of business and the frequent absence of adequate government regulations in the Global South (Kolk, 2014; Rasche, 2012; Ruggie, 2004; Scherer and Palazzo, 2007, 2011). In order to deal with inefficient government regulation, many companies have therefore adopted private CSR solutions in order to manage social and environmental challenges. Limiting business risk could mean using private governance to resist governmental or inter-governmental standards, in some cases, while in other cases, including those we study in Chapters 5 and 6, there is more of a synergy between governmental or inter-governmental standards and business strategy (Cashore et al., 2004). Moreover, others argue that CSR originates not with business but with public interest advocates such as NGOs that want to fill the regulatory vacuum created by the inadequacies of both national and international institutions to regulate corporations (Fransen and Burgoon, 2012; Kaplan, 2015; Moon and Vogel, 2008). These scholars view CSR as a set of activities through which society can undertake soft regulation of corporate conduct while norms of appropriate conduct are expected to 'ratchet' up over time (Cashore et al., 2004; Murphy and Bendell, 1999; Sabel et al., 2000; Waddock, 2008). In short, from this civil regulation perspective, CSR originates with public interest advocates (Kaplan, 2015). However, the central assumption remains that governments are absent from this new variety of CSR initiatives to address international governance problems.

Despite the weight of the argument about the centrality of business and civil society to global governance, as production has continued to grow increasingly global, many governments have found that private regulation of international business activities is insufficient. As Ruggie put it: a major reason for government CSR regulation is that 'private governance produces only partial solutions, and its own unfolding brings the public sector back in' (Ruggie, 2003: 28). However, the UNGC has also been criticized for offering firms a good cover behind the UN, but not requiring too many 'on the ground' changes (Kell,

2012). Rather than attempt coercive mandate as alternatives to private regulation, governments have adopted CSR regulation in order to enhance international competitiveness or to promote certain economic and political development goals (Midttun et al., 2006). Thus, government regulation of CSR has increasingly moved away from regulating domestic CSR programs to regulating the social and environmental performance of home country firms as they operate in a developing country context (Brown and Knudsen, 2015; Knudsen et al., 2015).

Although governments are using strong mandates to regulate some aspects of international business (e.g., the US and UK anti-corruption regulation), strong mandate is merely one end of a regulatory spectrum rather than the totality of regulation (Abbott and Snidal, 2000). The type of policies of interest to us include those described as softer forms of regulation, which do not stress detailed conformance requirements or punishments for failure to comply. Hence, we are primarily interested in government CSR policies where corporations are able to exercise choice as to whether to, and how to, conform. We are thus interested in comparing the different types of regulation that governments bring to CSR, the circumstances of these regulatory forms, and their interactions with one another.

In our discussion of domestic governance and CSR we highlighted that a key political economy literature exists that examines the interplay between historically and politically determined institutions and private CSR initiatives (see also Brammer et al., 2012). Turning to the literature on global governance and CSR, political economists have explored how domestic political institutions shape transnational CSR initiatives (Bartley, 2007; see also Bernstein and Cashore, 2002) or contribute to CSR outcomes (Distelhorst et al., 2015; Rodriguez-Garavito, 2005). Alternatively scholars examine how transnational CSR initiatives such as the ILO's Better Work Program have the potential (under certain conditions) to reinforce domestic labour regulation (Amengual and Chirot, 2016). Scholars also call attention to the limitations of organizations such as the UNGC and thus highlight the need for governmental capacity (Ruggie, 2003). Bernstein and Cashore (2002) analyse the conditions under which global governance can influence domestic policies to improve environmental effectiveness. We find, however, that notwithstanding some insights from adjacent fields (e.g. Bernstein and Cashore 2002; Ruggie, 2003) the role of national government is somewhat underspecified in this literature and in particular how government CSR initiatives play a role in a government's broader policy program.

So, our view is that in most of the CSR studies of the regulation of responsible business, the roles of national governments in these new, global governance arenas have been understated or more usually overlooked. In part this reflects a general assumption in the wider political economy literature that, axiomatically, the decline of national government is a cause or effect (depending on the theoretical perspective) of globalization (e.g. Daly, 1996; Friedman, 2005; Scholte, 2002; Wolf, 2005). But we also suspect that, in some cases, the novelty of the new forms of CSR regulation by inter-governmental organizations and multi-actor agencies, standards, and partnerships has resulted in the neglect of more familiar regulators, national governments, perhaps because many of these governmental activities are no longer in the familiar coercive mandate mode. So our book contributes to debates about global governance and CSR by bringing the national governments into our analysis, and investigating how and why governments regulate international CSR, that is, the behaviour of domestic companies abroad.

Global Governance and CSR – A Summary

The global governance literature highlights drivers of international CSR although mainly through private actors, be they corporate or civil society, but generally neglects the roles of government policies to support international CSR directly and indirectly. Thus we contribute to debates about governments, CSR, and international governance by highlighting the forms of policy that governments bring to CSR and their relationships with private initiatives designed to advance CSR and, in so doing, we explore how domestic CSR can have international implications. Focusing on ethical trade in Chapter 5 and tax transparency in extractives in Chapter 6, we illustrate the interrelationship between public and private CSR initiatives, the forms of government initiatives, and the interplay between the domestic and international spheres. Table 2.3 summarizes our classification of the literature on global governance and CSR and presents our expectations about this relationship.

To sum up, we develop our analytical approach from three distinct but related literatures. First, in the context of the CSR literature, we

Table 2.3 *Conceptualizations of CSR and Government in the Global Governance Literature: Expected Perspectives on Our Research Qestions*

Research questions	Government and CSR: dichotomous perspective		Government and CSR: related perspective	
	Express dichotomous view	Implied dichotomous view	Embedded related view	Agential related view
1. How do government policies support CSR?	CSR is defined as excluding the role of government	CSR is treated as if government has no role	International CSR is embedded in domestic political and economic governance	Government has limited agency in shaping international CSR
2. What roles do government policies play in supporting CSR?	Government role is not the focus		System centred	Problem/issue centred
3. Why do governments make policies for CSR?	Government role is not the focus		Motivation as per agential view: Legacy effect on CSR by structured actors' governance responsibilities	Changing societal expectations about the international role of business in society. Government views CSR as a means to achieve public policy goals
4. What are the interactions between different sorts of government policies for CSR? a. Between domestic and international policies for CSR? b. Between direct and indirect policies for CSR?	Government role is not the focus		Limited focus on public policies for international CSR BUT focus on international CSR. The literature focuses mainly on how international businesses and IGOS address problems and not on how governments develop public policies for CSR (neither direct nor indirect public policies for CSR)	

propose a 'related' perspective of government and CSR in which government has agency, albeit structured by embedded institutional settings. Second, from the domestic governance literature we build on the notion that governments possess a distinctive combination of regulatory resources. Third, with reference to the global governance literature, which highlights drivers of international CSR although mainly through private actors, we focus on the roles of government policies to support CSR directly and indirectly.

Analytical Approach

We present our analytical approach in three main parts. First, we introduce our overall framing of policies, which is the distinction between policies for CSR, directly and indirectly. Government policies that support a specific CSR initiative are considered to 'support CSR directly'. Public policies, which are not considered CSR policies, can nevertheless address the same problem that a CSR initiative is intended to ameliorate. Such public policies thereby 'support CSR indirectly'.

Second, we introduce the data on which we conduct our analysis. This consists of a panoramic overview of government policies for CSR directly in Europe, and three case studies of government and CSR. Third, we elaborate upon the research questions which guide our analysis. In the concluding section of this chapter we bring these parts together to provide an integrated framework.

Policies for CSR Directly and Indirectly

We make a distinction between policies that support CSR directly and those that do so indirectly on the basis of our empirical observation of the distinction. Governments make policies that directly create and support CSR initiatives, but they also make policies that are addressed to a problem that CSR initiatives focus on, and thereby indirectly support those CSR initiatives. So our contribution is to substantiate our observation of these two types of government policy for CSR, and to explore how they operate and interact.

Having introduced the distinction between policies which are aimed at CSR 'directly' and those that are for CSR 'indirectly', it behoves us to explain this novel perspective. Direct policies for CSR refer here to government policies specifically addressed to CSR initiatives such as CSR organizations and regulations. The terminology of direct and indirect regulation has been developed in the global governance literature by Abbott and Snidal (2000; Abbott et al., 2015). However, these authors focus upon how international governance organizations *regulate problems* either 'themselves' (i.e. directly) or via intermediaries (i.e. indirectly). In contrast our focus is upon how national governments *support* CSR either directly (i.e. by supporting CSR initiatives) or indirectly (i.e. by regulating the wider business environment in which CSR is enacted). This is not to say that we have no problem focus. On the contrary, we study the way the different policies for CSR address problems, specifically those of non-financial reporting, ethical trade, and transparency of payments in the extractives industry (see sub-sections that follow).

Indirect policies for CSR refer to government support for CSR, which is not focused upon a CSR initiative but upon the regulatory context of that problem to which the respective CSR initiative is addressed. By these means a government regulates the same problem to which a CSR initiative is addressed – and is thereby supportive of it – but this is not through direct support for the CSR initiative. It is, of course, possible that governments can unwittingly make policies, which shape the regulatory environment for CSR. However, our interest is in cases where the governments make these policies indirectly with awareness and cognizance of the respective CSR initiatives, and in which there are interactions between these different forms of policy and the CSR initiatives themselves. We suggest that these policies for CSR indirectly can include traditional government policies to regulate the environment in which companies operate, without coercing them to act in a particular way (in which case these would not be CSR policies but conventional business regulation). They can include policies which do not specify terms of compliance or punishment for non-compliance (a point elaborated upon in the sections that follow and in Chapter 3) or rules concerning the wider environment of business such as in other jurisdictions (a point elaborated upon in Chapters 5 and 6), and rules that pertain to one sphere of the business operations such as transparency (a point illustrated in Chapters 4 and 6). Although these forms of regulation often mandate behaviour, they do not themselves impose conceptions of responsible business and thus we describe them as for CSR *indirectly*.

Table 2.4 *Definitions of Public Policies for CSR Directly and Indirectly*

Public policy for CSR directly	Public policy for CSR indirectly
Government policy addressed to a CSR initiative (e.g. organization or regulation) directly. This can be in its initiation or in its operationalization, and the latter can be a one-off or an ongoing type of support	Government policy to address the same problem to which a CSR initiative is addressed. Government thus supports CSR indirectly by deploying its resources to regulate the wider institutional context of the CSR initiative and the problem in question

Whilst direct policies for CSR (i.e. those in which governments create, support, and supplement CSR initiatives) are reasonably well-understood at the domestic level (e.g. Campbell, 2007; Knudsen et al., 2015; Midttun et al., 2015; Steurer, 2010) there has been little attention paid to them at the international level. Moreover, there is no literature on indirect government regulation of CSR through policies which are addressed to a target problem which is shared with a CSR initiative but independently of it. Table 2.4 presents our conceptualization of government policies for CSR directly and indirectly, which we use in our analysis.

Although the two types of policies are presented here as separate and distinct, we should anticipate that governments could undertake direct and indirect support for CSR simultaneously or sequentially. This is a dynamic process: governments often adjust regulation based on feedback on how a regulatory initiative plays out. Furthermore, sometimes the direct and indirect initiatives develop in ways that reflect each other, and a degree of convergence can ensue.

Figure 2.1 is a graphic presentation of the relationships between government policies for CSR directly and indirectly. It depicts problems, which national governments cannot conventionally address directly because they lie outside their own jurisdiction. Instead, national governments can address the problem by directly supporting CSR initiatives, or they can change the regulatory context thereby supporting the CSR initiatives indirectly. The relationships captured in Figure 2.1 frame our analysis.

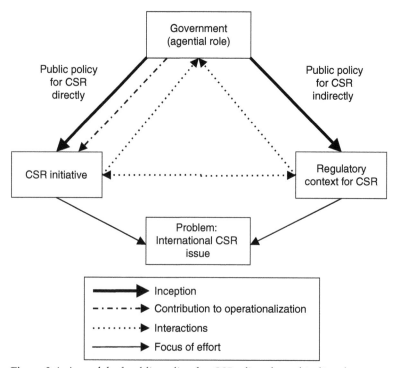

Figure 2.1 A model of public policy for CSR: directly and indirectly

For clarification, Figure 2.2 illustrates what we *do not examine* in this book. Our book *excludes* government policies which are addressed straight to international problems without intermediaries. The vertical arrow – unmediated public policy – illustrates the kind of public policy that we *do not* examine. The challenge for national governments is precisely that their jurisdictions are limited. There are cases where it could be argued that some national governments do make policies, which are unmediated (often referred to as 'Command and Control' regulation – see Abbott et al., 2015). The US Foreign Corrupt Practices Act and the UK Bribery Act are examples of such traditional regulations as they specify what compliance consists of and carry punishment for their transgression.

In contrast, we consider the way in which governments regulate an international CSR issue abroad. We examine public policies that directly shape international CSR initiatives and we examine public

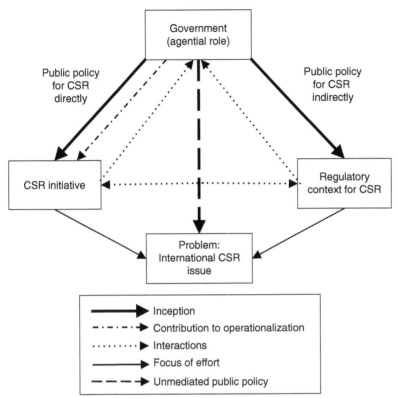

Figure 2.2 Public policy for CSR contrasted with unmediated public policy

policies that are not intended to shape CSR initiatives or organizations but that nonetheless build in support for CSR initiatives indirectly by means of their wider regulatory impact.

Our Data: A Panorama and Three Case Studies of Government Policies for CSR

Our approach to the question of national government policies for CSR is a layered one. We first provide a panorama of government policies for CSR directly. We do so by analysing government policies focusing on CSR in Europe, 2000–2011 (Chapter 3). This is to ascertain the relationship between government and CSR in general in these countries: do these governments make policies to support CSR, and if so, is this true of all or just some countries? On this basis we then identify the sorts of issues addressed – and specifically whether these include international CSR issues. We reveal the regulatory form that these policies have taken, ranging from endorsement, facilitation, and partnership, to mandate. We develop a typology of government regulation for CSR, particularly to identify those national governments which regulate CSR for a wide range of purposes and which deploy the full range of policies available for the cause of CSR.

We then embark on three case studies of government policy for CSR with a more in-depth qualitative analysis (Chapters 4–6). We have selected three main case studies of government and CSR in order to understand the following: the making and development of these policies; the interactions of domestic and international policy; and the interactions of direct and indirect policies for CSR. The first case study is the Danish non-financial reporting legislation – direct government adoption of a CSR rule – in which we investigate the relationship between domestic and international regulation for CSR (Chapter 4).

The second case study is of ethical trade in which we first investigate government support for a specific international CSR initiative directly (the ETI). We complement this with an analysis of policies that support CSR in ethical trade indirectly in the wake of the Rana Plaza disaster in Bangladesh in which Western governments sought to shape the regulatory environment of the Bangladesh textile and garment industries, and thereby shape the context for CSR. We also see how these governments supported and interacted with the work of two post–Rana Plaza CSR initiatives, the Alliance and the Accord, directly (Chapter 5).

The third case study is of transparency in the extractives sector in which we investigate government policies for a specific international CSR initiative directly (EITI). This study includes the policies of 'home' and 'host' governments in this sector. We also investigate how governments have shaped the regulatory context for the EITI indirectly in the form of the US Dodd–Frank Act Section 1504 and the EU Accounting Directive amendment (Directive 2013/34/EU), as well as the interactions of these with the EITI (Chapter 6).

As the purpose of our book is to offer a new interpretation of the roles of government in international CSR, our case selection fulfils four key criteria. First, all three cases relate to mainstream CSR issues that have been explored at great length in the literature albeit from different perspectives than the one we propose. Non-financial reporting has both been an expectation from many societal actors as well as a key mode by which corporations have come to demonstrate their CSR credentials. Ethical trade has been a key point of critique of MNCs by civil society in view of the parlous human rights and labour conditions in many international supply chains. Transparency of MNC payments, particularly in the extractives sector, has also been at the heart of critiques of business from anti-corruption and international development perspectives.

Second, we explore cases of public policy for CSR in contexts of relatively well-embedded government–CSR relations in which governments are continuously active in CSR policymaking rather than taking 'one-off' initiatives. Hence our cases are largely based around the Danish and the UK governments which, in our analysis of public policy for CSR (in Chapter 3), we describe as having 'systemic institutionalization' of CSR (see also Knudsen et al., 2015: 94), though several other national and international governments' (i.e. the EU) direct and indirect regulation of CSR also feature in our analysis.

Third, given our focus on the role of government in shaping *international* CSR we have selected cases accordingly. All three cases have clear but contrasting, domestic government–international CSR linkages. In Chapter 4 we see how the Danish Non-financial Reporting Act emerged from earlier regulation for CSR and also how it brought implications for the international activities of Danish companies. In the ethical trade case (Chapter 5) we see how the UK government (and later other governments) supported a fairly typical CSR partnership approach to a set of international CSR problems. In the transparency in the extractives sector case (Chapter 6), we see a rather more prominent role of government in an MSI, which nonetheless has clear CSR origins and continuing dimensions.

Fourth, we are interested in exploring the interactions between public policies for CSR ('directly') and public policies for CSR ('indirectly') that address the same problem. Hence we select two cases where we identify such interactions: ethical trade and tax transparency in the extractives sector.

Research Questions and Methods

We now turn to detailing the more focused research questions and associated methods, which enable us to address these objectives concerning direct and indirect public policies for international CSR. We structure this section by, first, discussing research questions addressed by aggregate analysis concerning direct government policies for CSR, and, second, by discussing research questions addressed by case studies (qualitative research method) concerning direct and indirect government public policies for CSR.

Direct Government Policies for CSR: Aggregate Analysis

First, we conduct an aggregate analysis of national policies for CSR in Europe. This enables us to identify policies and the issues to which they are addressed in order to justify our further analysis of policies addressing international CSR issues. It also enables us to answer the question in general terms as to what regulatory resources are deployed in policies to support CSR, directly.

Our focus is upon policies that Western European governments themselves refer to as 'CSR'. We define a policy as a governmental output or public action: 'the substance of what government does' (Dearlove, 1973: 2). This would be identified by the mobilization of public resources such as regulations, financial resources (negative or positive expenditures), organizational resources, or cultural/political resources. CSR policies are those designed to encourage responsible business behaviour but not to require it. This distinguishes CSR policies from straight out requirements for companies to behave in certain ways, which governments may also impose. However, this raises the question of how much regulation is needed for a policy to be a simple business regulation rather than a CSR policy, which would entail some level of corporate discretion as to whether or how to respond.

Our test for distinguishing public policies that shape CSR directly from simple command and control regulation is to answer the following questions:

1. Does the policy establish requirements for compliance?
2. Does the policy establish penalties for non-compliance?

If both questions were answered 'yes' we would not speak of public policies for CSR, but of command-and-control regulation.

We collected data on government policies for CSR from 2000 to 2011 and from twenty-two European countries. Data regarding CSR policies and responsible ministries were collected from an extensive web search and several published sources (see Knudsen et al., 2015). The policies were classified by expert researchers according to the responsible national government ministries from where they emanated. In many countries multiple departments may have had some relationship to CSR and these are recorded accordingly. These policies were then further coded as to whether the sponsoring ministries were responsible for issues that were: social, education, internal affairs, environmental, economic, treasury, energy, foreign affairs, and international development. This follows a method adopted in political science of using government departments responsible for public policy to identify the areas of public policy prioritized by governments. This could be in order, for example, to analyse the development of public policies in any single systems, to compare public policy settings among several systems, or to investigate policy convergence or divergence among multiple systems (Rose, 1976).

Thus we identified which ministerial departments of government or which ministerial portfolios (i.e. responsibilities officially attached to ministers serving in these departments) were assigned responsibility for CSR policies in each of the European systems. The identification of a ministry with a policy area, in our case CSR, enables us to establish the broad issue area to which CSR policies are directed. So, in sum, CSR responsibility by the ministries and ministers assigned provides an indicator of the broad issue area to which the government intends its CSR regulation to be directed.

Government Policies to Support CSR Directly and Indirectly: Qualitative Analysis

We now set out the research questions, which apply to public policies that support CSR directly and indirectly, and the qualitative research methods we deploy. Whereas in the aggregate analysis (refer to the previous section) the types of CSR issues to which national government policy is directed was a research finding, here in the qualitative analysis, we selected cases of national government policy for international CSR, directly and indirectly. In Chapter 4, we investigate the way an ostensibly domestic CSR policy (for CSR reporting) has international implications. In Chapters 5 and 6, we investigate two issues that are international, by definition, and examine government policies for CSR concerning ethical trade (which relates to labour rights and standards); and concerning transparency of payments between international companies and governments in the resources sector. In these cases we also investigate the forms of policy for CSR and are able to gain insights into the combinations of and relationships between different forms of regulation for CSR.

Research Question (1) How Do Governments Make Policies That Support CSR Directly: Through Endorsement, Facilitation, Partnership or Mandate?

We coded the respective policies according to the form of regulation that they represented. Hence we distinguished regulations for CSR which: endorse; facilitate; partner; or mandate CSR. This framework was developed by Fox et al. (2002) for the analysis of government policies for CSR in developing countries, and by Gond et al., (2011) in their conceptual investigation of the role of government in CSR configurations. We use it in our analysis of government policies for CSR in Europe (Knudsen et al., 2015 on which Chapter 3 is based). Other analyses of government policy for CSR use descriptive categories of policy which are nominal and combine regulatory style, issue focus, and intended styles of business–society relations (e.g. 'partnership; business in the community; sustainability and citizenship'; and Agora policies – as used by Albareda et al., 2007; and 'legal, economic, informational, partnering and hybrid policy instruments' as used by Steurer, 2009). In elaborating on Bernstein and Cashore's (2002) distinction between how governments regulate CSR, Auld et al. (2008, Table 1) distinguished new government roles in the 'new corporate social responsibility' depending on the nature of the new form of CSR. Hence they suggest that governments can require or encourage corporations to provide CSR information; they delegate or share responsibility in partnerships; they provide background facilitation for environmental management systems; they are often in the shadows for industry association codes of conduct; and tend not to use their sovereign authority responsibility in non-state-market-driven regulation.

In contrast, our framework uses a classificatory system which focuses on the type of government resource deployed, and which enables insights into the regulatory strength of the respective policies for CSR. This in turn allows us to address debates about soft and hard regulation prominent in business and society literatures (e.g. Scherer and Palazzo, 2011), and more broadly in economics (e.g. Stigler, 1971), law (e.g. Braithewaite et al., 2008), and political science (e.g. Moran, 1986).

In our schema governments can *endorse* CSR by means of official encouragement and the provision of the governmental imprimatur. Our 'facilitation' category of CSR regulation involves bringing capacity, subsidy schemes, and tax incentives. Governments can *facilitate* CSR by the deployment of organizational and fiscal resources to bring other actors together. The CSR regulation category of 'partnership' reflects government's ability to create and formally join *partnerships* with other actors for CSR, which usually pre-supposes endorsement and some facilitation. Our category of CSR regulation by *mandate* reflects the unique government resource of authority and this might be illustrated by a prescriptive definition of minimum standards for responsible business performance embedded within a legal framework. Governments can mandate CSR by use of legislation or delegated legislation. We note that this might be coercive (implying that the requirements for compliance with the regulation and punishments for failing to comply are clearly set out) or reflexive (implying that the regulation is designed to assist critical reflection and self-regulation (Braithewaite and Drahos, 2000; Teubner, 1983). One example is the Danish non-financial reporting act which when first introduced only required those companies (with a certain minimum turnover) to report their CSR if they conducted it. This will then have provoked companies to ask themselves 'do we conduct CSR and, if not, why not?' Scott captures the essence of reflexive regulation: 'This approach recognizes the "inner logic" of social systems and sets law the challenge of seeking to steer those social systems. A key aspect of this approach is re-casting the function of law from direct control to proceduralization' (Scott, 2004: 153).

Table 2.5 *Forms of Policy to Support CSR, Directly or Indirectly, and Their Regulatory Strength*

Form of regulation	Description	Regulatory strength
Endorse	Political support for CSR through general information campaigns and websites, political rhetoric, award, and labelling schemes	Low
Facilitate	Incentives for companies to adopt CSR through subsidies, tax incentives, or public procurement policies; brokering of agreements among business and civil society organizations	Medium
Partner	Collaboration of government organizations with business organizations to disseminate knowledge or develop/ maintain standards, and guidelines	Medium
Mandate	Regulation of minimum standards for business performance	High

(*Source*: Knudsen et al., 2015).

Thus, 'mandate' reflects the strongest regulation for CSR, requiring regulation and even legislation, and would usually also involve the other three forms of policy endorsement, facilitation and partnership. 'Facilitation' and 'partnership' policies reflect medium levels of regulatory strength, requiring governments to substantiate their commitment to encouraging CSR by, for example, providing financial and organizational resources. 'Endorsement' represents relatively weak regulation for CSR, for while it signals government approval of CSR, there are no further resources to redirect company behaviour, and CSR would remain at arms' length from government. All of these forms of regulation for CSR are explored in the subsequent chapters. These types are defined and distinguished in Table 2.5 and the regulatory strength we attach to these is also displayed.

Our approach is therefore in the spirit of that of Abbott and Snidal (2000), but also distinct. Abbott and Snidal argue that most international law is in fact soft in distinctive ways. Hard law is legally binding obligations that are precise (or that can be made precise through adjudication or the issuance of detailed regulation) and that delegate authority for interpreting and implementing the law. However, soft law is often preferable because it is easier to achieve and it can offer 'more effective ways to deal with uncertainty such as initiating processes that allow actors to learn about the impact of agreements over time' (Abbott and Snidal, 2000: 423). Soft law also facilitates compromise. The realm of soft law begins once legal arrangements are weakened along one or more of the dimensions of obligation, precision, and delegation. Rather than solely highlight hard or soft law, in focusing on government regulation of CSR initiatives, we consider the dynamic interactions between direct and indirect forms of government and CSR regulation. We unpack the non-mandatory types of regulation and distinguish their varying regulatory strengths. Moreover, we also recognize that even notionally mandatory policies can vary in their strength as noted in our distinction between laws which do and do not establish requirements for compliance and penalties for non-compliance. We illustrate this distinction in Chapters 3 and 4. Here we find that public policy which takes the forms of endorsement, facilitation, and/or partnering does not 'substitute' for mandatory regulation but rather they are inter-related.

There are a number of limitations to the analysis conducted for addressing Research Question 1 (Moon et al., 2012; Knudsen et al., 2015). First, despite a coding handbook and various research reliability checks, decisions about how to code national CSR policies rested with the respective researchers. They made judgements about the appropriateness of the CSR label to the policies and the designation of the regulatory types. Second, it is in the nature of aggregate studies to have a start and a finish date and thus, while our data are representative of CSR policies in the respective period, they give little sense of what preceded and succeeded these. We have conducted some additional research using secondary data such as EU Commission studies, research reports, and various academic articles. Third, and relatedly, the way in which our data were collected did not allow us to capture how the alternating parties in government may have used, or put into disuse, regulations initiated by their predecessors in the specified period. Fourth, the Knudsen et al. (2015) data analysis did not include CSR policies of the EU; however, in this chapter we integrate discussions of the EU's CSR regulation. Finally, this sort of analysis does not allow us to capture the interactions of governmental regulation with other sources of regulation of CSR. However, analysis of these sorts of interactions forms the core purpose of Chapters 5–6.

Government Policies to Support CSR Directly and Indirectly: Case Study Analysis

We now set out the research questions, which apply to public policies that support CSR directly and indirectly, and the qualitative research methods (case studies) we deploy. To recap, public policies that support CSR directly are those by which governments address one or more forms of regulation directly to a CSR initiative, be it at the initiative's inception or to its ongoing operations. Public policies that support CSR indirectly are those by which governments address the same issue to which CSR initiatives are directed, by affecting the regulatory context for CSR. In so doing, indirect public policies contribute to the effect of the CSR efforts to resolve the issue in question. Our chosen cases of indirect CSR regulation all reveal cognizance among the government regulators about the respective CSR initiatives' aims, achievements, and shortcomings.

Research Question (2) What Roles Do Public Polices Play in Support of CSR Directly: At the Inception of CSR Initiatives or in Contributing to Their Operations?

We operationalize our interest in the roles that government policy plays in shaping CSR initiatives by examining, when, in the development of CSR initiatives, governments bring their resources. First, we distinguish two stages at which governments may support CSR initiatives: at their inception and during their operations. Do governments play a role in supporting direct CSR at the inception of CSR initiatives or in contributing to their subsequent operations? In our case studies we therefore identify the forms of regulation deployed in each of these. Second, in the case of government policy for the operationalization of CSR initiatives, we distinguish ongoing, or *continuing*, support from occasional, one-off or *periodic* support. The continuing support would take the form of some long-term commitment, and the periodic support would be in the form of supplementation of CSR, usually for a special task or purpose. As we seek to reinterpret the role of government in shaping CSR we highlight the forms of government policy deployed to support CSR either at the inception of initiatives or in the support of continuing operations.

Research Question (3) Why Do Governments Make Public Policies to Support CSR?

As noted earlier, the analysis of the circumstances of government policy for international CSR is itself rather exploratory. It is our intention that our findings will inform the framing of subsequent research into these circumstances. We investigate the significance of broader policy objectives and commitments of respective governments for the policies for CSR. We also review the pressures acting upon the respective governments, be they in the nature of problems or in the political pressures from society and organized interests, or business, labour, or civil society. We investigate these questions in Chapters 4–6.

Research Question (4) What Are the Interactions between Different Sorts of Public Policy to Support CSR?

Our fourth research question explores the relationships between different sorts of policy for CSR. In particular, we focus, first, on the interactions of policies across different geo-political spheres, domestic and international. This arises from the problematic jurisdictional context of international problems for national governments and the significance of globalization for CSR noted earlier in this chapter. But in this context, our interest is in identifying how governments can obviate their jurisdictional constraints precisely to engage with CSR in its international context. Chapter 4 includes investigation of how the ostensibly domestic Danish Non-financial Reporting Act has extended to cover the international activities of Danish companies required to report under the Act. In Chapters 5 and 6 we also examine the ways in which international CSR initiatives feed back into domestic public policy.

Second, we focus on the relationships between policies for CSR which are direct and those that are indirect in Chapters 5 and 6 (Table 2.3 and Figure 2.1). The question here is how do these policies for CSR relate to one another? It could be that they are enacted in complete isolation of one another or that they are mutually reinforc-ing, or complementary to one another. Moreover we are interested here in how these types of policies also interact with the CSR initia-tives themselves. Put most simply, are these parallel types of business policy or do they together constitute a regulatory complex for business responsibility?

This investigation of different regulatory relationships is novel in the CSR literature, where government tends to be treated as a given, apart from the distinctions between different forms of CSR regulation addressed in our first research question (Fox et al., 2002; Gond et al., 2011; Knudsen et al., 2015). However, in the political science, law, and public policy literatures, these questions are more prevalent.

Our research questions are set out in Table 2.6, which distinguishes whether the questions concern policies supporting CSR directly or indirectly, and the chapters of the book in which these questions are addressed.

In addressing these research questions, we deploy a range of related research sources. First, we use the official records and documents of national governments and the European Union, including legislative debates, decisions (in the forms of bills and acts), and governmen-tal publications, including regulations and reports. Second, we refer to publications of international governmental organizations, such as the OECD, the United Nations, and the World Bank. Third, we use publications of other key CSR actors, including CSR organizations themselves, businesses, and non-government organizations. Fourth, we draw upon the extant secondary literature on our selected cases. These include journal articles and monographs in business, manage-ment, and the sciences. Fifth, we include reference to media coverage of the selected CSR initiatives and related issues. Finally, we draw on insights from selected interviews with key actors.

These sources were identified on the basis of bibliographic and internet searches. Likewise the records of these analyses were simply kept in the form of notes rather than in content analysis-type cod-ing frames. Taken together the evidence of these different sources was interpreted according to our authorial judgement.

Prior to examining these core cases for our study, we prepare the ground in Chapter 3 by investigating the general background of gov-ernment policies for CSR in European countries. Chapter 4 builds on this to provide an account of the development of domestic CSR

Table 2.6 *Research Questions Concerning Government Policies for CSR Directly and Indirectly*

Research questions	Types of CSR policies studied	
	Policies for CSR directly	Policies for CSR indirectly
1. **How do government policies support CSR: through endorsement, facilitation, partnership, or mandate?**	In Europe (Chapter 3) In Danish CSR reporting (Chapter 4) In ethical trade (Chapter 5) In transparency in the extractives sector (Chapter 6)	In ethical trade (Chapter 5) In transparency in the extractives sector (Chapter 6)
2. **What roles do government policies play in supporting CSR *directly*: as initiators or contributors to operations?**	In Danish CSR reporting (Chapter 4) In ethical trade (Chapter 5) In transparency in the extractives sector (Chapter 6)	
3. **Why do governments make policies for CSR?**	In Danish CSR reporting (Chapter 4) In ethical trade (Chapter 5) In transparency in the extractives sector (Chapter 6)	In ethical trade (Chapter 5) In transparency in the extractives sector (Chapter 6)
4. **What are the interactions between different sorts of government policies for CSR?** a) **Between domestic and international policies for CSR?** b) **Between direct and indirect public policies for CSR?**	In ethical trade (Chapter 5) In transparency in the extractives sector (Chapter 6)	In ethical trade (Chapter 5) In transparency in the extractives sector (Chapter 6)

regulation for non-financial reporting, and particularly on the use of mandates for CSR policy, and of how domestic CSR policies can have international effects. In Chapters 5 and 6 we turn to more manifest international agendas and examine the roles of national government policies in the selected international regulatory contexts of CSR, respectively regarding ethical trade and transparency in the extractive sector.

3 | Government and Corporate Social Responsibility: From Domestic to International Spheres

This chapter presents an overview of public policies for CSR in Europe. It draws upon previous collaborative work, which analysed European governments' policies for CSR for the period 2000–2011 (Knudsen et al., 2015) as well as upon a wider field of primary and secondary data. As the findings of the analysis of government policies for CSR contained in this earlier work motivated us to further consider the interactions of government and other actors in CSR, and the role of government public policies for international CSR, this chapter provides a fitting start to the empirical journey of the book.

The purpose of this chapter is to contextualize the questions that underpin the book (Table 2.6). Thus we first present our findings on the issue areas to which governments develop policies for CSR directly. The issues to which CSR is addressed have been a key point of comparative and temporal analysis of CSR (Chapple and Moon, 2005; Knudsen and Brown, 2014; Moon et al., 2017), as a well as a point of comparison in analysis of government and CSR (e.g. Albareda et al., 2007, 2008; Steurer, 2010). We provide a panorama of policies in twenty-two European countries over twelve years, and in so doing we demonstrate the significance of government policies for international CSR, the focus of Chapters 4–6.

In that light, we then address our book's first research question: *how do government policies support CSR: through endorsement, facilitating, partnership, or mandate?*

We investigate the forms of policy that these governments deploy for CSR directly comparing them according to their capacity to secure compliance, in this case of businesses. We therefore compare policies with 'weaker' capacity to secure compliance (i.e. endorsement); 'medium' capacity to secure compliance (i.e. facilitation, partnership); or 'stronger' capacity to secure compliance (i.e. mandate) and consider their overall balance (Table 2.5). We will also discuss the combined findings concerning CSR issues addressed and forms of public policy deployed in order to distinguish overall government approaches, ranging from 'selective support for CSR' to 'systemic institutionalization of CSR'.

In our discussion of these findings we also make observations about, first, whether the patterns for CSR issues and modes of public policies are broadly consistent across Europe or whether there are comparative configurations of CSR public policy. In other words we are interested in whether there is uniformity in the choice of issues to which public policies for CSR are directed, and in the selection of regulatory forms to that end, or whether certain types of political systems use distinctive blends of regulatory types. Second, we will discuss the relationships found between the spread of issues addressed by government policies for CSR and the forms of public policies deployed thereby. The findings of these analyses are brought together to provide an overall review of government policies for CSR in Europe in order to introduce the case studies that will be presented in the subsequent chapters.

The chapter opens with an introduction to European governments and CSR. Here we provide a brief introduction to European governments and to the research findings to date on the policies of national governments and the European Union on CSR.

European Governments and CSR: An Introduction

The main focus is upon national governments that are member states of the European Union,[1] thus excluding Norway and Switzerland. We do not include some very small EU members (e.g. Malta, the Baltic states). National governments are conventionally defined as having the monopoly of legitimate power within a given territory. This applies most obviously to unitary governmental systems. Our analysis also includes federal governmental systems (i.e. Austria, Germany) whose national governments share some authority with their constituent parts, known as 'Länder' (and in other systems as states, provinces, or cantons) and other systems in which there are shared legislative, executive, and judicial powers between national and sub-national authorities (e.g. the UK). However, we only include the CSR policies of their national governments. The national governments of the EU all constitute democracies and relatively 'developed' economies.

Notwithstanding these common features of the governments studied in this chapter, there are important differences among them. Most obviously, one group, the former East European countries, which had been dominated by the USSR until 1989, only recently joined the democratic capitalist camp, and the EU in particular (most did so in 2004 and Bulgaria and Romania in 2007). Greece, Portugal, and Spain ended their respective dictatorships only in the previous decade and joined the EU in 1981 (Greece) and 1986 (the Iberian countries).

Second, there are divisions within the longer-standing, democratic capitalist systems and these have in part been distinguished according to their political cultures and institutions, and their systems of economic governance, as well as geography. Accordingly, distinctions among 'national business systems' (Whitley, 1999) varieties of capitalism (Hall and Soskice, 2001), and 'diversity of capitalism' (Amable, 2003) have been used to group countries into the following types: 'Anglo-American' (comprising Ireland, UK); 'social-democratic/ Scandinavian' (e.g. comprising Denmark, Finland, Sweden); 'continental/neo-corporatist' (comprising Austria, Belgium, France, Germany, Luxembourg, the Netherlands); and 'Mediterranean' (comprising Greece, Italy, Portugal, Spain). We will reflect on whether and how government public policies for CSR reflect such country types.

We also discuss policies for CSR initiated by the institutions of the EU. These did not feature in Knudsen et al. (2015), but they do feature in Moon et al. (2012) on which we draw (see also Kinderman, 2013). This EU focus may seem counter-intuitive, as the EU is manifestly not a nation state – the focus of our argument. We readily concede that the EU is not a nation state but note that it shares with nation states features which are not shared by international governmental organizations (e.g. the United Nations, the International Labor Organization (ILO), the World Bank, the World Trade Organization (WTO)), nor by MSIs (e.g. the Marine Stewardship Council and the Global Reporting Initiative). In particular, the EU has defined powers with respect to particular territory, and these powers combine democratic, executive, and judicial features. As a result it is able to bring to bear the sorts of resources that we associate with government, in Rose's (1984) terms, 'laws, organization, budget' or in Hood's (1986) terms, 'advice, treasure, authority, organization'. Accordingly, the EU's ability to endorse, facilitate, partner, or mandate CSR is broadly comparable with that of national governments and quite distinct from the resources of other transnational governance entities such as international organizations or MSIs.

The literature on the subject of European government public policies for CSR to date is rather limited. Only a few reports and papers claim any EU-wide coverage, and there is a certain amount of selectivity in the choice of and attention to countries (see Alberada et al., 2007; Jackson and Bartosch, 2016; Knopf et al., 2010). Relatively few papers contain six or more countries, two of which were almost exclusively Western European (Rivera-Lirio and Muñoz-Torres, 2010; Steurer, 2010) and one of which was focused entirely on Central and Eastern European countries (Braendle and Noll, 2006). A few focused on two to four countries (Albareda et al., 2007 – Italy and UK; Albareda et al., 2008 – Italy, UK, and Norway; Midttun et al., 2015 – Denmark, Finland, Norway, Sweden). The remaining studies usually address only one country. Of those that addressed one country, twelve focused on the UK (including one which also compared the UK with China – Chambers, 2003); three on Spain; two on Germany and France; and one each on Austria, Italy, Slovakia, and Sweden. (This summary draws upon Knudsen et al., 2015: 82–83 and Moon et al., 2012: 13.) The focus on the UK may reflect the comparative accessibility of English-language sources for researchers from a variety of countries, although it is also consistent with the view that the UK government has been one of the leaders in public policies for CSR (Aaronson, 2002; Knopf et al., 2010; Vogel, 2005). There has not been a vast coverage of CSR policies from the EU other than from the European Commission itself (but see Fairbrass, 2011; Kinderman, 2013).

We now turn to our analysis of European national government policies for CSR in 2000–2011, looking first at the CSR issues to which CSR public policies are directed.

The Issues for Public Policies for CSR: From Domestic to International Spheres

In order to investigate a preliminary research question (i.e. prior to the four research questions that unite our whole study) concerning the issues addressed by public policies for CSR directly, we identify the ministerial departments and portfolios attributed responsibility for these CSR policies.

Thus we identified which ministerial departments of government or which ministerial portfolios (i.e. responsibilities officially attached to ministers serving in these departments) were assigned responsibility for CSR policies in each of the European systems in our study. This makes sense because in parliamentary systems government ministries are headed by ministers who receive a commission consisting of constitutional authority and who are responsible to their parliaments for these areas of policy. The identification of a ministry with a policy area, in our case CSR, enables us to establish the broad issue area to which CSR policies are directed. This contrasts with other indicators of government policy (e.g. legal, fiscal, public employment), which tend to be individually more skewed (e.g. a legal indicator may take little account of fiscal or public employment 'effort'). So, in sum, the specific CSR responsibilities that have been assigned to ministries and ministers provide an indicator of the broad issue area to which the government intends to direct its public policies for CSR. This method is discussed further in Knudsen et al. (2015).

Table 3.1 presents our findings. Although it does not present a chronological account of the spread of CSR policies across issue areas, our discussion will introduce some temporal character to the analysis with the support of secondary literature.

Table 3.1 indicates that in many countries there have been several ministries responsible for CSR. This is explained both by CSR responsibility being spread among different ministries at the same time, and by governments that have moved responsibility for CSR among ministries. Usually governments have assigned a CSR portfolio to a minister alongside other responsibilities. However, in some cases, governments have even assigned a dedicated CSR portfolio to a minister (e.g. Belgium, France, Poland, UK). In other cases, governments assigned a single ministry for a CSR-coordinating role (signaled in bold in Table 3.1).

In almost every European country CSR has been assigned to social and employment ministries and, moreover, these are usually the ministries to which CSR was originally assigned, including before our own analysis started. This was characteristically in the context of mass employment (e.g. the UK in the 1980s – Moon, 2005; Denmark in the 1990s – Morsing, 2005). However, there has been a subsequent widening of the range of domestic problems to which governments deploy CSR. This is signaled by the frequency of CSR being attached

Table 3.1 *Issue Areas of European Government Public Policies for CSR 2000–2011**

Ministry and Country	Social/ Employment	Education	Internal	Environment	Economic/ Trade	Energy	Treasury	Foreign affairs	International development	CSR
Austria	X			X	X					X
Belgium	X				X					
Bulgaria	⊗									X
Czech Republic				⊗		⊗				
Denmark	X	X		X	⊗	X		X		
Finland	⊗			X	X				X	
France	X			X	⊗			X		
Germany	⊗	X	X	X	X			X		
Greece	X		X	X						
Hungary	X			X		X				
Ireland	⊗			⊗		X		X		
Italy	⊗			X	X		X			
Luxembourg	X									
Netherlands				X	⊗		X			X
Poland	X			X	X					

60

Country						
Portugal	⊗				X	
Romania	X	X		X		X
Slovakia	X			X		
Slovenia	⊗	X		X		
Spain	X					
Sweden	X	⊗		X	X	X
UK	X	X	X	X	X	X

*As indicated by ministerial responsibilities. Ministries responsible for most government CSR policies are in bold and encircled. There were other ministries assigned CSR responsibilities which we have not coded:

Germany: The Federal Ministry for Family Affairs, Senior Citizens, Women and Youth is involved in training initiatives related to diversity and equality.

Netherland: The Ministry of Justice and of Transport, Public Works, and Water Management are involved in CSR-related policies.

Romania: The Ministry for Tourism is responsible for a tourism sustainable development project.

(*Source:* Knudsen et al., 2015: 91).

to environmental and then to economic ministries. By 2011, about two-thirds of national governments had Social and Employment, Environmental and Economic ministries (including Trade and Industry) with some CSR responsibility.

Most significantly from the point of view of our core interest in government public policies for CSR beyond their borders, Table 3.1 also indicates that several European governments (i.e. Denmark, France, Germany, Ireland, Italy, Sweden, and the UK) extended the reach of their public policies for CSR to ministries or ministerial portfolios for international matters (i.e. Foreign Affairs, International Development). We closely examine a case of how government policies for domestic CSR can extend to international CSR in Chapter 4, and cases of government policies precisely intended for international CSR in Chapters 5 and 6.

So our analysis reveals that governments direct their regulatory effort to a wide range of CSR issue areas – which are also public policy areas – from social, through environmental and economic, to international. Our conclusion here is that public policies for CSR are not simply a niche activity. Moreover, CSR is even assigned as part of a formal ministerial responsibility, and the portfolios we have identified with this CSR responsibility are widely spread at least in some countries.

We now turn to the question of how these CSR issues are regulated by government.

Forms of Government Public Policies to Support CSR Directly

In order to address our first main research question on how governments adopt public policies to support CSR issues we distinguished four forms of policy: endorsement, facilitation, partnership, and mandate (Table 2.5).

Our interest in the forms of public policies deployed in CSR enables us to investigate the ways in which governments approach CSR in an era of new governance. As was seen in Chapter 2, there is a weight of literature, which contends that rather than new global governance heralding the demise of national governments, in fact governments have found new ways of governing, which do not rely on their more traditional mode of authority to 'command and control' (Baldwin et al.,

2011). Our classification of public policies according to whether they reflect governments' power to endorse, facilitate, partner, or mandate (Fox et al., 2002; Knudsen et al., 2015) enables insights into how this broader regulatory mix is applied to CSR. Our analysis includes a discussion of different uses of mandate, reflecting the new ways of using 'reflexive regulation' (or 'soft' as opposed to 'hard' mandate) found in the new domestic governance literature (Ayres and Braithwaite, 1992; Teubner, 1983).

As indicated in Chapter 2 ('Analytical Framework'), we adopted the framework of Fox et al. (2002) to distinguish four types of policy to encourage CSR: 'endorsement, facilitation, partnering, and mandate' as this enables us to capture and compare different regulatory approaches.

CSR Endorsement Policies

Some of the earliest studies of CSR in Europe focused on the role that governments played in encouraging and legitimizing CSR through endorsement, particularly through speeches of high-profile government office-holders often characterized by moral injunctions for business to apply their CSR to public problems. For example, in 1981 UK secretary of state for the environment, Michael Heseltine, encouraged the Institute of Directors to address inner-city deprivation in the following terms: 'We (government) do not have the money. We do not have the expertise. We need the private sector again to play a role which, in Britain, it played more conspicuously a century ago than it does now' (Richardson, 1983: 1).

Accordingly, it was little surprise that we found that all European governments adopted *endorsement policies*. These came in a number of forms. In addition, to the simple injunction for business to take responsibility for particular issues, and to support and legitimize CSR through political rhetoric, governments invested in general information and education campaigns for CSR in particular to promote what they see as good practices. More focused forms of endorsement include websites about CSR and guidelines, and awards and labeling schemes to promote good practice.

Political rhetoric was often used in early or new phases of CSR development, including through high-profile speeches of ministers. For example, the Luxembourg minister of labour and employment,

François Biltgen, actively promoted CSR through speeches and more specifically by leveraging the Luxemburg 'tripartite model' – bringing together the diverse entities of government, labour, and corporate sectors to educate, inform, and drive support for the development of CSR within Luxemburg (European Commission, 2001). In his first address to the Labour Party conference as prime minister (1997), Tony Blair had expressed an intention to expand public–private partnerships in British schools. This call was echoed in 2003 by the minister for education, David Miliband:

> We cannot do this on our own. Education is a joint enterprise – between teachers and students but also between schools and the wider community. Business can sponsor Specialist Schools and Academies. Business can contribute to curriculum enhancement. Business can offer work placements and work experience. Business can offer mentoring and governor support. (quoted in Moon, 2005: 58)

The European Commission of the European Union has been particularly active in raising awareness about CSR, since its CSR Green paper 'Promoting a European Framework for Corporate Social Responsibility' (2001 – COM 366). The Commission formed a 'High Level Group' of Member States Representatives to share experiences, promote peer-learning systems, and develop best-practice guidelines. It subsequently set up a variety of more specialized expert groups in this vein (e.g. on CSR among Small and Medium-sized Enterprises, the Environmental Compliance Assistance Programme, the Committee on Transparency and Partnership).

To turn to the more focused forms of endorsement, in most countries government departments engage in knowledge dissemination activities. Others undertake more specialist contributions to CSR policy. For example, various German and UK ministries hosted websites related to CSR and sustainable development. In numerous countries there are policies to create national award schemes that reward companies for good social and/or environmental CSR programmes (Brown and Knudsen, 2015). The Austrian Federal Ministry for Social Security rewards the enterprise with the best equal opportunity and family-friendly policy (1999). In the UK, the annual Queen's award for enterprise includes a category for sustainable development. The Dutch Ministry of Economic Affairs operates a Transparency

Benchmark, which ranks companies' CSR reporting and publicizes the results. The European Commission sponsors a system of European Business Awards for the Environment.

Various EU member states have developed national label and logo schemes. The UK Sustainability Integrated Guidelines for Management (SIGMA) project provided a set of principles and a management framework to integrate sustainability issues into core processes and decision making. The Belgian Social Label was supported by the Ministry of Economic Affairs and overseen by the Committee for Socially Responsible Production to monitor company compliance with ILO labour standards in company supply chains. The Danish Ministry of Social Affairs sponsored a Social Index between 2000 and 2011. The Index provides a framework to score a company on employment-related issues, which can be undertaken by employees and management collaboratively. The EU Commission introduced directives on Eco-Design and Eco-Labelling designed to better connect consumer and business responsibility. The EU Eco-Management and Audit Scheme is a voluntary code to assist companies wishing to improve their environmental performance and is now used by over 4,000 organizations.

Notwithstanding national differences, what is clear is that European governments make great efforts to signal to business that they have general expectations of business responsibility, and that these contributions can also have issue/sector-specific value. While it might be countered that this is merely the stuff of 'parenthood and apple-pie' or a variant of the 'usual suspicion' that CSR is merely green-wash, our view is that business, and MNCs particularly, are generally attentive to the ways in which governments present social expectations of business. This is particularly true of MNCs who often rely on governments for licensing purposes and, in some sectors, for markets to deliver public services.

CSR Facilitation Policies

The facilitating role requires a stronger role for governments than entailed in policies which endorse CSR. Facilitation policies involve providing incentives or more tangible resources to companies which develop CSR (Fox et al., 2002; Knudsen et al., 2015). These policies typically involve the introduction of public procurement policies and the subsidies and tax expenditures to companies engaging in specified types of CSR.

We found some examples of tax incentives related to social and environmental activities throughout Europe. A common instrument here is the tax relief for general corporate charitable donations in Italy, Bulgaria, Poland, and the UK, for example. However, we also found more targeted policies for CSR such as incentive schemes to stimulate diversity and equal opportunities by granting tax relief or exemptions from employers' contributions for companies that employ previously long-term unemployed workers. The Netherlands and Belgium, for example, have tax relief schemes that aim to stimulate ethical or green investment by offering relief from income and dividend taxes on such investment. Some of the schemes are specifically designed to encourage CSR in small and medium-sized enterprises (SMEs) as, for example, the Belgium 'Plus award' scheme, which helps SMEs to develop CSR policies using various CSR tools such as audit and reporting standards.

Another type of scheme is one which offers tax relief for individuals and corporations as illustrated by the UK's Community Investment Tax Relief, which awarded tax relief to those investing in accredited Community Development Finance Institutions (CDFIs), which in turn provided finance to qualifying profit-distributing enterprises, social enterprises, or community projects (Brown and Knudsen, 2015). Some governments offer tax exemptions to employees who donate to charities through payroll giving schemes. These operate in countries as diverse as Sweden, Italy, Bulgaria, Poland, and the UK (Welzel et al., 2007). The point here is that the corporations still need to decide to facilitate such transfers through their payroll systems.

In addition to the tax relief approach to facilitating CSR, governments also use their considerable buying power for this purpose through public procurement policies for CSR.[2] These cover a very wide range of CSR activities from the employment of disadvantaged workers to the ethical sourcing of products. Steurer et al. (2008) found 103 sustainable procurement initiatives in EU member states in a 2007 survey, including educational activities, government-sponsored guidelines, and awareness campaigns. We found that the majority of EU governments used such schemes. An early example was the UK government, which introduced sustainable procurement specifications in 2003. In 2005 the UK government's Sustainable Development Strategy set out goals to make the UK a leader in the EU in sustainable procurement by 2009, and a Sustainable Procurement Task Force was created to measure progress against targets set for all government departments. In 2010 a voluntary supplier charter highlighted three priority areas for the public sector to concentrate on: SMEs; apprentices/youth unemployment; and resource efficiency (Sustainable Development Commission, 2011). Another example includes the Dutch government's creation of PIANOO, which is a sustainable public procurement network.

Moreover, the EU has policies for 'Green Public Procurement' and for 'Sustainable Public Procurement' (see Directives 2004/17/EC and 2004/18/EC) which, competition law notwithstanding, enable national, regional, and local governments of member states to develop purchasing criteria to encourage supply from green and sustainable sources. The 2008 EC Communication on Green Public Procurement provides a voluntary instrument for governments to assess the extent to which these directives have been applied, in the context of a stated goal that 50 per cent of all public purchasing should be made in compliance with the criteria in these directives.

CSR Partnership Policies

The partnering CSR policy role involves collaboration with firms or business associations, in which governmental roles vary from initiator and convener, to participant. Like policies to facilitate CSR, partnering requires a greater level of governmental commitment than endorsement, though they usually also entail endorsement and facilitation. Partnership approaches assist in disseminating knowledge about CSR and sustainability issues, and in some cases this extends to playing a key role in the development of guidelines, standards, or codes.

For example, the Austrian, German, and Italian governments introduced CSR multi-stakeholder forums. The German government set up the Federal Civil Participation Network (BBE) and the Working Group on Human Rights and Business, both with obvious CSR dimensions. The Irish government established the Sustainable Development Council. The Dutch government used a partnership approach in the fishing industry (with the North Sea Foundation and the World Wildlife Fund) to advance compliance of Dutch fisheries with the Marine Stewardship Council (MSC) standard, complemented by facilitation of companies seeking MSC certification through the use of grants. Numerous EU level MSIs exist for advancing responsible business, including the European Multi Stakeholder Forum, the business-led European Alliance on CSR, and the European Food and Sustainable Consumption and Production Round Table, which is co-chaired with the UN Environment Programme (UNEP) and food supply partner firms, and whose members include consumer and other non-governmental organizations.

Illustrative of partnerships used for public policies for international CSR, the French government initiated the Forum des Amis du Pacte Mondial (i.e. French signatories to the UNGC), and the Norwegian government established KOMpakt, a Consultative Body for Human Rights and Norwegian Economic Involvement Abroad. KOMpakt's purpose is to encourage respect for human rights, by awareness-raising, and to increase dialogue, information-sharing, and mutual understanding between business and/or industry organizations; trade unions, human rights organizations and research institutes; and the public authorities. Other examples include the Swedish government's formation of the Swedish Partnership for Global Responsibility, particularly to disseminate knowledge of the OECD Guidelines for MNCs and the UNGC Principles.

CSR Mandate Policies

Policies that mandate behaviour involve the specification of some minimum standard for business performance embedded within the regulatory framework (Fox et al., 2002). Mandating involves governments taking the most definitive role in CSR through regulations and decrees. However, as noted, in order to constitute CSR policies they must relax at least one of the 'command and control' elements which together are our defining criteria for 'hard' mandate. Rather they would typically offer either a flexible framework enabling choice (including the use of markets) or a regulated framework for rewarding conformance with some relatively open-ended criteria which are flexible and open to considerable interpretation. Thus this sort of soft mandate still allows some corporate choice, or discretion, as to how to or even whether to comply.

The common form of governmental mandate for CSR is through non-financial reporting legislation. The law on the New Economic Regulation of 2001 and a further decree in 2002 detail the reporting provisions for listed companies in France to encourage companies to establish the tools to measure their social and environmental impacts. Public policies also exist in France regarding senior management reporting on financial risks. Hungary's Recommendations on Social Responsibility of 2010 made by the Economic and Social Council also include a requirement for sustainability reporting in companies which are majority-owned by the government, and similar recommendations were included in the Swedish CSR reporting regulations.

Several governments including France, Belgium, and the UK have also legislated public pension fund reporting requirements. Since 2000, all UK asset managers have to report on the extent to which social, environmental, and ethical considerations are taken into account in their investment decisions in an amendment. Since 2010 they have been required to report on either their commitment to the government's Stewardship Code (2010) or to explain why this is not appropriate to their business model. The Danish non-financial reporting requirement (Knudsen and Brown, 2015) forms a central part of our first case of government public policies for international CSR (see Chapter 4). This includes a discussion of the Danish public policy in comparison with, and in relation to, the 2013 Amendment of the EU Accounting Directive concerning non-financial reporting, which itself follows from the EU Accounts Modernisation Directives requiring listed companies to report on non-financial social and environmental indicators (2005) and to provide a corporate governance statement in their annual report (2006).

The second most common mandating theme in CSR is environmental public policies, which took a variety of forms and focuses. Most of the relevant national CSR environmental public policies have followed from the requirements of the EU Emissions Trading Scheme (2005). This form of mandate combined national and sectoral carbon plans and emission caps within markets for carbon emissions that governments regulated through licensing schemes, funding, and monitoring and reporting systems. This pattern of regulation is accordingly emulated in the member countries. This can range from a simple reporting requirement for certain emissions (e.g. Ministry of the Environment of the Czech Republic, 2008); combinations of targets, a planning requirement on government, advisory boards, specific obligations on public bodies and promotional campaigns (e.g. the Irish Climate Change Response Act, 2010); sector-specific emissions reductions agreements (e.g. the Netherlands); to targets, a trading scheme and obligations, and powers to the government (e.g. the UK Climate Change Act, 2008).

So, in summary, we have found that governments are willing and able to use their powers to mandate behaviour for companies but they tend to do so in soft ways. For example, they may create markets, which companies are well used to (e.g. carbon trading); require a report or an explanation as to the absence of a report (e.g. the Danish Non-financial Reporting law, the UK Stewardship Code); create packages of required actions, thus signaling intent (e.g. the UK Climate Act); or impose obligations and powers on corporations to act in relatively unspecified ways.

Public Policies Without Coercion

Overall, we have found that European governments have been ready to make public policies to support CSR directly. The approaches they have used have been soft, particularly through endorsement, facilitation, and partnering. Usually, these modes of public policies are also mutually reinforcing, so that facilitation also entails endorsement, and partnering usually involves endorsement and facilitation. These forms of public policies rest on the resources other than that of the unique power to mandate supported by coercion. Rather they exploit softer governing resources: the legitimacy of governments (especially endorsement); their fiscal resources (e.g. to allocate subsidies and tax expenditures; to use their power of procurement); and their organizational resources (e.g. expertise within ministries; network capacities both within their respective countries and internationally). Even the instances of policies that support CSR directly through mandate tend to do so without recourse to 'command and control'. Although the burden of adopting public policies for CSR is through non-coercive means, some of these resources are more or less unique to governments and not easily substitutable. We further elaborate this position in the four following points.

First, democratic governments possess a unique legitimacy by virtue of their having been elected and being subject to future elections. Moreover, in democracies governments are also subject to the rule of law, and individual and other actors have considerable freedoms to criticize and challenge governments without fear of punishment. As a result, the legitimacy of democratic governments does not rest on their ability to exert their monopoly of legal force. Nor does it rest on a particular set of policies. Rather it rests on an electoral compact between the government and the governed whose legitimacy is only rarely widely questioned. This means that governments possess inimitable face value legitimacy, notwithstanding variations in the particular esteem in which any one party in government is held. Moreover, in many cases, governments are regarded as acceptable intermediaries between business and labour (particularly in neo-corporatist and tripartite traditions), or between business and civil society organizations (in some of the CSR-oriented MSIs and partnerships). This legitimacy means that the ability of governments to endorse a pattern of behaviour is usually relatively potent and allows them to draw attention to the benefits of exemplary CSR approaches without having to mandate them.

Second, though we often read of the increasing financial power of MNCs, governments retain unrivaled fiscal capacity. Many of the reports that companies are bigger than governments are based on spurious comparisons of wealth. And while it is conceded that by some measures corporations appear to rival governments' financial resources (e.g. VandenDolder, 2013), the ongoing fiscal capacity of most democratic governments to tax and spend remains a singular resource. This enables governments to not just endorse best practice, but also to assist companies or associations, which are endeavouring to develop a new CSR approach or product through subsidies or tax benefits. Moreover, such is the scale of their financial resources that governments are able to adjust incentive structures and even create new markets (e.g. for green products and technologies) without having to make new rules.

Third, the organizational capacities of governments can assist the facilitation and partnership of CSR initiatives by virtue of the ability to deploy their own staff to administer CSR initiatives (e.g. in local economic development programmes – Moore et al., 1985); or coordinate partnerships (e.g. Extractive Industries Transparency Initiative – Chapter 6); or to provide expert knowledge such as through the use of embassies for the benefit of international CSR networks (e.g. in the Ethical Trading Initiative – Chapter 5). Again, while MNCs are often well endowed with organizational capacity, this rarely rivals that of modern democratic governments.

Fourth, governments have occasionally used the resource of mandate in soft ways, often to highlight best practices (e.g. social and environmental reporting) or to 'nudge' (Thaler and Sunstein, 2008) companies towards more responsible behaviour (e.g. in environmental policy). This is distinct from the command and control use of mandate to coerce behaviour, which would be definitionally incompatible with CSR policy. The soft mandate can be used to create new incentive structures for responsible business behaviour and to establish obligations upon corporations. This can include using a CSR framework to require companies to conform with other governments' reporting requirements (Chapter 4) or to report whether or not a company has CSR policies, which 'nudges' a company to consider the implications of reporting that it has none.

Together, the use of the resources of legitimacy, fiscal and organizational capacity, and the ability to regulate, however softly, add up to an inimitable array of resources for governing CSR. Although inimitable, these resources have been deployed in ways that are consistent with CSR's underlying assumption of 'discretion'. In 2014 the European Commission published an overview of national public policies on CSR in the European Union from 2011 to 2013. The report shows more examples of endorsement, facilitation and partnering, and mandate. Most important are the examples of mandatory policies. In the Netherlands companies must demonstrate a commitment to CSR when they apply for government funding. Belgium and the Czech Republic have followed France in implementing a legislative requirement for socially responsible investment for asset management companies which require them to state how they take into account sustainable development criteria in their investment and voting policies. France, Sweden, and Spain have adopted legislation to cap remuneration of senior executives in state-owned enterprises (European Commission, 2014).

We now turn to ask whether these findings hold true across Europe and, if not, how do national governments differ in their approaches? We therefore investigate whether all European governments make policies to support CSR directly in the same ways (i.e. the 'how' question for which we use 'forms of public policies' as our indicator) and whether they do so to address similar or different issues (i.e. the 'what' question for which we use ministerial responsibilities as our indicator).

A Typology of European Public Policies to Support CSR

Our findings are of marked comparative contrasts in the strength of policy deployed to support CSR directly. The countries most likely to deploy the full range of regulatory measures (i.e. endorsement, facilitation, partnership, mandate) are the Scandinavian countries – France, Germany, Italy, and the UK. The mid-range regulatory measures (facilitation and partnership) tend to feature more in Scandinavia, Northern Europe, and the UK than they do in the Mediterranean and former Communist countries. The countries, which only tended to deploy policies of endorsement, are the Mediterranean and the former Communist countries.

So there is some fit of breadth of policy application (i.e. the range of issues to which CSR is addressed) and the strength of government policy deployed for CSR among the national business systems. The Scandinavian countries, France, the UK, and Northern European countries are much more closely associated with wide deployment of different regulatory of modes, particularly facilitation, partnership, and 'soft' mandate. The Mediterranean and former Communist countries tend to be more closely associated with endorsement policies more selectively applied, particularly to social and economic issues.

Table 3.2 integrates these findings on the breadth of the policy application and strength to present a framework for government policies to support CSR. The strength of government policy ranges from endorsement to facilitation and partnership and to mandate. The breadth of policy application ranges from 'partial' (e.g. concentrated on social and economic issues') to 'broad' (e.g. also including internal affairs, environment, trade, foreign affairs, international development). At the top left of Table 3.2 there is one extreme, 'selective support' (i.e. endorsement and partial policy application). This is characterized by the Mediterranean countries minus Italy and some of the former Communist countries, notably Bulgaria and the Czech Republic. At the bottom right of Table 3.2 there is the other extreme, 'systemic institutionalization' (i.e. all forms of public policies deployed – endorsement, facilitation, partnership, and mandate – and broad policy application). This is characterized by the Scandinavian countries, Northern Europe, and the UK.

This finding is significant for our analysis in the following chapters in two ways. First, the case studies of policies for CSR directly

Table 3.2 *A Framework for Government CSR Policies*

		Breadth of policy application	
		Partial	Broad
Strength of government policy	Endorse	Selective support	Systemic support
	Facilitate Partner	Selective steering	Systemic steering
	Mandate	Selective institutionalization	Systemic institutionalization

(*Source*: Knudsen et al., 2015: 94).

that we examine in Chapters 4–6 are all centred on countries whose government policies for CSR are described as 'systemic institutionalization'. In other words, we have selected cases, which reflect involvement of national governments for which policies for CSR have become both commonplace and significant. Second, as the analysis unfolds in Chapters 5 and 6, particularly, other governments become involved in support of international CSR both directly and indirectly, and this enables some further comparison of approaches.

Discussion

We have provided a clear picture of the government policies to support CSR directly in Europe, in answer to our preliminary question about the CSR issues towards which government policies are directed. We found that the most common area is social/employment (and there are additional target issues of education and 'internal'); followed by the environment; and the economy. In addition, there are governments, which have made CSR policies in relation to foreign affairs and international development, a theme of Chapter 4 and the particular focus of Chapters 5 and 6. But not all European governments have applied CSR policies to this full range of issues (Table 3.1): some of the Mediterranean and East European policies have been mainly focused on social issues; and the full range has been applied only by seven countries, mainly from Scandinavia and Northern Europe (including the UK). So our main focus on government policies for international CSR is validated: about a third of the European countries appear to have such policies and these appear to be the countries whose policies we label 'systemic institutionalization' at the respective national level.

Turning then to our first research question concerning how governments adopt public policies that support CSR, we find that European governments deploy a range of public policy forms from endorsement to mandate. Endorsement appears to be the most frequently employed mode of policy. A narrower range of national governments employs facilitation and partnership policies. These bring greater government resources, some of which are unique, and which also tend to reflect long-term involvement of government in CSR. Mandate-type policies bring the sine qua non of national governments – the ability to legally coerce – and they have been mainly used in the field of non-financial reporting and environmental impacts. A yet narrower range of governments has used mandate policies, and these are mostly in Scandinavia and Northern Europe (including the UK).

Therefore although the phenomenon of public policies to support CSR is found across Europe, there are variations in governmental approaches, specifically in the range of issues addressed and in the forms of policy deployed. Combining our two sets of findings on the varying strength of CSR policy employed and the varying breadth of issues to which CSR is applied by governments enables us to address the question of whether there is a relationship between the types of policy instruments chosen and the types of issues to which the policies are addressed.

We can distinguish some overarching trends when we aggregate CSR policies across all countries based on our findings (summarized in Table 3.1). Social/employment issues such as CSR training and skills provision are most often addressed through endorsing (e.g. information provision, labels), while human and labour rights are often addressed through partnering-type policies (e.g. multi-stakeholder forums). Limited facilitating policies also exist for social issues through tax incentives for corporate philanthropy. Environmental issues, such as energy efficiency and climate change, are addressed in an even wider range of policy types, ranging from endorsing (e.g. information provision, labels) through to facilitating (e.g. 'green' investment schemes) and mandating (e.g. climate change public policies). Several types of policies address social and environmental issues through endorsing (e.g. awards) or facilitating (e.g. public procurement). Corporate governance issues, such as CSR reporting or bribery, are mainly addressed through mandating-type policies, although we found less evidence of this type of policy overall. Finally, policies addressing issues with a more economic focus such as Socially Responsible Investing (SRI) and fair trade tend to be addressed through partnering-type policies (fair trade) and mandating (SRI). In summary, we see social issues being addressed through policy forms that require limited government involvement, corporate governance/economic issues being addressed through policy forms requiring strong government involvement, while government involvement in environmental issues ranges broadly across policy forms.

However, there is some variation in these policies among countries. Mediterranean and former Communist country governments tend to use the weaker sorts of public policies, particularly endorsement, and they tend to confine this to a narrower set of, particularly social, issues. This confirms Albareda et al.'s (2007) description of the 'agora model' of CSR in Spain, Greece, Italy, and Portugal, which was designed to involve a broad range of stakeholders to develop a social consensus around CSR policies by means of endorsement through public debate. This may reflect the relatively weak institutional frameworks extant on which basis facilitation, partnering, and mandate might have been premised.

In contrast, the UK, Scandinavian, and Northern European countries tend to also use the stronger forms of public policy than solely endorsement, specifically facilitation and partnership, and even 'soft' mandate. Moreover, they tend to use these regulatory means for a much wider range of CSR/public policy issue areas, including international issues, than do their Southern and Eastern European counterparts. Close relationships between business, labour, and government have been the hallmark of public policy in many of these countries. The case of the UK is more surprising as it is usually categorized as neo-liberal (Kinderman, 2012), such that one would expect government to rely primarily on market mechanisms to elicit social benefits from business. Kinderman's (2012) explanation is of the mutual government and business legitimation exercises in a neo-liberal context. But former UK minister for CSR, Margaret Hodge (2006), explains the government policies for CSR in much more strategic terms in order to improve business accountability as a vehicle for social justice and for international competitiveness for companies and the UK. This signals the sort of 'systemic institutionalization' (Table 3.2) of CSR policies with wider public policies.

Our analysis is not designed to explain either the trend of government policies for CSR in general, its issue focus, its mainly soft, but variable, regulatory strength or its cross-national manifestations. We can, however, interpolate our findings with some of the secondary literature in order to consider these questions. Looking first at general explanations, Moon (2002) offered three reasons for government interest in making policies for CSR based on his analysis of government and CSR in the UK and Australia in the context of the development of 'new governance' (see Chapter 2). The first is substitution for government effort, such that CSR can take some of the burdens of government off an 'over-loaded' government. Second, he identified 'complementarity' such that CSR enhances the work of government and makes it more effective or more efficient. Third, he suggested that governments may also be engaged in a legitimation exercise, whereby through drawing on CSR – and thereby, business – governments are legitimizing themselves with companies. However, these motivations may not be mutually exclusive, and a single government CSR public policy may be animated by all three motivations. We address the question of government motivation in Chapters 4–6 when we consider 'why' governments adopted public policies for CSR.

Equally, government motivations may vary across Europe. Our sense is that the countries which we describe as fitting within the 'systematic institutionalization category' (Table 3.2, i.e. Northern Europe, Scandinavia, the UK) may be more likely to be motivated by the opportunities that CSR affords to complement public policy. This is certainly the interpretation that Midttun et al. (2015) attribute to the Norwegian and Swedish government's efforts to integrate CSR policies with their social democratic international agendas.

Finally, our analysis was not designed to assess the effectiveness of these policies for CSR. Our main emphasis has been on the development of policy processes. There is no reason to assume that all these policies were successful, even by the criteria used to justify them by governments. Moreover, policies devised for legitimation purposes may well serve those objectives but have less effect on the ostensible problems addressed. One analysis of a wide range of public policies for CSR (Welzel et al. 2007) singled out Germany, the UK, Denmark, Sweden, and France as having followed 'good policy options'. Moreover, it names Denmark's National Action Plan for Corporate Social Responsibility and Germany's Public Private Partnership

Program as innovative examples of public policies for CSR. This gives a particular justification for our case study in Chapter 4 of the Danish National Action Plan, and the CSR reporting requirement, in particular, to which we now turn.

Notes

1 Austria, Belgium, Bulgaria, Czech Republic, Denmark, Finland, France, Germany, Greece, Hungary, Ireland, Italy, Luxembourg, the Netherlands, Poland, Portugal, Romania, Slovakia, Slovenia, Spain, Sweden, and the UK.
2 Please note that public procurement policies were coded as 'endorsement' public policies in Moon et al. (2012). Here, and in Knudsen et al. (2015), we code them as 'facilitation' as on reflection we see these policies, like subsidies, as re-shaping markets, and thus better described as 'facilitation' rather than endorsement alone.

4 | Government and Non-financial Reporting: Public Policy in Denmark

In contrast to the panoramic view of European government policies to support CSR directly (Chapter 3) our focus in Chapter 4 is on the ways in which these policies develop. We explore this issue through the means of an extended case study of Danish policies for non-financial reporting. We are particularly interested in the dynamics of government policymaking for CSR. This case illustrates that public policymaking can take the form of succession from one policy to another rather than of 'innovation' and 'termination' or at the other extreme, of simple policy 'maintenance' (Hogwood and Peters, 1982; Pierson, 2000).

In this chapter we examine the development of government policy for CSR in Denmark. We focus on government policies that address CSR issues *directly* (in Chapters 5 and 6 we shall examine government policies for CSR that address CSR both directly and indirectly). While in Chapters 5 and 6 we consider as examples of direct public policy for CSR the support for specific CSR organizations, such as the ETI and the EITI, here we consider the adoption of a mandatory non-financial reporting regulation (also known as CSR or environmental, social, and governance reporting). Furthermore, in contrast to the adoption of the ETI and the EITI that are CSR initiatives, which are mediated by other actors, the non-financial reporting rule is unmediated by other actors. The purpose of the chapter is to show the political process that led the Danish government to regulate CSR directly in the form of mandatory non-financial reporting. In so doing we highlight two key issues: (1) Public policies for CSR are dynamic and their regulatory form changes over time such as from soft forms of public policies to mandatory regulation; (2) The focus of public policies for CSR changes over time such as from domestic to international CSR. We argue that the development of public CSR policy in Denmark is mostly a story of policy succession whereby the Danish government has sought to bring in business as a key contributor to solving social problems traditionally handled by the state exclusively although the CSR priorities of the Danish government have substantially altered over time.

We select this case for three main reasons. First, after the UK (Moon, 2005), Denmark was, in the early 1990s, one of the first European countries where business adopted policies that were explicitly referred to as CSR (Matten and Moon, 2008). Significantly from the perspective of our study, these policies were led by the government (Morsing, 2005; Vallentin, 2013) eager to directly deploy CSR for its own public policy objectives concerning countering unemployment. Since then Denmark has been a front-runner country when it comes to public policies for CSR (Buhmann, 2010; Cooper, 2009; Knudsen and Brown, 2014; Midttun et al., 2012; Vallentin, 2013) and the Danish government's approach to regulating CSR can be characterized as 'systemic institutionalization' because of a systemic spread of CSR policies that are relevant to government policies broadly, and that are intended to advance CSR across a wide range of issue areas (Knudsen et al., 2015; see also Chapter 3). Second, the theme of non-financial reporting is a key one in the development of CSR worldwide and brings with it expectations of accountability both to companies' stakeholders and to societies in general. It incorporates a wide range of social, environmental, and governance themes, and therefore cuts across the full range of issues that companies address through CSR, and of the modes by which they do this. Third, through the case study methodology we deploy, we are able to examine a key theme for our study, the relationship between what are ostensibly domestic government policies for CSR, and their implications for international CSR.

The research questions that we address in this chapter are adapted from the ones that we set out in Chapter 2 (see Table 2.6 excluding Research Question 4b concerning the interactions of direct and indirect policies for CSR, which we address in Chapters 5 and 6):

1. *How does Danish government policy support non-financial reporting: through endorsement, facilitation, partnership, or mandate; and how do these forms of public policies interact?*
2. *What roles do government policies play in supporting non-financial reporting directly: as an initiator or as a contributor to operations?*
3. *Why does the government make policies for non-financial reporting?*

4. *What are the interactions between different sorts of policies for CSR?*
   a. *Between domestic and international policies for CSR?*

We also consider the adoption of non-financial reporting in the European Union (EU) and explore its implications for the Danish non-financial reporting legislation in addressing Research Question 4a on the relationships between domestic and international regulation for CSR.

But before we address these questions we first provide some background on non-financial reporting and why and how it emerged as a CSR issue. Second, we examine a range of public policies in other countries for non-financial reporting in order to establish an international context for the analysis of Danish non-financial reporting.

Non-financial Reporting as a CSR Issue – Demand for Greater Business Accountability

Corporations face increasing criticism for imposing social and environmental costs on the communities where they operate. As a result, societal demands have arisen for greater 'transparency of corporate social and environmental impact, together with delivering enhanced levels of accountability to organizational stakeholders' (Owen and O'Dwyer, 2008: 385). The first companies to face such demands and to engage in non-financial reporting were very large companies in 'exposed' sectors such as extractives, consumer brands, and pharmaceuticals (Owen and O'Dwyer, 2008; Spar and LaMure, 2003). Non-financial reporting began with a focus on environmental issues. As Owen and O'Dwyer (2008) point out, the growth of environmental reporting and the development of its practices followed increasingly critical scrutiny of corporations following several major environmental catastrophes including Bhopal (the 1984 gas leak in India that is considered the world's worst industrial disaster), the Sandoz Rhine spill (a 1986 fire at the Sandoz agrochemical storehouse in Switzerland that resulted in toxic agrochemicals being released into the Rhine river), and Exxon Valdez (an oil tanker that in 1989 struck Bligh Reef in Prince William's Sound, which resulted in a massive oil spill on the south coast of Alaska).

Environmental reporting came to involve issues such 'as an environmental policy statement, disclosure of quantified targets; detailed performance and compliance data; a description of the environmental management systems in place' (Owen and O'Dwyer, 2008: 389). In the 1990s, business – and in particular large international corporations – also came under increasing scrutiny for their social impact. A wide range of stakeholders including consumers, civil society organizations, and the media demanded that corporations should be more accountable about the social, environmental, and governance impacts of their business activities (Herzig and Kühn, 2017; Iannonou and Serafeim, 2014; Vogel, 2008). For example, many firms operating in or sourcing from developing countries were increasingly held responsible for a range of issues such as labour rights and human rights that were previously seen as outside a firm's sphere of influence (Vogel, 2008). Environmental reporting has been expanded to also include social dimensions (along with economic factors) in so-called triple bottom-line reporting (Elkington, 1997). The social dimensions in reporting range from overviews of community programmes, to diversity and training initiatives, to labour and human rights issues in a company's global supply chains (Global Reporting Initiative, 2016a). In addition to environmental and social issues, governance issues have also come to be included in non-financial reporting such as information about the ability of common stockholders to vote on important issues, criteria for board member selection, and remuneration of the top management team (Global Reporting Initiative, 2016a).

Investor pressure for CSR has contributed to the growth of non-financial reporting. According to Dyck et al. (2015), investors with over $59 trillion in assets under management around the world have pledged to follow the UN Principles for Responsible Investment (PRI), requiring, among other things, that they incorporate environmental, social, and governance issues into their investment analysis and decision making. An important premise behind the push for environmental and social issues to be integrated into the investing process is that these issues may pose substantial risks to firms and the wider communities in which they engage. Such risks may cause institutional investors, as owners of a large fraction of major corporations, to compel managers to reduce CSR risks. The Danish government, in addition to mandating large firms to undertake non-financial reporting, has also mandated institutional investors to engage in socially responsible investing (Danish Government, 2008).

Before turning to the role of government policies for non-financial reporting, we highlight that with the rise in non-financial reporting various guidelines have emerged from multi-stakeholder initiatives (MSI) or from international government organizations. Key international reporting principles or guidelines include MSIs such as the Global Reporting Initiative (GRI), the UNGC, and the UN guiding principles on business and human rights. UNGC is the world's largest corporate sustainability initiative with more than 9,000 businesses and a further 4,000 other societal actors from more than 140 countries (United Nations Global Compact, 2016). Furthermore, the Organisation for Economic Co-operation and Development's (OECD) guidelines for multinational enterprises constitute recommendations by OECD governments to enterprises that operate in or from the territories of the forty-four countries that adhere to the guidelines. Finally, in 2010 the International Organization for Standardization (IOS) launched the ISO 26000 – an international standard for organizations' social responsibility.

A 2013 KPMG International Survey of Corporate Responsibility Reporting found that sustainability reporting has become a mainstream activity, with almost three-quarters of the 4,100 companies surveyed producing CSR reports, and 78 per cent of these referring to the GRI guidelines (KPMG, 2013: 11). The KPMG survey also found that 93 per cent of the world's largest 250 companies issue a CSR report, of which 82 per cent refer to the GRI guidelines (GRI, 2013; KPMG, 2013: 11). The GRI was founded in Boston in 1997 and is today headquartered in Amsterdam. The roots of the GRI lie in the UN non-profit organizations such as the Coalition for Environmentally Responsible Economies (CERES) and the Tellus Institute, with the support of the UNEP in 1997. Although the GRI is independent, it collaborates with UNEP and the UNGC. The GRI guidelines were most recently revised in May 2013 when G4, the fourth generation of the guidelines, was launched. The launch marked the culmination of two years of stakeholder consultation and dialogue with hundreds of experts from across the world from a wide variety of sectors, including companies, civil society, labour organizations, academia, and finance (GRI, 2016b). The G4 Framework includes references to other recognized reporting frameworks and is designed as a consolidated framework for reporting performance against different codes and norms such as the OECD guidelines for multinational enterprises and the UNGC principles. The GRI also includes specific sector reports that include information about sector-specific sustainability challenges.

While much of this growing trend in reporting is voluntary, KPMG concludes that the introduction of reporting requirements by governments and stock exchanges has also played an important role in driving corporate transparency and accountability. In 2014 Ioannou and Serafeim found that 'While less than 100 firms reported such information twenty years ago, by 2013 more than 6,000 companies around the world were issuing sustainability reports' (2014: 1). According to KPMG, government requirements have resulted in almost 100 per cent reporting rates in countries such as Denmark as well as in France and South Africa (KPMG, 2013). In short, company reporting on non-financial activities has become so widespread that according to the KPMG, 'To report or not to report? The debate is over' (KPMG, 2013: 10).

Public Policies for Non-financial Reporting in an International Context

We turn next to public policies for non-financial reporting. While this chapter focuses on Denmark, we highlight four aspects of government involvement in non-financial reporting that apply more generally: first, public policies for sustainability reporting are not a new phenomenon. For example, since 1977 French companies with more than 300 employees have been required to file a 'bilan social' (a social balance sheet), reporting on 134 labour-related or human resource management indicators. In the United States, while there is little public policy on sustainability reporting, apart from rules regarding hazardous waste and toxic chemicals disclosure, the New York Stock Exchange requires listed companies to publish a code of business conduct and ethics. In China the state-owned Assets Supervision and Administration Commission issued a directive in January 2008 encouraging state-owned companies to report on responsible business activities. In 2012 the Securities and Exchange Board of India (SEBI) issued a circular on Business Responsibility Reports, which requires the hundred largest listed companies by market capitalization to report annually on their social responsibility (Krichewsky, 2014).

Malaysia and South Africa have also adopted non-financial reporting requirements (Ioannou and Serafeim, 2014).

Second, countries differ regarding whether it is governments or stock exchanges that issue non-financial reporting requirements. In Europe in particular, governments have been the main drivers of non-financial reporting whereas outside Europe, stock exchanges have played a key role in fostering CSR reporting (Initiative for Responsible Investment, the Hauser Institute for Civil Society, Kennedy School of Government, Harvard University, 2014). Stock exchanges communicate with investors about listed firms. In contrast, governments communicate with the broader society, and government non-financial regulation often covers a wider range of companies (such as public enterprises, cooperatives, or smaller firms).

Third, extensive variation exists regarding the content of public policies and the degree of specificity of regulatory requirements. For example, in 2001 France became the first country in Europe to enact a comprehensive corporate non-financial reporting requirement. Article 116 of the French New Economic Regulations required publicly listed companies to include information on forty different environmental, social, and governance indicators in their annual reports. Since 2008 Swedish state-owned companies have also been required to publish a sustainability report following the GRI guidelines (Van Wensen et al., 2011).

Finally, the shift from domestic to international CSR has happened across most countries. The UK government, known as a frontrunner country for government involvement in CSR (Brown and Knudsen, 2015), has adopted a range of domestic as well as international CSR initiatives. For example, in 2005 the government focused on reducing waste within the UK grocery sector, and in 2013 the focus was on supporting the implementation of the UN Guiding Principles for Human Rights as they apply to the actions of British firms abroad. In 2005, the UK government passed a statute requiring approximately 1,300 publicly listed companies on the main board of the London Stock Exchange to prepare an annual Operating and Financial Review and Directors Report (OFR) which included reporting on the social and environmental impact of the business (this paragraph on non-financial reporting relies on Daniel Kinderman (2016, unpublished). The OFR, however, was withheld by the then chancellor Gordon Brown in November 2005 in order to reduce administrative costs on business. The 2006 Companies Act specifies directors' duties and the non-financial reporting requirements for companies listed on the main board of the London Stock Exchange. Section 172 lays out directors' duties, which include that they must have regard to their impacts on employees, the community, and the environment, while Section 417 requires a Business Review in which directors specify how they have addressed their duties. In 2013 the Business Review was replaced by a Strategic Report that highlights materiality and also required listed companies to report on gender diversity, human rights, and green-house gas emissions.

Non-financial Reporting in Denmark

Mandatory non-financial reporting requirements aimed at improving the CSR performance of corporations constitute an important exam-ple of how governments mandate CSR activities in their home country firms' activities abroad through promoting certain CSR behaviours in their subsidiaries and supplier companies. However, the Danish government policies for CSR did not start out with a focus on the international CSR activities of Danish firms. We begin this section by highlighting that the Danish government's CSR initiatives start-ing in the 1990s initially addressed social and employment policies in Denmark. Long-term unemployment had remained a problem for many years despite the adoption of a wide range of public initia-tives to assist with skill upgrading, training programmes, and so on (Bredgaard, 2004). The Danish government was therefore eager to try new types of solutions and sought to involve business as a key con-tributor to reducing long-term unemployment (Knudsen and Brown, 2014; Vallentin, 2013). As we shall see, the Danish government has continued to involve business in developing new solutions to social problems as the government's CSR agenda shifted from domestic social and employment programmes and towards the adoption of public policies for non-financial reporting, as well as from a domestic to an international focus.

Foundations of Government Policy for CSR

The Danish government introduced CSR policies in 1994, when the Minister of Social Affairs Karen Jespersen from the Social Democratic

Party launched the campaign 'It concerns us all'. The campaign identified social responsibility as domestic social inclusion (Ministry of Social Affairs, 2001). The campaign for a more socially inclusive labour market suggested that employers had a social responsibility to ensure that workers were not simply laid off if they suffered from work-related physical or psychological problems. Instead employers should seek to organize work in such a way that workers could continue to be employed. Karen Jespersen's 'Inclusiveness Regime' (Vallentin, 2013) also encouraged companies to recruit people with other problems than unemployment (Bredgaard, 2004; Knudsen and Brown, 2015). It had become clear that the public sector had failed to prevent unemployment and social exclusion for people with other problems than unemployment, and Jespersen therefore wanted to involve the private sector in finding new socially inclusive solutions. The so-called Inclusiveness Regime came into being under the Social Democratic government headed by Poul Nyrup Rasmussen. In 2003 the ministerial responsibility for CSR shifted to the Ministry for Employment to highlight the ministry's growing focus on developing regular employment opportunities for people with other problems than unemployment (Knudsen and Brown, 2015).

We next explore the shift in public policy emphasis from domestic social and employment initiatives to a trade and an international CSR agenda. We focus in particular on the government's development of public policies for non-financial reporting which mainly addresses international CSR challenges. According to Vallentin (2013), the Social Inclusiveness regime was replaced by an (international) Competitiveness Regime under the Liberal Conservative government headed by Prime Minister Anders Fogh Rasmussen who came to power in 2001 and who won second and third terms in 2005 and 2007. However, the political rule change was not the only driver of the change in government policies. The shift from domestic social and employment inclusion to an international CSR agenda was one that took place across a wide range of European countries as well as at the EU level driven by factors such as globalization pressures and growing media attention (Knudsen et al., 2015). In 2007 the ministerial responsibility for CSR shifted once again and this time to the Ministry of Economic and Business Affairs (in 2011 the ministry was renamed the Ministry of Business and Growth following the coming to power of Helle Thorning-Schmidt's Social Democratic coalition government together with the Social Liberal Party and the Socialist Peoples' Party). This shift signalled that CSR made a gradual but radical transition from social and labour market policy to economic policy whereby international competitiveness became the new mantra in the governmental approach to CSR (Knudsen and Brown, 2015; Morsing et al., 2007; Vallentin, 2013).

The 'Action Plans for Corporate Social Responsibility'

The Danish government's 'Action Plan for Corporate Social Responsibility' published in May 2008 subscribes to the notion of strategic CSR as conceptualized by Porter and Kramer (2006), who argue that value creation should be the guiding principle in CSR (Danish Government, 2008). Kramer indeed provided consultancy services to the Danish government when it was developing a new programme for CSR (Pedersen et al., 2013). The government strongly endorses CSR as a way to achieve international competiveness and contribute to economic and political development. The Action Plan described how globalization leads to new challenges for companies that cannot be solved by governments alone. The Action Plan therefore aimed at strengthening the competitiveness of Danish firms through CSR (Danish Government, 2008). So while the Danish government sought to enhance business accountability, the government's motivation reflected a positive expectation that CSR as a business strategic consideration would contribute to increased international competitiveness.

On 16 December 2008 the Danish Parliament (Folketing) passed an amendment (§ 99a) to the Danish Financial Statements Act accounting for CSR in large businesses (http://csrgov.dk). According to the Act all large businesses – private and public – must include information about CSR in their annual report. The requirement concerns all companies in accounting class D. Class D companies have securities traded on a regulated market in EU/EEA member states and state-owned public limited companies. Accounting class C applies to medium-sized and large companies as well as private limited companies. Companies in class C shall report if they exceed at least two of the following criteria (Danish Business Authority, 2010): (1) total assets/liabilities of €19.2 million; (2) net revenue of €38.3 million; (3) an average of 250 full-time employees. In total about 1,250 Danish corporations in accounting class C and 175 companies in class D are required to file a report.

The Danish Parliament mandates CSR by requiring a large firm to report on the following: (1) its social responsibility policies, including any standards, guidelines, or principles for social responsibility the business employs; (2) how the company translates its social responsibility policies into action, including any systems or procedures used; and (3) the company's evaluation of what has been achieved through social responsibility initiatives during the financial year, and any expectations it has regarding future initiatives. If the company has not formulated any social responsibility policies, this must be reported. The CSR report must be included in the management review section of the annual report. Alternatively, the company can report on CSR in an appendix to the management review, as a supplementary report to the annual report, on the website of the company, or as a UNGC or PRI communication on progress report. It was still voluntary for companies to work with CSR. In short, the Danish disclosure requirements constitute a mode of 'comply or explain' (or, 'report or explain'). The Act only requires companies to report on the initiatives that they have adopted (Danish Business Authority, n.d.).

As we show in further sections, while the 2008 legislation was vague on reporting requirements, its motivation was to promote international CSR, for example, by encouraging (but not requiring) firms to join the UNGC and support international labour, human rights, environmental, and anti-corruption principles. We view this form of mandatory requirement as a 'soft' form of mandatory public policy. Therefore companies had a choice whether they wanted to undertake CSR and in that sense CSR was still voluntary which was a key demand from the Confederation of Danish Industries (DI) and from the Danish employers' association (DA). Government thus endorsed CSR but also facilitated it by providing financial support for the Danish UNGC network (Buhmann, 2010; Parliamentary hearings).

The Danish government embarked on its *second* round of mandatory non-financial CSR requirements when in 2012 it adopted a new action plan entitled *Responsible Growth*. According to Vallentin, *Responsible Growth* mostly considered CSR as a global concern and offered 'continued provision of courses and guidance in adherence to international principles, promotion of the UN Global Compact' (2013: 42). However, this new Action Plan also represented a new approach to CSR. Vallentin (2013) terms this an 'Accountability Regime' as the non-financial reporting requirement was expanded to require reporting on initiatives to reduce the impact of climate change as well as initiatives to better protect human rights. Firms must explicitly state in their reports what measures they are taking to respect human rights and reduce their climate impact. We note here that the issue of human rights protection has a clear international component. International principles are key for the Danish 2012 CSR Act. The Act makes references to the 2011 UN Guiding Principles on Business and Human Rights and the 2011 update of the 'OECD Guidelines for Multinational Enterprises: New Guidelines to Protect the Environment, Human Rights and Social Development' (Danish Government, 2012).

The 2012 Action plan comprises four programmatic focus areas: (1) to strengthen the respect for international principles; (2) to increase responsible growth through partnerships; (3) to increase transparency; and (4) to use the public sector to promote a good framework for responsible growth. Regarding strengthening the respect for international principles the government adopted a new initiative in the form of a mediation and grievance mechanism for responsible business conduct to ensure that Danish companies comply with the OECD Guidelines for Multinational Enterprises. The Mediation and Grievance Institution (MGI) has been made into law effective since November 2012. The MGI is intended as a framework for mediation, dialogue, and conflict resolution. It is set up as an MSI representing labour, business, and civil society organizations as well as academia. The MGI serves as an independent public body that deals with complaints related to the OECD Guidelines perpetrated in Denmark or involving Danish businesses (or other Danish organizations) and their business relations such as suppliers. Anyone can register a complaint. However, the MGI cannot force companies to participate in mediation. According to Vallentin then (2013: 43), 'the only stick at its disposal is publicity'. This means that if the involved parties in a complaint are not able to resolve the dispute on their own then the results of the mediation attempt will be made public. The multi-stakeholder approach to problem solving is a common way for social partners and civil society actors to interact in Denmark. The multi-stakeholder approach reflects an institutional context with high union density and collective bargaining, and labour and employers have a long tradition for voicing differences and working them out (Hassel et al., 2016).

Summing up, then, according to Vallentin (2013: 43), 'the work of the MGI is to merge respect for international principles with increased transparency'.

The Impact of the EU Directive on Non-financial Reporting

In 2013 the government adopted its *third* round of mandatory non-financial reporting requirements when it revised the Danish non-financial reporting regulation such that Denmark would fulfil the new EU directive on non-financial reporting. On 16 April 2013, the European Commission adopted a proposal to enhance business accountability on social and environmental matters. On 29 September 2014 the EU Council of Ministers adopted the directive on the disclosure of non-financial and diversity information by large companies. The directive requires all listed and some unlisted companies with more than 500 employees to include in their annual reports statements on their policies and actions relating to environmental and social issues, human rights, and the fight against corruption. The directive allows companies to use existing frameworks to report non-financial information – such as the UNGC (European Commission, 2013). This measure is part of the Commission's efforts to improve corporate governance in Europe, and was announced by the Commission in the Single Market Act Communication in April 2011 (European Commission, 2011), in the communication 'A Renewed Strategy 2011–2014 for Corporate Social Responsibility' issued in October 2011 (European Commission, 2011), and in the Action Plan for Company Law and Corporate Governance, adopted in December 2012 (European Commission, 2012). EU member state legislation had to be in place by the end of 2016 and effective from the financial year of 2017.[1]

The new directive applies to large public-interest entities (listed companies, banks, insurance undertakings, and other companies that are so designated by member states) with more than 500 employees. The scope includes approximately 6,000 large companies and groups across the EU. Companies should disclose in their management report relevant and useful information on their policies, main risks, and outcomes relating to at least environmental matters, social and employee aspects, respect for human rights, anti-corruption and bribery issues, and diversity in their board of directors. The EU directive requires that companies undertake a more elaborate explanation of their CSR

activities compared to the Danish requirements. Article 1 of the directive also establishes that the non-financial statement shall include: (1) a
brief description of the undertaking's business model; (2) a description
of the policies pursued by the undertaking in relation to those matters, including due diligence processes implemented; (3) the outcome
of those policies; (4) the principal risks related to those matters linked
to the undertaking's operations including, where relevant and pro-
portionate, its business relationships, products, or services which are
likely to cause adverse impacts in those areas, and how the undertaking manages those risks; (5) non-financial key performance indicators
relevant to the particular business. Member states have two years to
transpose the directive into national legislation and start reporting as
of their financial year 2017.

The directive provides companies with some flexibility to disclose
relevant information in the way that they consider most useful, or
in a separate report. Companies may use international, European,
or national guidelines, which they consider appropriate. Companies
will disclose information on policies, risks, and outcomes as regards
environmental matters, social and employee-related aspects, respect
for human rights, anti-corruption and bribery issues, and diversity
on boards of directors. In this sense the breadth of the public policy
went beyond the 2012 Danish regulation that highlighted the environment and international human rights. The EU's motivation for
adopting the directive stressed (international) corporate competitiveness. For example, vice president of the European Commission in
charge of Internal Market and Services, Michel Barnier, said: 'I am
pleased that the Council has adopted this directive, which will drive
the long-term performance of the EU's largest companies by significantly improving their accountability and, concretely, the disclosure of
material non-financial information. Companies, investors and society
at large will benefit from non-financial reporting. This is important for
Europe's competitiveness and the creation of more jobs' (European
Commission, 2014). Table 4.1 provides a chronological overview of
Danish legislation on non-financial reporting.

Policy Processes for Non-financial Reporting

In order to get a sense of the role of the Danish government in regulating non-financial reporting we first consider the role of the government

Table 4.1 *Chronological Overview of the Danish Act on Non-financial Reporting*

Year	Extent of Danish non-financial reporting requirement (amending the Danish Financial Statement Act)
2008	§99a. Businesses must account for their policies on CSR, or state if they have none
2012	§99a. Businesses must account for their policies to respect human rights and reduce climate impact
2015	§99a. The EU directive requires that large public-interest entities (listed companies, banks, insurance undertakings, and other companies that are so designated by member states) with more than 500 employees should disclose in their management report relevant and useful information on their policies, main risks, and outcomes relating to at least: 1. Environmental matters 2. Respect for human rights 3. Social and employee aspects 4. Anticorruption and bribery issues 5. Diversity in their board of directors (3–5 are in addition to the Danish 2012 requirement)

in the inception of non-financial reporting and next the role of the government in the operationalization of the public policy. The Ministry of Economic and Business Affairs (Økonomi- og Erhvervsministeriet) was responsible for presenting the legislative proposal for non-financial reporting. It organized a hearing process with key stakeholders including members of parliament, business associations, unions, and civil society actors (Ministry of Economic and Business Affairs, 2008). There was a broad consensus among all stakeholders that the proposal was a good idea although there was disagreement as to the form of reporting with the Confederation of Industry pushing for a flexible approach and civil society organizations pushing for specific reporting requirements.

The Confederation of Danish Industries (DI) and the Confederation of Danish Enterprise (Dansk Erhverv) stated that social responsibility was of increasing importance for Danish companies and in particular constituted an important competitive element. Both organizations stressed that CSR should be voluntary and therefore welcomed that although public policy required companies to report on their CSR activities it did not mandate companies to undertake CSR initiatives. Furthermore, business associations welcomed that the public policy did not require a particular format for non-financial reporting but that companies were free to choose how and what they would report. The Confederation of Danish Industries expressed concern that the proposal would impose undue 'administrative burdens' on firms. However, the Ministry of Economic and Business Affairs had calculated the total administrative burden for the affected 1,100 companies to require a total of 2,745 hours a year at a cost of about DKK 600,000 (about USD 100,000) (Ministry of Economic and Business Affairs, 2008). This figure does seem rather low given that it would mean a cost per company of less than USD 100. In contrast civil society organizations such as Save the Children stated that it would prefer more detailed and specific reporting requirements.

So the Danish government's focus on CSR shifted from a major emphasis on domestic social policy to international competitiveness and political and economic development which echoed the shift in UK ministerial responsibility for CSR from employment and social affairs, to the Ministries of Economic and Business Affairs, Foreign Affairs, and International Development. In the Danish case we see a shift in the government's CSR focus to international challenges such as human rights in global supply chains. In other words, the Danish government is issuing new requirements that pertain to the activities of Danish corporations outside of Denmark and in particular in the Global South.

Regarding its contribution to the operationalization of the initiative, the Danish government privileges certain international organizations in their CSR framework. For example, the National Action Plan for CSR specifically recommends that companies report according to the UNGC guidelines and that institutional investors follow the UN PRI. The Danish government has also funded a UNGC business network. The stated purpose in the National Action Plan is to enable Danish firms to meet CSR demands from large international customers. No mention is made of particular sectors and their international business needs nor is there any mention about challenges in particular regions such as Africa or Asia. These issues were addressed from the Ministry of Foreign Affairs. This is in contrast, for example, to the UK government's initiatives that highlight the particular needs of vital sectors in the UK economy (e.g. extractives and retail), as well as seek to address the challenges involved in the global reach of British firms. In short, the Danish government explicitly uses CSR policies as a new form of industrial policy bringing on board international organizations and initiatives. The political process involved a wide range of social partners, but the outcome really reflects what leading companies in terms of CSR (such as Novo Nordisk) were already doing to ensure social responsibility. With regard to non-financial reporting Novo Nordisk has been a frontrunner in issuing an integrated annual report (triple bottom-line reporting) that includes economic, social, and environmental indicators, first reporting on their environmental impacts in 1989 and providing their first integrated report in 1993 (Brown and Knudsen, 2012).[2]

Danish Government Motivations

Why did the Danish government regulate non-financial reporting? The government and key businesses and business associations saw a business opportunity in branding Danish firms as socially responsible as a way to market products and services, recruit employees, and attract investors. In short, the main rationale for the Danish government in promoting mandatory non-financial reporting was to promote the international competitiveness of Danish firms (Brown and Knudsen, 2015; Vallentin, 2013). In a Brief ('Høringsnotat') from 7 October 2008, the Ministry of Economic and Business Affairs sums up the responses and provides the government's comments. We consider the supply side (the position of the government) and contrast it to the demand side for CSR.

Regarding the supply side, the Danish government sums up its position in the following manner (authors' translation – Ministry of Economic and Business Affairs, Brief, 7 October, 2008): 'It is a key goal for the government to ensure that Danish companies to a greater extent can benefit from being in a global leadership position when it comes to CSR.' The government continues (authors' translation): 'The largest 1,100 or so companies that will need to report are those companies that are already facing demands from their customers and other stakeholders.' The intention is that legislation will 'create greater openness about the CSR initiatives undertaken by Danish corporations … this can contribute to making Danish companies and Denmark well known for responsible growth which will benefit

Danish business more generally. In addition, increased openness will strengthen the ability of shareholders, customers and other stakeholders to be aware of and relate to the CSR initiatives of Danish companies' (Brief, page 2). The government further noted that the reporting requirements are voluntary in the sense that it is up to the companies and investors themselves 'to determine if and how they engage in CSR. Companies and investors are only required to state if they are working with CSR and if they are then they must provide information about how they carry out the work' (Brief, page 2).

In *Responsible Growth* (the government's Action Plan for Corporate Social Responsibility 2012–15), the government further stated that corporate social responsibility is an element of competitive strength and 'should be regarded as an integral part of the work and development of Denmark's industrial policy' (Danish Government, Responsible Growth, 2012: Preface). In addition, the government sees corporate social responsibility in the form of improved protection of human rights in developing countries 'as a natural component of its political development strategy' (Danish Government, Responsible Growth, 2012: 5).

Regarding the demand side, seventy public bodies, business associations, and civil society associations were asked to comment on the proposal for an amendment to the Financial Statements Act to adopt non-financial reporting. Twenty-four of these provided a response. Business, the labour unions, and civil society actors generally supported non-financial reporting regulation. The Confederation of Danish Industries (Dansk Industri) and the Confederation of Danish Enterprise (Dansk Erhverv) recognized that CSR was of increasing importance for Danish firms and critical for ensuring their competitiveness. In addition organizations such as the Danish Confederation of Trade unions (Landsorganisationen i Danmark) and Save the Children also welcomed the proposal and supported the government's goal of promoting business-driven CSR (Ministry of Economic and Business Affairs, 7 October 2008). The Confederation of Danish Industries and the Confederation of Danish Enterprise expressed concern that non-financial reporting would be mandatory. They argued instead that CSR should be voluntary 'because it is important to ensure a flexible framework for how corporations report about their activities' (authors' translation, Ministry of Economic and Business Affairs, Notat, page 1, 7 October, 2008). Leading Danish companies such as

Novo Nordisk and the government therefore contended that Danish firms should be prepared to meet growing demands for CSR policies from international buyers, institutional investors, and other key stakeholders (Knudsen and Brown, 2015).

Interactions between Domestic and International Policies for CSR

We turn to consider interactions between domestic and international mandatory non-financial reporting requirements. The Danish government adopted non-financial reporting regulations, which highlight international CSR principles before the EU adopted its non-financial reporting directive. The Danish government was particularly interested in promoting the UNGC principles including international labour and human rights as well as anti-corruption. In *Responsible Growth* the government stated, 'The Government wants to support the Global Compact Secretariat and Global Compact's local networks in selected developing countries' (Danish Government, 2012: 7). The Danish government also encouraged the EU Commission to propose an addendum to the accounting directive on CSR reporting in annual reports so that companies are obliged to report in their financial statements whether or not they have a policy on corporate social responsibility (Danish Government, 2012: 11). However, in implementing the EU directive, Denmark set stricter criteria than its European counterparts concerning which companies are required to report on their non-financial activities.

Denmark has designated as 'public-interest entities' all 1,100 firms required to undertake non-financial reporting according to the 2008 National Action Plan (European Commission, 2016). According to the EU requirement, only about fifty Danish companies would be required to report (interview, Danish Ministry of Business and Growth, 30 August 2016). Therefore by this comparison of the number of firms required to report, Denmark is 'over-implementing' the EU directive (interview, Danish Ministry of Business and Growth, 30 August 2016). The broad range of CSR issues included in non-financial reporting is a stark contrast to a study on CSR reporting of 142 Danish companies in 2008 and 2009 (Pedersen et al., 2013). This study showed that reporting was dominated by environmental and climate issues and social conditions in Danish companies whereas international issues such as human rights and labour rights in global supply chains were much less likely to be covered (Pedersen et al., 2013). However, the Pedersen et al., 2013 data were collected only one year after the adoption of the National Action Plan when many companies were not yet focusing on international CSR in their reporting. In another study from 2014 the consulting firm COWI on behalf of the Danish Business Authority investigated the extent and nature of CSR reporting in 170 large Danish firms (COWI, 2014). The COWI study found that 96 per cent of the companies provided information about whether they have a strategy for CSR or not. And, 77 per cent of these companies report that they have a strategy for CSR while 23 per cent do not have a CSR strategy. Regarding the requirement to report specifically on human rights and climate impact, 66 per cent of the firms comply with the legislation by stating whether they have a human rights strategy or not and 72 per cent report on whether they have a climate strategy or not. Most companies place the CSR report in the management review section of the annual report, but 31 per cent of firms refer to one of the international guidelines or standards such as the UNGC, PRI, or the GRI (COWI, 2014). In short, firms today are more likely to focus on international CSR issues following the 2012 Danish Action Plan and the EU directive that both highlight international CSR issues such as human rights.

Discussion

This chapter has addressed the relationship between national government and international CSR in the context of societal demand for greater accountability of how corporations impact social and environmental conditions. Danish government used regulatory resources in the form of endorsing non-financial reporting; it has supported partnerships such as the UN initiative for social responsibility in the fashion industry; it has undertaken facilitation by promoting and financially supporting the UNGC network in Denmark and the use of the UNGC framework for reporting. The Danish government has taken a lead in contributing to supporting key international CSR organizations such as the UNGC (through its network in Denmark), the GRI, and the UN Guiding Principles. It has also supported the OECD Guidelines for International Enterprises by setting up a Mediation and Complaints Handling Institution for Responsible Business Conduct. Finally, the government has mandated non-financial reporting in three steps: the 2008 National Action Plan for CSR, the 2012 revision of the Action Plan that made reporting on human rights and environmental impact mandatory; and finally following the EU 2015 non-financial reporting directive, the Danish government has adjusted reporting requirements such that they are aligned with the EU directive notably mandating reporting on such issues as anti-corruption and bribery.

The Danish government's policy for non-financial reporting emerges as part of a succession of policies for CSR lasting over twenty years. In this context, the government played a key role in the inception of the new reporting requirement. The government has endorsed the UN Global Compact reporting framework and contributed to the operationalization of the Danish Global Compact network through financial and administrative resources. The Danish government has supported the adoption of an EU directive for non-financial reporting. The EU directive has imposed new reporting requirements on Danish firms – specifically requiring companies to report on anti-corruption measures, for example. Figure 4.1 provides an overview of how the Danish government plays a role in regulating direct CSR in the form of non-financial reporting aimed at enhancing business accountability.

Public policies in support of non-financial reporting have shifted from being non-coercive in terms of what government responsibilities are to being more coercive as companies are required to submit a report. The government has played a key role in driving CSR forward by adopting mandatory non-financial requirements. While reporting requirements at first were left to each company (with a recommendation to report according to the UN Global Compact guidelines), reporting requirements have become a bit more specific as companies must report on initiatives to reduce the impact of climate change as well as initiatives to better protect human rights. Thus, the mandatory reporting requirements also influence CSR organizations such as the UN Global Compact and help underpin them as key CSR organizations for Danish firms.

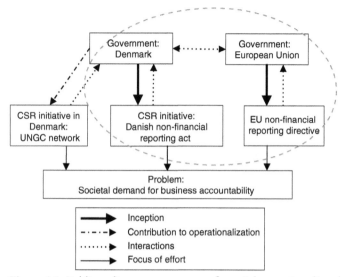

Figure 4.1 Public policy to support non-financial reporting directly in Denmark

The 2012 Action Plan and its focus on 'Accountability' (Vallentin, 2013) resulted in more specific reporting requirements, and according to some observers signals a more restrictive as opposed to supportive stance towards business (Vallentin, 2013: 42). In contrast the 2008 Action Plan with its open-ended and highly flexible reporting demands has been interpreted as an example of reflexive law intended to stimulate the ability of corporations to engage in internal reflection and contribute to creating social responsibility through self-regulation (Buhmann, 2010). The Danish government has retained an element of corporate discretion as companies can choose which form their report should take. We provide an overview of the answers to our research questions 1–3 in Table 4.2.

We found a clear shift from a domestic social and employment inclusion emphasis to a focus on the international activities of Danish firms and their suppliers. We see that over time the Danish non-financial reporting requirements have become more specific in terms of the issues that must be reported on. This development is underpinned by the EU reporting requirements. Table 4.3 provides an overview of interactions between domestic and international regulation.

Table 4.2 *The Danish Government's Policy to Support Non-financial Reporting Directly*

Research questions 1–3	Policies to support CSR directly
1. How does Danish government policy support non-financial reporting: through endorsement, facilitation, partnership, or mandate; and how do these forms of public policies interact?	*Endorsement* Promotion of non-financial reporting by government *Facilitation* Financial support for the UN Global Compact network and recommendation that companies report according to the UNGC principles *Partnership* A range of initiatives such as supporting the first UN initiative for social responsibility in the fashion industry *Mandate 1 (International competitiveness)* NFR reporting by large firms is the law (2008) *Mandate 2 (Accountability)* 2012 revision of the Danish National Action Plan *Mandate 3* EU 2015 non-financial reporting directive
2. What roles do government policies play in supporting non-financial reporting directly: as an initiator or as a contributor to operations?	Government *initiates* non-financial reporting after extensive consultation with labour, business groups, and civil society actors Government *contributes to operations* of the Danish UN Global Compact chapter (ongoing – via support for the UN Global Compact)
3. Why does the government make policies for non-financial reporting?	International competitiveness International political and economic development

The Danish government and the EU still leave business some choice in how they report on CSR issues although reporting requirements are gradually becoming more specific. It remains to be seen how non-financial reporting will affect business accountability. More and more

Table 4.3 *Interactions between Domestic and International Public Policies for Non-financial Reporting*

Research question 4	Direct policies for CSR
What are the interactions between domestic and international public policies for non-financial reporting?	Shift from domestic to international regulatory focus Interactions between Danish reporting requirements and EU directive

companies report on CSR but the impact of non-financial reporting is less clear. Does it provide an international competitive advantage for European firms? Does it contribute to political development in less developed economies? Is Denmark more competitive as a result of 'over reporting' on CSR and as a result of its history of engaging in direct CSR?

Notes

1 Directive 2013/34/EU of the European Parliament and of the Council of 26 June 2013 on the annual financial statements consolidated financial statements and related reports of certain types of undertakings, amending Directive 2006/43/EC of the European Parliament and of the Council and repealing Council Directives 78/660/EEC and 83/349/EEC (Directive 2013/34/EU) as amended by Directive 2014/95/EU of the European Parliament and of the Council of 22 October 2014 amending Directive 2013/34/EU as regards disclosure of non-financial and diversity information by certain large undertakings and groups (Directive 2014/95/EU).
2 A study of the impact of the Danish CSR reporting law found that companies have generally adopted the practice of non-financial reporting. It also found that reporting practices were rather homogenous, which could suggest that the law has resulted in a box-ticking mentality (Pedersen et al., 2013).

5 | Government and Ethical Trade: The Ethical Trading Initiative and Responses to Rana Plaza

This chapter investigates the research questions set out in Chapter 2 concerning the role of government policies in relation to the regulation of what is a long-standing societal issue, ethical trade. Ethical trade is a term that emerged in the 1990s to refer to the ethical sourcing of products (Blowfield, 2010). Ethical trade is trade that is characterized by high labour standards such as the avoidance of child labour and forced labour, the adoption of good health and safety standards as well as workers enjoying the right to organize freely (The Ethical Trading Initiative Base Code at www.ethicaltrade.org/eti-base-code). We shall see, however, that ethical trade has a longer history. This chapter starts out by introducing ethical trade as an issue of societal concern and one which has become a key CSR issue. The chapter then investigates how government policy has interacted with CSR initiatives in this area.

The section titled 'Government Policies for Ethical Trade – The Ethical Trading Initiative' focuses primarily on government policies for CSR initiatives *directly*, their forms, government roles, explanations, and regulatory interactions. In particular we examine the UK government and the UK Ethical Trading Initiative (ETI), as well as the Norwegian and Danish governments and their respective ETIs (IEH – Initiativ for Etisk Handel (Ethical Trading Initiative Norway) and DIEH – Dansk Initiativ for Etisk Handel (Ethical Trading Initiative Denmark)). We focus on the ETI because of its substantial company membership, its longevity, and its broad impact. The creation of the IEH and the DIEH illustrates the internationalization of the idea of ethical trade as a focus for CSR (a theme echoed in our subsequent analysis of responses to the Rana Plaza factory collapse with varying governmental roles therein). The chapter also highlights how the ETI, the recipient of direct government support, interacts with wider government policies to promote labour standards such as through public procurement that rewards membership of the ETI (indirect government support for CSR). Furthermore, we also show how the IEH and the DIEH are now central to the policies of the Nordic Council of Ministers for ethical trade.

The section titled 'Government Policies for Ethical Trade in the Bangladesh Garment Sector Post–Rana Plaza' highlights government ethical trade policies in response to the 2013 Rana Plaza factory collapse in Bangladesh. Rana Plaza was the deadliest accident in the garment sector killing 1,129 garment workers and injuring more than 2,500. The severity of the accident resulted in a massive response by governments, buyers, NGOs, international government organizations, as well as Bangladeshi producers. The section on Rana Plaza focuses primarily on US and European government policies to support CSR *indirectly* by impacting on the Bangladeshi institutional context for ethical trade. However, it also considers government policies that *directly* support CSR initiatives. These CSR initiatives are the Accord on Fire and Building Safety in Bangladesh (the Accord) and the Alliance for Bangladesh Worker Safety (the Alliance) that were designed to address the root causes that led to the Rana Plaza factory collapse.

The concluding discussion of our research questions straddles the material covered in the two main sections and brings the analysis together to highlight the regulatory forms of government policies for ethical trade; the roles of government in direct support of CSR initiatives (i.e. the ETI, DIEH, IEH, Accord, and Alliance); the explanations of these policies; and the interactions between different sorts of government regulation, specifically between the regulation of CSR at home and abroad, and between direct regulation of CSR and indirect regulation of CSR through government policies to shape the wider institutional environment.

This chapter investigates *direct* government policies for ethical trade focusing on the UK ETI, the Norwegian and Danish ethical trading initiatives, the Accord and the Alliance. The chapter also considers *indirect* government policies for CSR including actions taken by Western governments to pressure the Bangladesh government to improve working and safety conditions in the garment factories, mainly through diplomacy, including the Sustainability Compact,[1] as well as threats of trade sanctions.

The research questions addressed in this chapter are summarized in Table 5.1 and will structure the concluding discussion.

Table 5.1 *Research Questions on Government Policies to Support Ethical Trade Directly and Indirectly*

Research questions	Types of policies	
	Direct policies for ethical trade	Indirect policies for ethical trade
1. How do government policies support CSR: through endorsement, facilitation, partnership, or mandate?	UK ETI Norwegian and Danish Ethical Trading Initiatives Accord Alliance	Government policies to effect institutional context of post–Rana Plaza ethical trade in Bangladesh
2. What roles do government policies play in supporting CSR *directly*: as initiators or contributors to operations of CSR initiatives?	UK ETI Norwegian and Danish Ethical Trading Initiatives Accord Alliance	N/A
3. Why do governments make policies for CSR?	UK ETI Norwegian and Danish Ethical Trading Initiatives Accord Alliance	Government policies to effect institutional context of post–Rana Plaza ethical trade in Bangladesh
4. What are the interactions between different sorts of policies for CSR? a. Between domestic and international policies? b. Between direct and indirect policies?	UK ETI Norwegian and Danish Ethical Trading Initiatives Accord and Alliance Government policies to effect institutional context of post–Rana Plaza ethical trade in Bangladesh	

But before we address these questions focusing on our two cases (Ethical Trading Initiatives and post-Rana Plaza initiatives) we provide some background on ethical trade and its emergence as a CSR issue.

Ethical Trade as a CSR Issue

Although there are some distinctive features of the contemporary ethical trading initiatives, which we will examine in further sections, ethical trade has been a matter of longer-term societal concern. Perhaps this is best illustrated in the case of the slave trade, which was one of Britain's most profitable business sectors in the eighteenth century. Nevertheless a climate of social opinion gathered force, which found that slavery was immoral. This materialized in the creation of such pressure groups as the Anti-Slave Movement, or Abolitionists (1783), and the Committee for the Abolition of the Slave Trade (1787). These organizations mobilized public opinion and pursued judicial and parliamentary initiatives, which led to the Slave Trade Act (1807). This made slave trade illegal in the British Empire, and was followed by the Anti-Slavery Act (1833), which made slavery itself illegal. At this time slavery was mainly regarded by civil society as a problem which government regulation could and should resolve. Yet some business leaders allied themselves with the anti-slave trade and anti-slavery movements as illustrated by Wedgwood's production of a porcelain cameo of a slave bearing the motto 'Am I Not a Man and a Brother?' which he donated for distribution to the Society for the Abolition of the Slave Trade. The emblem became the most famous image of the campaign worn by fashionable ladies as a brooch or hairpiece much as more contemporary campaigners wear NGO-sponsored T-shirts.

A more modern instance of ethical trade, or, more accurately, its withdrawal, is the case of apartheid in South Africa. Although the anti-apartheid movement targeted Western governments variously to pressurize and isolate the South African government because of this matter, from the 1960s onwards it also started targeting investors and companies, which did business in or with South Africa. Business initiatives also addressed the question. An early example was the Sullivan Principles specifically requiring equal treatment of black South Africans with white workers by Western employers. At their peak the Principles were adopted by more than 100 multinational corporations but because of the illegality of such employment practices in South

Africa', most of these corporations, under pressure from NGOs and governments alike, simply divested rather than working to apply the principles to address 'unethical trade'. However, there was also a much wider 'disinvestment campaign in South Africa', in North America, Western Europe, and Australasia, which focused on companies operating, and universities which invested, in South Africa. The adoption of the 1986 UK Anti-apartheid Act went further and mandated certain restrictions on trade with South Africa. Evaluations of these and other trade boycotts differ, but our point to note here is that companies withdrew trade if the alternative would be to 'trade unethically'. These themes of ethical trade being used 'positively' to improve worker conditions in respective supply chains, and 'negatively' through threats of its withdrawal (some of which are followed through) will feature in our more contemporary analysis below.

In the United States, a key theme in ethical trade has been to create a level playing field for the relatively high wages enjoyed by American workers by preventing cheap imports made under poor working conditions. For example, in 1947 the US established an Office of International Labor Affairs as a means to formally institutionalize the international directives of the Department of Labor. It was replaced by the Bureau of International Labor Affairs (ILAB) in 1959. ILAB includes, for example, an Office of Child Labor, Forced Labor and Human Trafficking as well as an Office of Trade and Labor Affairs. ILAB leads the US Department of Labor's efforts to ensure that workers around the world are treated fairly and are able to share in the benefits of the global economy. ILAB's mission is to improve global working conditions, raise living standards, protect workers' ability to exercise their rights, and address the workplace exploitation of children and other vulnerable populations. 'Our efforts help to ensure a fair playing field for American workers and contribute to stronger export markets for goods made in the United States' (emphasis added) (dol.gov). More than thirty years ago, for example, ILAB noted that protecting labour standards abroad through trade helps protect American workers: 'By helping other countries and international organizations better understand the problems facing workers throughout the world, international labor standards are strengthened, strengthening American worker protections' (Marshall, 1981).

However, spurred by the 1999 Seattle demonstrations against the World Trade Organization, the past two decades have seen a remarkable growth in the concern with ethical trade both among critics of business and among those who seek to use business for social improvements (by which we include governments and civil society, particularly church and non-governmental organizations) (Knudsen, 2002). As Naomi Klein noted in the second half of the 1990s, 'North Americans could not turn their televisions on without hearing shameful stories about exploitative labor practices behind the most popular, mass-marketed labels' (2000: 327 quoted in Hughes et al., 2007: 500). Companies now use the term 'ethical trade' in managing and communicating their responsible sourcing policies (e.g. the UK retailer, Sainsbury's Supermarkets, has an Ethical Trade Code of Conduct (2013)).

The emergence of an ethical trade movement has arisen in parallel with two related trends, fair trade and sustainable sourcing. 'Fair' trade and 'ethical' trade are terms which have emerged over the past few decades and are now axiomatic in the CSR and international social development lexicons. Notwithstanding our describing these concepts as CSR issues, they owe their emergence to a variety of mainly Western social movements (Jenkins et al., 2002). Despite evidence of and prospects for convergence (Smith and Barrientos, 2005 – on which this section draws) their origins are rather distinct.

Fair trade is concerned principally with equity in the terms of trade, mainly relating to fair prices for producers. It grew out of sales of handicraft and some consumable products sold in dedicated, often charitable, shops, and was mediated by social movements, churches, and charities themselves. Fair trade acquired a major surge in scale once labels were developed, which could be exploited by major supermarket chains, eager to signal their ethical claims. This followed the first fair trade label of Max Havelaar and the emergence of the Fair Trade Labelling Organizations International consisting of member national initiatives.

In contrast, ethical trade is primarily concerned with labour practices using, for example, the United Nations Declaration of Human Rights and International Labor Organization (ILO) standards, to underpin what is now a variety of labour standard codes. The codes are mediated by standards and partnership bodies (e.g. SA 8000, the Fair Labor Association, Worker Rights Consortium, Social Accountability International, Worldwide Responsible Apparel) which develop systems and standards; training and development programmes; and transparency, certification, and inspection systems for business use. The ethical trade movement emerged following the NGO reports of exploitative supply chain conditions (e.g. Oxfam, 2004) that began to be identified as a business risk for retailers. As a result business and NGOs shared a motivation to develop systems, which guaranteed supply chain standards, particularly labour standards. In the United States this was led by Levi Strauss who, with Oxfam, pioneered a monitoring and engagement initiative with a supplier in the Dominican Republic (Zadek, 2001). Subsequently, Levi Strauss joined the US Apparel Industry Partnership (AIP), a coalition of business, civil society actors, and trade unions in 1997. In 1999, the AIP was re-constituted as the FLA. The role played by the Clinton administration in initiating and supporting the AIP is illustrative of our theme of the role of government in CSR (www.fairlabor.org/about-us/history – accessed 5 January 2017, Fair Labor Association, 2012) although it is also a relatively rare American instance of this kind, as we shall see in the discussion in later sections and in Chapter 6. Other ethical trade initiatives include the Worldwide Responsible Accredited Production, Fair Wear Foundation, International Labor Rights Forum, Institute for Global Labour and Human Rights, and, of course, the ETI, to which we shall shortly turn.

Ethical trade systems have expanded their criteria from labour standards, narrowly understood such as limiting working hours, to embrace some of the issues addressed by the fair trade movement. They often include criteria reflecting community and environmental concerns, hence the term 'sustainable sourcing', which is commonly used to combine environmental responsibility with responsibility for the livelihoods of, for example, agricultural producers and their families and communities. As a result, many corporations such as supermarkets or food and textile brands include fair trade products and employ ethical trade sourcing systems and labels, along with systems and labels of sustainable development (e.g. Forest Stewardship Council, International Federation of Organic Agricultural Movements, Marine Stewardship Council). So ethical trade is a long-standing issue for society, for government, and for business. It has recently become a particularly prominent issue for business strategy, management, and accountability among Western retailers, which are attempting to manage their responsibilities for their supply chain labour standards (Locke, 2013). Moreover, like CSR more widely, ethical trade has important overlaps, in this case with fair trade and sustainable sourcing movements. The demands of these movements have now penetrated markets such that ethical trade can be a factor in buying decisions of consumers and retail buyers. Ethical trade is thus one element of what Moon (2014) describes as the 'socialization of markets', a key factor in the growth of CSR, whereby market decisions entail social criteria. The main focus of ethical trade is on cross-border relationships, which multinational corporations and civil society organizations are adroit at crossing, but which are conventionally seen as a jurisdictional barrier for governments, which brings us to the role of the UK government in the ETI (Blowfield, 1999; Jenkins et al., 2002).

Government Policies for Ethical Trade – The Ethical Trading Initiative

This section is divided into three parts: an introduction to the UK-based ETI; an analysis of UK and other governments' policies for the ETI and similar organizations; and a summary.

The Ethical Trading Initiative

The ETI is a CSR-based multi-actor partnership embodying standards or principles for the sourcing of resources or products from developing countries into more developed consumer markets. It is designed to improve labour standards, as well as to raise wider social and environmental standards, in developing countries. However, it has also become a key reference point for companies seeking to identify and address shortcomings in their supply chains, as well as to communicate their commitments to addressing these.

The ETI is a non-profit and civil legal entity and describes itself as 'a leading alliance of companies, trade unions and NGOs that promotes respect for workers' rights around the globe' (ETI, 2015). By virtue of its membership it is also referred to as a multi-stakeholder initiative (Hughes, 2001). Member companies adopt the ETI Base Code, which is grounded in international labour conventions, particularly of the ILO, and addresses issues of: (1) Labour being free; (2) Freedom of association and the right to collective bargaining being respected; (3) Working conditions being safe and hygienic; (4) Child labour not being used; (5) Living wages being paid; (6) Working hours not being excessive; (7) No discrimination being practised; (8) Regular employment being provided; and (9) No harsh or inhumane treatment being allowed (ETI, 2016).

Member companies need to make annual reports on their sourcing operations against this code and they are able to manage these as they prefer, but with the benefit of the best-practice training and education that the ETI provides. Unlike some other, mainly US, ethical trade approaches there is no certification or transparency requirement on the member companies. There are random inspections by civil society organizations and social auditors, which get reported back to the ETI board. The ETI also provides training courses (ETI, n.d.) to support member and non-member companies which want to develop their ethical trade capacity. Companies failing to comply can have their memberships suspended or terminated. There is evidence that the ETI can act as an effective regulatory mechanism as the threat of suspension can provoke improved labour standards (e.g. for clothing retailer Primark, see Butler, 2010). However, the main contribution of the ETI is its more participatory and consensus-based approach to gradual improvement.

The significance of the ETI in the field of ethical trade can be captured in a number of ways: its membership and growth; its impacts on companies and workers in global supply chains; and its impact on wider regulation of ethical trade.

First, the ETI has grown in terms of the number, size, and significance of companies involved. It now claims about 80 member companies and a number of others which are in the foundation stages of membership. The member companies have a combined turnover of about £166 billion. The significance of these companies is that their combined supply chains are estimated to include nearly 10 million workers worldwide who are thereby covered by the Base Code (IOD PARC, 2015). Although the membership now includes all the major UK retailers, many companies initially hesitated to join. Zadek comments on the symbolic importance of Marks & Spencer's membership, the company having initially decided to rely on its own history as a responsible company and its own systems (Zadek, 2001: 40). The ETI also includes several leading retailers and brands from outside the UK (e.g. The Gap, C&A, H&M).

The ETI also has a significant civil society membership, including the UK's leading international development NGOs (e.g. Oxfam,

CAFOD (Catholic Agency for Overseas Development), Fairtrade Foundation, Save the Children. Finally, the ETI's membership includes the UK national confederation of trade unions, the Trade Union Congress (TUC), and the world bodies of national union federations, the International Trade Union Confederation, and the Council of Global Unions. As many commentators have noted (e.g. IOD PARC, 2015; Zadek, 2001) the ETI has provided a 'safe space' for dialogue among these groups who otherwise might have found themselves in more antagonistic relationships. However, a point of critique has been around the absence of representation of workers from the Global South or other organizations representative of workers (Hale, 2000).

Second, the ETI has had a significant impact on the wider regulation of ethical trade. The ETI has influenced the regulation of ethical supply chains through CSR norms beyond the UK companies (Schaller, 2007: 27). The ETI 'crossed the domestic boundaries, first, because its outlook and methodology is a source of inspiration that is referred to in CSR documents stemming from the European Union (EU) institutions' (Voiculescu, 2006: 373–74). This theme of inspiration was also evident in the emergence of the Norwegian and Danish ethical trading initiatives, both of which are loosely modelled on the UK's ETI. The IEH was formed in 2000 by the Norwegian Church Aid, the Federation of Norwegian Commercial and Service Enterprises, the Norwegian Confederation of Trade Unions, and Coop Norway. The DIEH was launched in 2008. It was modelled on the IEH and, thus indirectly on the ETI, as a multi-actor initiative (including eight business associations, more than forty individual companies, and public bodies). It differs from the ETI in retaining a closer focus on the retail sector and, like the IEH, uses partner engagement around its Guidelines incorporating key United Nations and ILO conventions and documents rather than operating an equivalent of the ETI's Base Code. At the time of writing, these three ethical trading initiatives are exploring closer cooperation.

Third, the impacts of the ETI on the issue of ethical trade can be assessed in terms of its effects on member company behaviour and on the labour standards and associated problems in their supply chains. Blowfield and Murray (2008) note that the ETI has had various types of impact: improving the knowledge of its member organizations about how to monitor labour conditions among suppliers; improving knowledge about what to monitor; raising member companies' awareness of labour rights issues; increasing the overall level of monitoring of overseas' suppliers; building the capacity of companies and others to implement voluntary labour standards (2008: 324–25; see also Barrientos and Smith, 2005, 2007).

Together, these member companies have a major potential impact by virtue of their supply chains including about ten million workers. In 2010, for example, ETI member companies reported that they had collectively adopted 133,000 actions to improve workers' conditions in supplier companies (ETI, 2015). Certainly, the ETI has been associated with benefits for supply chain workers, particularly health and safety (e.g. fire safety, emergency procedures, use of chemicals), reduced working hours, avoiding child labour, meeting minimum pay standards, benefits for families, education, access to social security, improved managerial awareness of codes and national regulations (Barrientos and Smith, 2006). However, the ETI has been criticized for failing to sufficiently address particular ethical trade target issues. The list of issues here usually includes freedom of association and discrimination concerning certain groups of workers, particularly women, migrants, and temporary workers (e.g. Barrientos and Smith, 2006). The recent external evaluation of the ETI concluded that the positive impacts had been confined to the more visible aspects of the Base Code such as 'child labour, and health and safety' (IOD PARC, 2015: ii). More generally, this report concluded that the impact of the ETI on some supply chains has been too slow; that learning about making improvements to supply chain conditions has been too weak; that a clear business case for positive action here has been inadequately adumbrated; and that trade unions are insufficiently engaged and supported at the local level (echoing Barrientos and Smith, 2006).

Another point of critique is that the ETI needs more regulatory strength to achieve its ethical trade goals (e.g. Robinson, 2009). One source of stronger regulation usually cited is 'international organizations', but these too are generally characterized by precisely the lack of authority that is identified with the ETI unless they are backed by national governments (e.g. the Organisation for Economic Co-operation and Development (OECD), the EU). This brings us back to national governments.

Policymaking Processes and the Ethical Trading Initiative

Now we turn to the place of government in the development of ethical trade, focusing mainly on the case of the UK government and the ETI. We first consider *how* governments make policy for ethical trade. Illustrative of the general point about the social salience of ethical trade issues, the ETI emerged against a backcloth of NGO and media critique of retail corporations for the abject working conditions in their supply chains (Hughes, 2001). This led to concern among businesses, which had long only focused on their community responsibility, about the risks to their businesses that these criticisms entertained. In this context companies became interested in systems that might enable them to address these problems effectively and collaboratively (Blowfield, 1999; Diller, 1999). Two corporations, Littlewoods and Sainsbury's, took a particular interest in the deliberations of NGOs and trade unions that were seeking to develop ways of monitoring and verifying supply chain labour standards (Hughes, 2001). At this point the Department for International Development (DfID) took an interest in these issues, and the Secretary of State for International Development, Clare Short, launched the ETI in 1998.

But the UK government contribution had already gone further than mere endorsement of the ETI. Preceding the official launch, it had also ensured that the ETI initiative was possible by facilitating the integration of the ETI's founding business, NGO, and trade union members, who might at that time have otherwise considered themselves as 'strange bedfellows'. The impact of this is captured by Guy McCracken from Marks & Spencer, Britain's biggest clothing chain, who reported that 'the group had been persuaded by contact with organizations such as Oxfam and Christian Aid. The more we got to know about it the more we liked the evolution of international standards and felt we had got something to contribute' (Roger, 1999).

The ETI was among the first initiatives to be included in the Blair Labour government's CSR agenda and has its roots in a Government White Paper titled 'Eliminating World Poverty: A Challenge for the 21st Century' (HMG, 1997). The ETI initiative highlighted how ethical trade could contribute to international economic development whereas in the United States a main emphasis was on creating a level-playing field for US workers. The UK union movement supported ethical trade and collaborated with UK retailers. The TUC stated, 'The

ETI is an experiment based on good faith of all involved, not least the DfID. It is not a social project, nor another version of free trade' (Memorandum submitted by the TUC to the House of Commons, February 1999). In contrast to the US discussion about the need for labelling (see further sections) the position of the UK government was that 'there is no need for a comprehensive social labelling' (House of Commons, 1999).

So what *roles* did UK government policies play in ethical trade? As indicated earlier, DfID played a key role in the inception of the ETI through facilitation of the ETI in its formative stages and endorsement at its launch. However, its support for the ETI did not end with the key inception role. Rather the government was motivated to take a much closer interest in what emerged as the ETI by contributing to its operations on a continuing basis, mainly in the form of endorsement and facilitation. These contributions to the ETI's operations were critical in its early stages, particularly in the form of the provision of organizational and fiscal resources. These acted as a pump-primer for company membership contributions, and also provided tangible assistance to the ETI in host countries. As a result of bringing these resources, the UK government indirectly contributed to the development and agreement of the Base Code.

The Conservative/Liberal Democrat coalition government (2010–15) and the Conservative government (2015–2017), which succeeded the Labour government, continued to endorse and facilitate the ETI. For example, the Minister of State for International Development in the coalition government, Alan Duncan, 'urged companies and other stakeholders to engage with the ETI to improve supply chains in the Bangladesh garment sector'. He described the ETI as 'a central partner (nb though there was no formal partnership[2] – the authors) in enabling the government to work closer with businesses to improve working conditions in supply chains' (ETI, 2013 – we will turn to the Bangladeshi garment sector in another section). This confirms that the UK government continued to aspire to contribute to ethical trade, and that the ETI was identified as a key vehicle to this end. Under the 2015 majority Conservative government, the Secretary of State for International Development, Justine Greenwood, commented that through the ETI 'I am determined that Britain will continue to play its part in improving the lives of employees in the developing world' (ETI, n.d.). The government provided continuing support to the ETI's operations through a tranche of £1.3 million core funding for the period 2011–14, and further funding until the end of 2016. This core funding from DfID has been recently extended until 2019 to the tune of £5 million. DfID continues to lend its own organizational structure of regional and country offices (ETI, n.d.), and retains observer status on the ETI board. These periodic contributions have proved vital for establishing an open sharing of views and a constructive dialogue on major development issues between the business and not-for-profit partners. We can conclude then that the UK government not only played key roles in the inception of the ETI through endorsement and facilitation, but also has continued to facilitate the ETI's operations on a continuing basis by means of these same forms of policy.

In addition, the ETI also receives periodic forms of government support. This includes funding from the UK Foreign and Commonwealth Office for projects on workers' rights in Turkey and on the integration of the United Nations General Principles on Business and Human Rights in the Chinese Restructuring of Manufacturing programme. It also receives funding for projects in Bangladesh from the Ministry of Foreign Affairs of Denmark. However, the dependence of the ETI on government has declined gradually over its twenty-year lifetime. Together, members' fees (the overwhelming majority of which is from companies) now make up about half of the total budget.

Having detailed the forms of regulation that the UK government brought to the ETI, the next question is *why* the government makes policy for ethical trade. We highlight a bundle of related reasons. First, as noted in our account of the history of ethical trade this issue has had periodic social salience, and this was the case in the late 1990s in the UK, activated by NGOs and media accounts of working conditions in the supply chains of UK companies. Moreover, shortly before the ETI was launched, the UK government had requested the Competition Commission to make an investigation into the market power of UK supermarkets. Although the Commission reported that UK supermarkets broadly speaking acted competitively, it did criticize them for their ill treatment of suppliers. This led to new regulation and a re-organization of supermarkets' buying practices to reflect this more ethical approach. Yet, although the government could regulate ethical supply inside the UK borders, this option was not open for the international supply of UK retailers – an issue that the Blair government was concerned about – and the consensus-seeking approach was therefore an obviously attractive option (Hughes, 2001).

Second, the approach of the NGOs, unions, and companies to the issue of ethical trade was very much in accord with the formative idea of the Blair government, 'The Third Way' (Giddens, 1998), by which it was intended that governing became a collaborative endeavour with business and organized labour. Hughes et al. (2007) note that the UK government contributed to the emergence of the ETI because of the success of its approach reflecting a consultative and accommodative style as the 'national-institutional context' (2007: 495) in the UK, which included trade union involvement. They draw upon Amin (2004) to depict the UK government's role as 'decentred' because the stakeholders engage with each other as well as with it, the government (Hughes et al., 2007: 496).

Third, not only did the ETI fit the characteristics of the idea of the Third Way, but it also focused on a substantive issue of international development, which had been given an increased status by the Blair government, illustrated by the appointment of the Secretary of State for International Development, Clare Short. Moreover, Clare Short described the government's motivation as seeing this voluntary initiative as being about 'applied international development policy' (authors' interview with Clare Short, 27 November 2014). Later this involvement in the ETI was also incorporated in the government's account of its international policies for CSR by the then minister for CSR, Margaret Hodge (2006).

It might be asked why, if the government was so committed to the idea of the key parties – business, labour, and civil society – deliberating over the issue and coming to a harmonious agreement on how to address the ethical trade issue, it then effectively took a lead in the negotiations? The answer is that the different parties were so divided that an agreement appeared very far off. Important ideological differences, as well as strategic and tactical ones, existed between the actors. The leading brands (e.g. ASDA, Premier Brands, The Body Shop, Littlewoods, Sainsbury's), were mainly concerned with resolving problems of their supply chain legitimacy (authors' interview with Clare Short, 27 November 2014). The unions were more concerned with establishing clear and defensible labour rights, and the civil society groups with positive international development. It was the government then, which facilitated discussions among leading retail companies, trade unions, and NGOs. Although these non-governmental actors had had an interest in a collective approach to identifying and managing their supply chain responsibilities, the government's facilitation role in the negotiations proved critical. It enabled mutual suspicions to be overcome by virtue of its imprimatur as an authority in the negotiation of the ETI's organizational model among business and civil society representatives. This role was also underpinned by other forms of facilitation in the shape of initial financing of the ETI organization. This was vital as companies, who now provide the burden of the ETI's funding, were then too suspicious and, perhaps, pessimistic to put their money up front. There were also secondments of government staff to the ETI secretariat, again reflecting the initial absence of any other organizational capacity. A DfID official was appointed as an ETI board member in the early years, reflecting a close relationship, though this position was later designated as of 'observer status' (Zadek, 2001).

The first eighteen months were spent negotiating the Base Code which Zadek described as a

difficult process; serious differences between the organizations involved surfaced, were worked through, and solutions found. At various stages, organizations from all four constituencies (retailer businesses, NGOs, organized labour, government) were prepared to leave the table over particular issues ... every organization changed during the process ... the ability to build this learning into the core of their respective organizations, enabled the initiative to move forward. (2001: 101)

Government was thus the critical factor in the successful emergence of the ETI. Commentators also credit the NGO Oxfam, the supermarket Sainsbury's, and the ETI Secretariat with key roles in these early stages.

We close with some preliminary reflections on the *interactions* between different sorts of government policy support for the ETI and its Scandinavian counterparts. The ETI is legally a civil initiative, not a governmental one, but our first conclusion is that it may not have come into existence without government, or at least it might have taken much longer to emerge, or yet that it might have looked rather different. Once in operation, the ETI has acquired an international status illustrated by its emulation in Norway (the IEH) and Denmark (the DIEH). Although, in contrast to the UK model, the Norwegian and Danish initiatives do not reflect governmental involvement in their inception or in the form of continuing support for operations, the IEH and the DIEH have enjoyed periodic interactions with their respective governments. Moreover, numerous public bodies (e.g. universities, municipalities, health authorities) have joined the IEH (IEH, n.d.). The Danish international development agency, DANIDA (Danida, 2013), operating under the Ministry of Foreign Affairs, was active in endorsing the DIEH's launch and development, and later contributed part of the DIEH's periodic funding, including for the DIEH's participation in an ETI project on social dialogue in Bangladesh (see further sections). So endorsement and facilitation relationships were evident between the Danish government and the DIEH.

Government policy itself has been informed by these ethical trading initiatives – a form of reverse policy support. While the UK government directly supported the ETI, the Norwegian government indirectly supported the initiative by adopting new legislation to ensure that public procurement criteria included the principles adopted by the IEH. Furthermore, the IEH and the DIEH support government public policy following the Nordic Council of Ministers' launch of the Nordic Strategy on Corporate Social Responsibility in 2013. One of its three priority areas is 'addressing risks and opportunities in global value chains', and the Danish and Norwegian ETIs were commissioned by the Council to run the initiative as well as to facilitate similar organizations in Finland, Sweden, and Iceland.

Finally, the ETI has contributed to the extension of mandatory regulation of labour standards in UK supply chains. It played a major coordinating role to enable business and trade union negotiations with the government about proper labour standards for temporary workers in the lead up to the Gangmasters (Licensing) Act (2004). This Act was set up to prevent the exploitation of workers, particularly by debt bondage or forced labour in the fresh produce sector. Businesses, which provide labour in the sector, need to be licensed. Subsequently, the ETI was heavily involved in the development of the regulation, which extended this Act, and became known as the Modern Slavery Act (2015) to address slavery and trafficking in the UK (LeBaron and Rümpkopf, 2017). The ETI claims special responsibility for the inclusion of a Transparency in Supply Chains clause, and for the scope of the powers of the Gangmasters Licensing Authority to be extended to enable it to monitor and regulate labour in all sectors, rather than just in agriculture and food (ETI, 2015). In other words, the government-supported ETI interacts with the wider regulation of employment in the UK.

National Government and the Ethical Trading Initiative: Summary

Our analysis has revealed various direct relationships between the UK government and the ETI. The UK government was critical to the formation of the ETI in endorsement and facilitation in order to broker an agreement among the then mutually suspicious civil society and business organizations. Although in the early years of the ETI it retained a close relationship, as the ETI found its feet and grew stronger, the UK government's role has settled on one of more arms-length endorsement and facilitation of the ETI's continuing operations. It is not possible to precisely attribute responsibility for the ETI's subsequent development, but it has emerged as a significant CSR initiative in terms of its longevity, its membership and scope, and regulatory effect. Significantly, the Scandinavian ETIs, while not recipients of their respective government support at their inception, have been supplemented by endorsement and facilitation from the Danish and Norwegian governments.

The interactions between the ETI and the UK government have not been simply one-way. The ETI was brought in by the UK government to assist in the drafting of its Modern Slavery Act (2015) by virtue of its expertise in supply chain labour regulation and the legitimacy that it has acquired among civil society and business organizations. This not only represents evidence of mutual regulatory support between this CSR organization and government, but also a case of a domestic role for an organization ostensibly established for international purposes. Most significantly, the investment that the government made in establishing the ETI as a CSR/multi-stakeholder initiative regulatory organization served its own purposes when it came to developing its mandatory regulation for slavery within its own national jurisdiction, further illustrative of CSR's regulatory reach.

Hughes et al. (2007: 508) capture the significance of the ETI in comparison with similar US initiatives in which national government played a much more modest and short-lived role than its UK counterpart. First, that there is a single UK ethical trade initiative is itself a major achievement in contrast to the multiplicity of US initiatives (e.g. Fair Labor Association (FLA), Worker Rights Consortium (WRC),

Social Accountability International (SAI)). This can be at least partly attributed to the UK government's distinctive endorsing and facilitating roles, reflecting its unique legitimizing, fiscal, and organizational resources. Second, it can be partly attributed to the success that the DfID had in finding a consensus among the key parties in the initiation stages, again reflecting the underlying legitimization and promise of further resources (Hughes, 2001: 429). The significance of our findings on government and CSR organizations for ethical trade for our broader research objectives will be considered in the concluding chapter, Chapter 7.

Government Policies for Ethical Trade in the Bangladesh Garment Sector Post – Rana Plaza

Our discussion of the ETI focused primarily on government policies to support CSR directly although we also considered indirect government support for the ETI through, for example, public procurement. We now turn to an analysis of government policies that support ethical trade directly and indirectly and how these policies can interact. Our investigation centres on government policy responses to ensure ethical trade following the 2013 Rana Plaza factory collapse in Bangladesh. We first describe the Ready Made Garment (RMG) sector and its economic importance in Bangladesh and then investigate the Rana Plaza disaster. We investigate government policies that support two key CSR responses to the Rana Plaza disaster *directly*: the Accord and the Alliance. We complement this investigation with an analysis of government policies that support ethical trade through CSR in Bangladesh *indirectly*. These policies consist of efforts by Western 'home' country governments to shape the regulatory context of the RMG industry in Bangladesh consistent with the objectives of the Accord and the Alliance. We conclude with a discussion of interactions between government policies for ethical trade in the RMG sector in Bangladesh, indirectly and directly.

The Bangladesh Garment Sector and the Rana Plaza Factory Collapse

Bangladesh is the second-largest garment producer in the world behind China. The industry is of key economic importance as it accounts for more than 80 per cent of exports from Bangladesh (European Commission, 2016) and it is a major employer providing at least four million jobs (Knudsen, 2017). Bangladesh is a poor country with an annual GDP per capita just short of $1,000 and is struggling to fulfil the needs of its large population of 160 million people (bbs.gov.bd). Bangladesh has reached its position as a key RMG producer because of its extremely low wages (the minimum monthly wage is 68 USD, which is only a quarter of China's minimum wage). The sector is characterized by fierce international competition and a constant pressure to reduce costs.

The RMG sector became important to the Bangladeshi economy in the 1970s. In 1971 Bangladesh had gained independence from Pakistan, and was referred to as an 'international basket case' (Rahman, 2004: 17). Bangladesh was so dependent on foreign aid that the international community feared that Bangladesh would never be able to survive without it (Rahman, 2004). However, the garment sector started growing after the introduction of the 1974 Multi Fibre Agreement (MFA). Under the MFA, the United States and the EU restricted imports from developing countries in an effort to protect their own domestic industries. Under the agreement, developed countries such as the United States, the UK, France, and Germany were assigned a quota for how much could be exported to them. However, countries such as Bangladesh that were classified as having Least Developed Country status enjoyed favourable trade access. The result of the MFA was that companies from the Newly Industrializing Countries moved their production to Bangladesh to take advantage of Bangladesh's favourable access to the European and North American markets. One notable example was Daewoo Corporation of South Korea, which when faced with a restricted export quota after the MFA, began a collaboration with Desh Company in Bangladesh to produce RMG goods. Daewoo provided machinery, training, and expertise to Desh Company, and the result was a tremendous growth in Desh's export value (Rahmann, 2004). Similar collaborations soon spread across Bangladesh.

However, working conditions throughout the Bangladeshi garment sector have been notoriously bad, and factory fires and building collapses have plagued the sector. Most notably, in April 2013, the Rana Plaza building collapsed resulting in the biggest number of fatalities in the RMG sector to date. At first, the Bangladesh government downplayed the event. Sheikh Hasina, the prime minister of Bangladesh, stated that 'Anywhere in the world, any accident can take place' (CNN, 2 May 2013). However, it soon became clear to the Bangladeshi garment manufacturers that many large international buyers were pushing for significant improvements in building safety and worker rights such as freedom of association and the right to collective bargaining (interview, Bangladesh Garment Manufacturers and Exporters Association (BGMEA), 28 July 2015; Manzur, BA thesis, 2016; interview, AFL-CIO, 29 November 2016; interview, Solidarity Center, 29 November 2016). Governments, institutional investors, and international organizations also demanded improvements in working conditions. In short, as a consequence of the disaster, Rana Plaza brought the country's apparel industry under intense scrutiny, inspiring national governments, the EU, the ILO, and apparel retailers to establish monitoring initiatives to improve working conditions. Advocacy organizations such as the Solidarity Center and trade unions from the United States and Europe, in particular, played a key role in driving regulatory changes (Knudsen, 2017).

Our analysis focuses, first, on the CSR organizations incepted in response to Rana Plaza, the Accord, and the Alliance, both of which aimed to improve worker safety standards, and on the support that governments provided directly. We then analyse the indirect ways in which governments supported these initiatives through regulating the institutional environment of the Bangladesh RMG industry precisely to improve worker rights and safety standards.

Government Policies to Support CSR for Ethical Garments Trade in Bangladesh Directly

We first consider *how* governments supported CSR directly in the aftermath of the Rana Plaza tragedy. The Accord and Alliance are the two key CSR initiatives that were adopted in the aftermath of the disaster to establish better working conditions and help ensure ethical trade in garments. Their main focus is on improving fire, electrical, and building safety.

The Accord is dominated by European firms, although the US firm PVH was one of its founders. The Accord is a multi-stakeholder initiative like the ETI and, significantly, the ETI urged its members that source from Bangladesh to join the Accord (interview, ETI, 24 September 2016). As a result there is substantial overlap in company membership between the two initiatives. A total of fifty-two ETI members are garment manufacturers and retailers. Of these fifty-two ETI firms, 40 per cent (twenty-one firms) are also members of the Accord. German companies dominate the Accord with sixty-three companies followed by thirty-one UK companies and twenty-two US companies. The Accord is legally binding, meaning that companies which sign can be sued in their home country under contract law if they fail to meet the Accord requirements (to date no lawsuit has taken place). The Accord is governed by a Steering Committee with equal representation of the signatory companies and trade unions with a neutral Chair provided by the ILO. The Accord covers more than 1,600 factories, 200 brands, and 2 million workers (Accord, 2013).

The Alliance is a business-only initiative that consists of primarily US companies (twenty-nine in total), with a governing board comprising prominent leaders from major US brands as well as other business representatives. US retailers such as Wal-Mart and the Gap would not sign the Accord due to liability fears and concerns about potential anti-trust violations from working closely with competitors.[3] Instead a group of North American apparel retailers and brands founded the Alliance as an internally binding, five-year undertaking with the intent of improving safety in Bangladeshi apparel factories. It has 687 factories and covers about 1.1 million workers. Companies such as the Gap and VF Corp played a key role in setting up the Alliance. The Alliance was organized in 2013 through the Bipartisan Policy Center, which was brought in to add credibility to the business-led initiative with discussions convened and chaired by former US Senate majority leader George Mitchell (D-ME) and former US senator Olympia Snowe (R-ME) (Alliance, n.d.-a).

Next, we turn to the question of the *roles* of Western government policies in supporting directly these two CSR initiatives. In contrast to the ETI (mentioned earlier), governments did not play a formal role at the inception of the Accord or of the Alliance. However, they supported the Accord and Alliance initiatives through a range of public policies such as endorsement and facilitation by offering financial support and providing technical support to improve building safety. For example, in 2015 the US government through USAID donated USD 20 million not only to the Accord and Alliance (USD 16 million – of which went to the Alliance), but also to factories that are not supplying to Accord or Alliance buyers, and which the Bangladesh government therefore regulates under its National Tripartite Action Plan (USAID, 2015).

The Accord and Alliance are formally expected to end in 2018 when the Bangladeshi government is scheduled to take over the responsibility for supervising fire, electrical, and building safety for all factories in Bangladesh. However, foreign retailers that we talked to did not expect the Bangladeshi government to be ready to take over the supervisory duties for the Accord and Alliance factories (authors' interviews in Bangladesh, Summer 2015 and 2016). Indeed, the Bangladesh government has been critical of the Accord and Alliance stating that they are 'a noose around our neck' with many costly requirements (*Daily Star*, 2015). Accordingly it began remediation of non-Accord and non-Alliance factories only in August 2016 (only 101 factories had been inspected on 12 August 2016). As a result it is likely that Western governments may well provide support to the Accord and the Alliance beyond 2018.

The next question that arises is *why* Western governments got involved in making policies to support direct CSR in the form of the Accord and Alliance. The main driver for the policies was the scale of the Rana Plaza disaster. As it was the largest disaster in the RMG sector in the history of garment production worldwide, it functioned as a game changer (Manzur, 2016). Clothing brands, in particular, feared a negative backlash from customers, civil society actors, and investors (Reinecke and Donaghey, 2015), and the Bangladeshi government came under tremendous pressure to act. The BGMEA feared that if another disaster were to happen then international buyers would leave Bangladesh for good.

Policies to Support CSR for Ethical Garments Trade in Bangladesh Indirectly

In addition to the support that governments in advanced industrialized countries have given to the Accord and Alliance *directly*, governments have also been involved in developing policies for CSR *indirectly*. By indirect government policies for CSR we refer to policies which are not aimed at supporting the Accord and the Alliance directly but, rather, are intended to address the same social problem (poor working conditions in the Bangladeshi RMG sector) to which the Accord and the Alliance and the government policies to support them are directed.

We first examine *how* governments regulate ethical trade indirectly after the Rana Plaza tragedy. We start by focusing on US and EU trade policies that have been used to push for a reshaping of the regulatory environment for working conditions in the RMG sector in Bangladesh. We also consider initiatives to improve working conditions by the Bangladesh government.

The United States has a long tradition of using trade policy to promote social change in countries from which it imports (Burgoon, 2001). In June 2013, President Obama adopted a foreign trade policy initiative, suspending Bangladesh's trade benefits under the Generalized System of Preferences (GSP) in view of insufficient progress by the government of Bangladesh in granting workers internationally recognized worker rights (Sokou and Schneider, 2013). Prior to Rana Plaza the Obama administration had already initiated an investigation into violations of worker rights in Bangladesh and, following the 2012 Tazreen Fashions factory fire, into safety in the Bangladeshi industry (US Department of Labor, 2013a). The investigation followed a filing in 2007 by the AFL-CIO – the umbrella federation of US unions – with the US Trade Representative's Office requesting that the US withdraw GSP access for Bangladeshi products because of the Bangladeshi government's failure to ensure a safe working environment for workers and to guarantee the rights of workers to organize (Executive Office of the President, Office of the US Trade Representative, Public Hearing for US Generalized System of Preferences (GSP), 28 March 2013). Following the Rana Plaza collapse, the United States used the lack of progress for working conditions in sectors other than ready-made garments, such as the shrimp industry, to revoke GSP with the intention of pushing for a wider overhaul of workers' rights in Bangladesh (interview, US State Department, June 2015). The GSP arrangement waived tariffs on imports into the US, but textiles and apparel were not affected because they were not included in the GSP. While the amount of trade covered in the GSP arrangement was limited (USD 34.7 million out of the USD 4.9 billion worth of goods imported into the US from Bangladesh in 2012 – Quelch and Rodrigues, 2014a, 2014b), the end to GSP status has been a blow to Bangladesh's image (authors' interview, US Trade Representative's Office, 6 June 2015) and has made the Bangladesh government anxious that the EU might also close off special access trade in the form of the EU's 'anything but arms' bilateral trade agreement with Bangladesh (authors' interview Bangladeshi Minister for Industry, 26 April 2016). Furthermore, the Bangladeshi government was interested in getting duty-free access for its RMG products to the US market as duties were 15 per cent and it was concerned that the end to the GSP would make this goal impossible (MacDonald, 2013). The EU Commission is solely responsible for adopting trade agreements on behalf of all EU member states. The EU promotes a policy of non-conditional trade access (i.e. duty free-and quota-free) through its 'Everything but Arms' program for Bangladesh (European Commission, 2013). However, the EU has stated that lack of progress to improve conditions for workers will lead the EU to block trade access (authors' interview, EU Commission DG Trade, 26 November 2014). Since Rana Plaza, the EU and the US closely monitor initiatives to improve working conditions through regular meetings in the Sustainability Compact.

After the US government ended GSP access for Bangladeshi products and as a result of the monitoring by the Sustainability Compact, the Bangladeshi government adopted several new pieces of legislation to improve working conditions. First, the NTAP was adopted by the Bangladeshi government (the Ministry of Labour and Employment – MoLE), 'worker organizations', and employer representatives, in which the ILO plays a key supervisory role. A national committee (NTC) is in charge of implementing the NTAP (Khan and Wichterich, 2015). The Committee consists of the secretary of the MoLE; the president of the Bangladeshi Employers' Federation; the vice president of the Bangladeshi Garment Manufacturers and Exporters Association (BGMEA), the first vice president of the Bangladeshi Knitwear Manufacturers & Exporters Association (BKMEA); the chairman of the National Coordination for Workers' Education (NCCWE); the chairman of the Bangladeshi National Council.

The 'Tripartite partners' first met on 15 January 2013 in a meeting organized by the MoLE and the ILO where they committed to working together to develop the NTAP by the end of February 2013 (ILO, 2013). The MoLE endorsed the NTAP on 24 March 2013. The NTAP was primarily a plan undertaken by the national actors and the ILO, and initially focused on fire safety. After the Rana Plaza collapse, following consultation with and pressure from the ILO, the Committee added 'structural integrity of buildings' to its plan which was formally implemented on 25 July 2013. The objectives of the Plan of Action are:

1. 'To identify activities that the tripartite partners agree fall within their individual and/or collective responsibility and need to be implemented to ensure an integrated approach to promoting fire safety and structural integrity in Bangladesh, in particular in the RMG sector.'
2. 'To provide entry points for other stakeholders that wish to support implementation of the Plan of Action, as well as provide a platform for coordination for stakeholders that wish to initiate additional fire safety promotion activities.'

The Bangladeshi government also adopted amendments to the Bangladesh Labour Act of 2006 (15 July 2013) to improve labour standards (i.e. freedom of association; a minimum wage increase; election to the Worker Participation Committees by secret ballot). Since the 2013 Labour Act was amended, the EU Commission regularly follows up to track progress. The Labour Act is considered a key supportive element for the Accord and Alliance because it allows workers to speak up about unsafe working conditions without the risk of being fired. Before the Rana Plaza factory collapsed, workers were aware that there were cracks in the building, but they were told to report to work regardless (Human Rights Watch, 2013). In the wake of the disaster, steps were taken to ensure that workers' rights would be protected and that they would be free to refuse to enter a potentially dangerous work place. The Amended Labour Act is a key component of securing better workers' rights (Clean Clothes Campaign, 2014; *The Huffington Post*, 2015). It is not clear, however, how strictly these new regulations have been implemented. Tim Ryan from the Solidarity Center estimates, for example, that one in two applications to establish a trade union are turned down by the government (Tim Ryan, Solidarity Center, public presentation, Harvard Law School, 24 September 2016).

We now turn to the question about government motivations for undertaking indirect policies for CSR. *Why* did the US and European governments make policies for CSR and why did the Bangladeshi government undertake legislative reforms to improve working conditions? As we discussed earlier, when focusing on US and European government support for the Accord and the Alliance (direct CSR) it was the scale of the disaster that pushed governments to act. When Rana Plaza happened, the 2007 AFL-CIO case submitted to the US Trade Representative's Office was still pending. The massive scale of the disaster led President Obama to act quickly. Although the Bangladeshi government had been reluctant to undertake legislative reform it became clear that it had to improve its image if it wanted to stay internationally competitive as a major RMG exporter. The need to avoid another Rana Plaza was a consistent theme in all the interviews that we conducted with Bangladeshi government officials in the summer of 2015 and 2016. Changes had to be made in order to secure market access and to stay competitive internationally. In short, Rana Plaza was 'a game changer' (Manzur, 2016).

We end the section on Rana Plaza and ethical trade with some preliminary conclusions about *interactions* between different sorts of policies for CSR in the wake of the disaster. First, we see interactions between domestic and international government policies for CSR. For example, the US government indirectly supported ethical trade in Bangladesh by ending GSP trade access in order to push the Bangladeshi government to improve workers' rights. Both the EU and the US government have also undertaken a range of partnerships with the Bangladeshi government and the ILO to improve working conditions in Bangladesh. Second, we see links between direct and indirect government policies for CSR with the EU and US governments directly supporting the Accord and the Alliance thereby acting as a legitimizer for other corporations to join. Western governments have also indirectly supported ethical trade and the Accord and Alliance by seeking to pressure the Bangladeshi government to improve working and safety conditions in the garment factories, mainly through diplomacy including in the form of meetings in the Sustainability Compact as well as the use of trade sanctions.

National Government and Responses to the Rana Plaza Disaster: Summary

Although neither of the two main CSR responses to the Rana Plaza disaster reflected government policies at their inception, governmental support has been provided *directly* for their operations. Both the Accord and the Alliance have received supplementary support for periodic operations from various governments, in the form of endorsement and facilitation. This support has enhanced the legitimacy of the respective CSR organizations among their own members and their immediate stakeholders in their home countries and in Bangladesh, although the extent of the support from Bangladeshi governmental authorities is less clear. However, support from the Bangladeshi government is critical given the aspiration of the Bangladeshi government to assume responsibility in 2018 for the administration of electrical, fire, and building safety as stated in the Accord and Alliance (US Department of Labor, 2013b).

The other way in which governments, particularly the US government, have acted to support these CSR initiatives *indirectly* is also critical. The US government has put pressure on the Bangladeshi government through diplomatic means and by revoking trade access until workers are allowed to freely organize. As a result the institutional context for the work of the Accord and the Alliance has been transformed and extended to include a wider set of working condition initiatives than electrical and construction improvements as well as fire prevention. The United States and the EU have also pushed the Bangladeshi government to improve labour rights and standards and remuneration. The pressure on the Bangladeshi government is not simply from two international 'voluntary initiatives' but also from key governments. Fire, electrical, and building safety has clearly improved in Alliance and Accord supplier factories since 2013. In fact, since the Rana Plaza factory there have been no fatal accidents caused by fires or building collapses in the RMG industry. However, the situation for labour more broadly remains precarious with extremely low wages and a weak union movement, which, overall, still organizes less than 1 per cent of the total national workforce. Interviews with the US Trade Representative's Office and the US State Department in December 2016 also revealed that according to US authorities the Bangladeshi government has not made changes to improve working conditions that would justify a reinstatement of GSP.

Public Policies for CSR in Ethical Trade: Discussion

We now turn to a combined discussion of the development of ethical trade in our two cases. We have presented a story where the UK government is a vital contributor to the inception of the ETI, a model of multi-actor regulation of international CSR. The UK government has subsequently supported the ETI's operations, both on a continuing basis (through multi-year core funding) and periodically (through project finance). Significantly, the Norwegian and Danish governments have emulated these support roles in relation to the respective Scandinavian ethical trade initiatives. Although these governments were not central to the inception of the initiatives, they have supported them through continuing facilitation in the form of periodic funding and related regulatory support such as the Norwegian public procurement criteria that include ethical trade principles. These three governments have contributed to further developing the ETI by shaping ethical trade and assisting in the development of new governance models with the participation of a range of stakeholders and governance by mutual agreement, learning, and transparency. Corporations in the UK, Norway, and Denmark are regulated by a decision-making process where the ultimate sanction is the reputational damage of exclusion. Suppliers in developing countries are regulated through the power of collective business action legitimized by civil society participants and by the governmental endorsement, facilitation, and partnership that underpin the initiative.

Moreover, the CSR initiatives in the form of the ETI, IEH, and DIEH have also been deployed by these three governments in the development of their own policies, as illustrated by the contribution of the ETI to the UK Gangmasters and Modern Slavery regulations and the central place that the IEH and DIEH have in the policies of the Nordic Council of Ministers for ethical trade.

We also offer some observations regarding interactions between direct and indirect government regulation of CSR in the garment sector in Bangladesh. The main objective in the wake of the Rana Plaza tragedy was to ensure that workplaces were made safe. As a consequence, factory buildings had to be constructed in such a way that they would not collapse; electrical wiring had to be improved; and new fire safety measures included installing certified fire doors in all doorways from the factory to the stairwells as well as automatic fire alarm systems, ensuring adequate and unobstructed fire exits, and removing excess flammable materials in work areas. However, as large buyers from advanced industrialized countries dominate the Accord and the Alliance, other measures had to be taken to improve working conditions in Bangladeshi factories that are not supplying buyers from the Global North. The EU and US governments have, for example, pushed the Bangladeshi government to adopt new legislation modelled on the Accord and Alliance requirements in order to cover the entire RMG sector. In addition, the EU and the US governments require that workers are made aware of their right to refuse to enter a factory that they suspect could be unsafe. In September 2016 US secretary of state John Kerry met with leaders of Bangladesh garment unions in Dhaka, where he emphasized workers' ability to freely form unions as key to workplace safety (Solidarity Center, 2016). 'Enhancing worker safety has to be paired with strengthening workers' rights', Secretary Kerry told a group of sixty garment workers and allies. The United States and the EU have funded a wide range of projects to improve social dialogue and freedom of association. Only about 200 factories in Bangladesh have factory floor union representation, and the largest union federations typically have only around 30,000 union members. Between 2006 and 2008 unions were even illegal. It is also not uncommon that union representatives are threatened by employers and in extreme cases murdered (Khanna, 2011). In short, governments facilitate the work of the Accord and the Alliance by adding financial support and offering technical and organizational expertise. We have also seen in the wake of the Rana Plaza disaster that the US government has supported the objectives of the Alliance and the Accord through trade policy while the EU has threatened to end trade access. In response to these threats, the Bangladeshi government used its power to mandate behaviour through safety at work regulation and easing restrictions on labour unions.

In this light we can reflect on the nature, timing, and motivation of the government involvement in CSR. Our conclusions concerning government direct and indirect support for the general CSR initiatives for ethical trade are summarized in Table 5.2.

First, with respect to the forms of policy that governments have applied in their support of CSR initiatives (Research Question 1) we find that the UK, Norwegian, and Danish governments have done more than simply endorse the ETI, EIH, and the DIEH. They have brought more substantive financial and organizational resources to bear in the form of facilitation and partnership. Regarding the issue of

Table 5.2 *Government's Direct and Indirect Public Policies for Ethical Trade*

Research questions	Types of policies	
	Direct policies for ethical trade	Indirect policies for ethical trade
1. How do governments support ethical trade: through endorsement, facilitation, partnership, or mandate?	*Ethical Trading Initiatives* UK government endorses *and facilitates the ETI* Norway and Denmark governments and Nordic Council of Ministers *endorse, facilitate and partner* with IEH and DIEH *Post–Rana Plaza* US government *endorses and facilitates* the Alliance but also the Accord and the National Tripartite Action Plan (i.e. through USAID) EU/European governments *endorse and facilitate* the Accord and the National Tripartite Action Plan	US government ends GSP trade access for Bangladeshi goods (*mandatory policy*) EU Commission '*anything but arms*' bilateral trade agreement (*mandatory policy*) is used by the EU to ensure progress by Bangladeshi government Bangladeshi government adopted: 1. Amendments to the Bangladesh Labour Act of 2006 (2013) 2. 2013 National Tripartite Action Plan on Fire and Safety
2. What roles do government policies play in regulating ethical trade *directly*: as initiators or contributors to operations of CSR initiatives?	*Initiation:* UK government played a key role in the initiation of ETI (securing agreement and providing initial resources) *Contributor to operations:* Ongoing: UK government played a key role in ETI Periodic: UK government support for the ETI Periodic: Danish government support for DIEH Periodic: Norwegian support for IEH	N/A

(continued)

Table 5.2 (*cont.*)

Research questions	Types of policies		
	Direct policies for ethical trade		Indirect policies for ethical trade
	Periodic: US government support for the Alliance, Accord and NTAP		
	Periodic: EU gvernment support for the Accord		
3. Why do governments make policies for ethical trade?	High social salience of ethical trade issues in late 1990s		Rana Plaza was a 'game changer' which led the Obama administration to revoke GSP access
	Pressure on government to regulate supermarket supply chains' ethical standards		Bangladesh government saw a need to improve working conditions in order to compete internationally
	Public policy interest in multi-stakeholder approaches to governance and to the issue of international development		
	Corporate and civil society desire for agreement on ethical standards – but mutual suspicions		
	Governments in United States, UK, Europe focused on improving situation in Bangladesh (game changer due to the scale of the Rana Plaza disaster)		

See Table 5.3 for an overview of Research Question 4.

the timing of the government regulation for CSR (Research Question 2), in the UK case, this was at the initiation of the ETI as well as in the form of continuing support for operations. In the Nordic cases, this was for periodic support for operations. We also noted that the ETI received periodic support for operations in the form of project finance from other governmental bodies.

We find European and the US governments providing similar periodic facilitation support to the Accord and the Alliance (Research Question 1) on a periodic basis (Research Question 2). We also find the US and the EU governments using their power of mandate in the form of trade policy to support CSR indirectly by seeking to change the regulatory context of the RMG sector in Bangladesh. This is through pressure on the Bangladeshi government to use its power of mandate to adopt new legislation (Research Question 1).

Our discussion of the motivations (Research Question 3) for government policy for CSR-inspired ethical trade focused on the UK and its role in shaping the ETI. We found a number of related factors. First, there was the general salience of the issue, which was compounded by the UK Competition Commission report. This not only contributed to the salience of the issue, but also specifically identified a governmental regulatory responsibility/opportunity. This issue was related to a government agenda that prioritized the issue of international development along with a commitment to an 'ethical foreign policy' (Haufler, 2001: 64). The multi-stakeholder character of the ETI reflected the ideological positioning of the Blair government in the Third Way (Giddens, 1998). Operationally, there was also a 'pull' factor for a prominent governmental role given the combination of a common commitment to an agreement, but also mutual hostility and suspicion among and between the main parties: the companies, the NGOs, and the trade unions. These last two points also help us to understand the relationships among the main actors underpinning the role of government. There was a shared commitment of all actors for a solution, yet there was a need for an 'honest' broker which the non-governmental actors agreed only government could fill. Moreover, once government adopted that role, it proved effective in persuading other corporations of the legitimacy of the fledgling ETI leading them also to join. We have also seen that governments from the United States and the EU have pushed for safer working conditions and have played a key role in providing finance and expertise for the Accord and the Alliance.

Turning to our Research Question 4, we found evidence on important interactions between national and international, and direct and indirect government policies for ethical trade. Table 5.3 provides an overview of different forms of policy for ethical trade (national and international as well as direct and indirect). Figure 5.1 provides an overview of key interactions.

Our two cases illustrate that government involvement in CSR includes interactions between the domestic and the international levels. We also see that government involvement in direct and indirect CSR leads to interactions between these two sorts of policies. First, the UK-initiated ETI has become increasingly international having been emulated in Denmark and Norway. Second, international community coalition of international companies as members of the Accord and Alliance as well as international organizations such as the ILO and domestic governments in countries such as the United States and the UK have put pressure on the Bangladeshi government to improve building safety in the readymade garment sector. Policies to support CSR directly are linked to indirect government initiatives. For example, the UK government's role in the initiation of the ETI is linked to a broader international development agenda where trade is used as a lever for promoting international development. In Bangladesh, government programs from the EU and the United States supported the CSR initiatives (the Accord and the Alliance). After President Obama ended GSP access for Bangladeshi exports, the US government has adopted a range of initiatives to support the Alliance (and also to some extent the Accord) as well as a range of initiatives and programs in Bangladesh in order to improve working conditions.

In the case of the ETI we found that the UK government gave great support to the inception and continuing operation of the initiative, and then also drew on the ETI's Base Code in the formulation of its own regulation of casual and migrant workers. The ETI is a multi-stakeholder initiative, and the government played a role as an honest broker between business on the one hand and union and civil society actors on the other (Knudsen, 2017). The UK government involvement also serves as a legitimizer for other corporations to join as government involvement signals that the initiative is important and represents a broader set of goals than business interests. Through two pieces of legislation the UK government (under Labour and Conservative administrations), has introduced relatively coercive regulation for

Table 5.3 *Interactions between Different Sorts of Government Policies for Ethical Trade*

Research question 4. What are the interactions between different forms of government policy for ethical trade?	Case: ETI (mainly direct government support)	Case: Ethical trade in the garment sector in Bangladesh (mainly indirect government support)
a. Between domestic and international policies for ethical trade?	The ETI expanded from the UK to other countries including Norway and Denmark The IEH and DIEH are deployed to internationalize ethical trade among Nordic countries	US government uses trade policy to promote workers' rights EU and US government partnership with Bangladesh government and ILO
b. Between direct and indirect policies for ethical trade?	Governments *directly* support CSR: as 'honest broker' between actors, and as 'legitimizer' for other corporations to join ETI Government *indirect* support for CSR: 1. CSR initiatives supported by government inform wider mandated government domestic policies: UK Gangmasters (2004) and Modern Slavery (2015) Acts mandate labour standards that ETI companies sign up for 2. Norwegian government public procurement criteria included IEH principles	Governments *directly* support CSR: as 'honest broker' between actors, and as 'legitimizer' for other corporations to join Accord and Alliance EU and US governments operate *indirectly* to shape the Bangladeshi institutional context

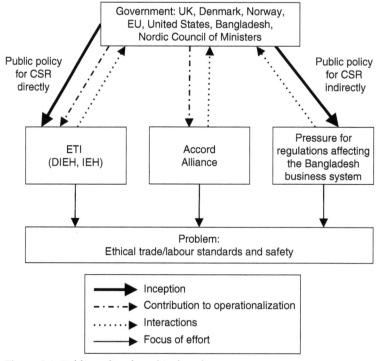

Figure 5.1 Public policy for ethical trade

employment standards within the UK, which not only reflected elements of the ETI Base Code but also served to strengthen the place of ethical standards in the UK employment field, including for migrant labour (UK Gangmasters (2004) and Modern Slavery (2015) Acts). Second, the Norwegian government's amendment of its public procurement criteria to include principles of the EIH offers a powerful example of the interaction of indirect and direct government policies for ethical trade (McCrudden, 2007).

Ethical trade has been a long-term social issue in the UK and other Western countries. The issue has achieved high salience in the past two decades as a CSR issue. In short, pressure has been put upon companies to regulate themselves and their supply chains, particularly in respect of labour rights and standards and remuneration. Companies have responded with various forms of institutionalization of ethical trade, be it through their own associations, partnerships, and standards, and through multi-stakeholder initiatives, which include civil society organizations of NGOs and trade unions of which the ethical trading initiative is a prominent example. These developments have rightly attracted attention as new forms of business regulation. Yet our analysis has shown that notwithstanding the new regulatory roles that such initiatives represent (e.g. Blowfield, 1999; Barrientos and Smith, 2006; Locke, 2013), the roles of government have been underestimated.

Certainly, the roles of government in this context are not all familiar ones. The forms of national government regulation we have surveyed represent counter-intuitive contributions to international governance. Through directly empowering the ETI, the UK government has been able to support some of the UK civil society and business aspirations for international ethical trade. Similarly, numerous governments have directly supplemented the more recent CSR initiatives – the Accord and the Alliance – in response to the Rana Plaza disaster. These forms of government support for CSR initiatives tend to emphasize softer forms of regulation.

Nonetheless, governments have used their harder power of mandate in their indirect support for CSR, notably in deploying trade policy as a means of exerting pressure on the Bangladesh government to support the ambitions of the Accord and the Alliance. Governments have supported CSR initiatives by effecting the institutional environment in which CSR initiatives operate. Clearly, the various roles of government in supporting CSR for ethical trade have not emerged solely as a result of business and civil society desire for governmental involvement and support. The UK Labour government (1997–2010), so crucial to the ETI's formative period, had also articulated an approach to public policy, which entailed collaboration with business and labour and other civil society organizations as represented in the idea of the 'Third Way' (Giddens, 1998). This had coincided with distinctive commitments to an 'ethical foreign policy' associated with the foreign secretary (Robin Cook), and a more conspicuous role in international development signalled by the first ever Cabinet appointment of the secretary of state for international development, Clare Short. Prior to her support for the ETI, Ms Short had also supplemented the Fair Trade Foundation by means of endorsement and facilitation. Likewise the Danish and Norwegian governments have long been known for their commitment both to internationalism and an approach to policymaking, which stresses consensus among, and collaboration with, business and labour actors. So we can conclude that government support for ethical trade initiatives serves a number of governmental purposes. It enables the governments to assist in elite-level interactions with key constituents, domestic multinational corporations, and leading labour and civil society organizations. It allows them to pursue their own policy objectives with the advantage of cooperative relations with the very actors pivotal in the respective sector – in this case international business.

We will elaborate on the theoretical and strategic significance of our findings in Chapter 7.

Notes

1 The Sustainability Compact is an agreement adopted on 8 July 2013 that brings together the European Union (EU), Bangladesh, the United States, and the ILO accompanied by employers, trade unions, and other key stakeholders with the common goal of improving working conditions and the respect of labour rights in Bangladesh's ready made garments industry to ensure that the Rana Plaza tragedy is not repeated. To do this, the Compact builds upon the National Tripartite Action Plan (NTAP) on short and long-term commitments related to three inter-linked pillars: 1) respect for labour rights; 2) structural integrity of buildings and occupational safety and health; and 3) responsible business conduct (ILO, 2013).

2 We define a partnership as 'involving collaboration of government organisations with firms or business associations, in which public sector bodies can function as participant or convener' (Knudsen et al., 2015: 4).

3 American companies face a higher risk of litigation than overseas competitors, largely because the court systems differ significantly (Knudsen, 2017). Unlike the system in the United States, courts in Europe generally prohibit class-action lawsuits, do not allow contingency fees for lawyers who win cases and require losing parties to pay legal fees for both sides. Those policies often discourage lawyers and plaintiffs from filing lawsuits.

6 | Governments and Tax Transparency: The Extractive Industries Transparency Initiative, Dodd–Frank, and the European Accounting Directive Amendments

In this chapter we explore the role of governments in addressing a long-standing issue of transparency in payment of taxes and charges by, usually Western, companies in the extractive sector to their host, usually developing country, governments. We introduce the issue of resources sector transparency in the context of the so-called resources curse for many developing countries. We see particularly how the transparency aspect of the resources curse has changed from an international development issue to emerge also on CSR agendas. The chapter then turns to investigate the role of government policies to support CSR in this area. Our focus here is on two sorts of government policies, first those in support of the EITI directly, and, second, those that support it indirectly in securing such transparency by re-shaping the regulatory contexts in which the EITI operates. This is support to CSR indirectly through governmental initiatives, namely the US Dodd–Frank Act (2010) and the European Accounting Directive Amendments (2013).

With respect to the government policy that directly supports the EITI, our focus here is upon the UK and Norwegian governments, which have nurtured and underpinned the EITI, and upon the EITI member governments which regulate transparency according to the EITI principles and its standard in their own jurisdictions. We then turn to our analysis of government support for the EITI indirectly by adopting public policies that address the wider issue of transparency in this sector. Here we investigate the roles of government in addressing this governance issue through the USA Dodd–Frank Act Section 1504 (2010) and the 2013 amendments to the EU Accounting Directive (1978). A concluding section summarizes and integrates the findings of the foregoing sections on the EITI and on the Dodd–Frank and EU Accounting Directive, focusing particularly on the interactions between the types of public policies deployed for transparency in the resources sector, between domestic and international policies; and between policies for CSR, direct and indirect. The research questions for this chapter (derived from Table 2.6) are set out in Table 6.1.

Prior to these analyses of two forms of government policy for transparency of payments in the extractives sector, we present the broader context of the issue of tax transparency in the extractive industries: the 'resources curse' and how the issue of transparency in the resources sector has grown from an international development issue to also become a CSR issue for which at least partial responsibility is attributed to, and claimed by, corporations.

From the Resources Curse to Transparency as a CSR Issue

The issue of transparency of tax payments in the context of wider international development issues, known as the resources curse, has emerged as a major concern for civil society organizations. The term the 'resource curse' was coined by Auty (1993) and applied to countries which are rich in natural resources and often appear unable to or fail to turn this endowment into economic and social wealth (see also Sachs and Warner, 2001). There are disagreements about why this happens with arguments varying from ineptitude to wilful expropriation of financial resources (Rosser, 2006; Ross, 1999; Stevens, 2005). Moreover, there are exceptions to the curse among more developed economies (e.g. Norway) and as well as developing economies (e.g. Botswana, Chile, Malaysia).

The basic story of the resource curse goes that inflows of foreign capital increase the value of resource-rich economies' currencies; as a result these countries are unable to develop other competitive export markets (e.g. in agriculture, manufacturing); and the extractive industries themselves draw in other financial and labour resources without pay-offs of human capital development and entrepreneurialism for the host societies (Frynas, 2009a: 134–35). So, although much of the focus has been upon the failure of governments in resource-rich countries to translate the revenue from taxes and charges upon the extractive industry, the large international corporations are a vital link in the economic paradox that makes for the curse. Moreover, it has been argued that, host governmental corruption apart, Western

Table 6.1 *Research Questions on Government Policies to Support Transparency of Payments in the Extractives Sector, Directly and Indirectly*

Research questions	Types of policies	
	To support transparency of payments in the resources sector directly	To support transparency of payments in the resources sector indirectly
1. *How do government policies support transparency of payments in the extractives sector: through endorsement, facilitation, partnership, or mandate*	EITI	Dodd–Frank Act (2010) Section 1504 European Accounting Directive amendments (2013)
2. *What roles do government polices play in supporting transparency of payments in the extractives sector: as initiators or contributors to operations of CSR initiatives?*	EITI	
3. *Why do governments make policies to support transparency of payments in the extractives sector?*	EITI	Dodd–Frank Act (2010) Section 1504 European Accounting Directive amendments (2013)
4. *What are the interactions between different sorts of policies to support transparency of payments in the extractives sector?* a. Between domestic and international policies? b. Between direct and indirect policies?	EITI and host country governments EITI Dodd–Frank Act (2010) Section 1504 and international business European Accounting Directive amendments (2013), UK Government and international business	

Note: the Direct and Indirect cells are merged for question 4 as the answers to these integrate findings.

MNCs systematically dodge tax obligations in developing countries and exacerbate fiscal losses to host societies (e.g. Oxfam, 2000; Action Aid, 2008).

Many resource-rich countries not only suffer the problems of the economic paradox explained but also such related problems as civil war and other violent conflicts (e.g. in Angola, the Central African Republic, the Democratic Republic of Congo, Liberia, Sierra Leone – see Collier and Hoeffler, 1998). Underlying these conflicts are long-standing governance problems, of which opacity of payments is merely a part. Karl (2005) concludes that such resource-rich countries are 'the most authoritarian and the most conflict-ridden in the world' (2005: 21). They are characterized by poor systems of political accountability that explain the failure to turn payments made by extractive industry corporations to secure wider national benefit (Frynas, 2009a). There are also yet-wider governance short-comings arising from the resource curse, notably the failure or inability of developing country govern-ments to adequately regulate the often deleterious environmental, workplace, and community impacts of MNCs operating mines and wells.

In the last two to three decades, attention has turned to the roles of international corporations as contributors to the resource curse. Gradually international extractive industry corporations have taken some social responsibility initiatives when operating in resource-rich developing countries. Frynas comments that oil companies

engage more with communities than multinationals in many other sec-tors ... (are associated with a) remarkable growth of corporate codes of conduct and social reporting ... (and) have embraced major international CSR initiatives such as ... the Extractive Industries Transparency Initiative. (2009b: 4)

Companies have long been associated with efforts to address the consequences of the resource curse, typically supporting commu-nity education and health, entrepreneurial development schemes, and local sourcing (Frynas, 2009b: 11; see also Fortanier and Kolk, 2007; Muthuri, Moon, and Idemudia, 2012). Nevertheless these CSR commitments, have often been criticized variously for being poorly integrated into company strategy, poorly evaluated, creating depend-ency cultures, and to be mainly motivated by reputation management (Blowfield, 2005; Frynas, 2009a, 2009b).

Moreover, as a spokesman for one company observed:

For years, it's been assumed that traditional CSR work has been the limit of the oil companies' impact in developing countries. In fact that sort of spend is low compared to the sums of money paid in taxes and royalties to government and the money we spend with local companies in the supply chain. (George Cazenove, Head of Media Relations Tullow Oil, 2014)

In this context, Frynas (2009a, 2009b) identified a further area of responsibility that extractive corporations could and should take to reduce the resources curse, and that is to better assist host countries by addressing the underlying causes of the resource curse, their governance shortcomings. He illustrates the possibilities here with reference to the ways that BP had stated in 2006 that it was prepared to:

Engag[e] in policymaking processes and offer assistance, as appropriate, on the development and implementation of policy agendas, which include for consideration addressing poverty alleviation, revenue management, and domestic energy. (cited in Frynas, 2009b: 15)

Other scholars are more critical on this count, and Jenkins and Newell (2014) cite a range of estimates of taxation foregone in developing countries through non-paid corporate taxes (principally through transfer pricing, manipulation of asset ownership, and financial manipulation) though they note the problems concerning the reliability of the underlying data.

Hence the issue of transparency of payments – or its absence – emerged as an item in the international development and international justice agendas. This was illustrated in the formation in 1993 of Transparency International (TI), a 'global coalition against corruption' in all sectors. TI has chapters in more than 100 countries and combines research and publications (e.g. data on national and business sector transparency) with promotional campaigns. A decade later a campaign for transparency of payments, specifically in the extractives sector, the Publish What You Pay (PWYP) was founded in 2002 by six London-based NGOs (CAFOD, Global Witness, Open Society Foundation, OXFAM, Save the Children, TI):

We believe that increasing transparency in the extractive sector will enable citizens to hold governments and companies to account for the ways in which natural resources are managed … Our mission is for a more transparent and accountable extractive sector, that enables citizens to have a say over whether their resources are extracted, how they are extracted and how their extractive revenues are spent. (Publish What You Pay, n.d.-a)

Indicative of the scale of civil society concern with transparency in the extractives sector, PWYP now has more than 800 organizational members across more than 50 countries, in 35 of which there are national coalitions affiliated to the PWYP campaign (Publish What You Pay, n.d.-b). The Global Alliance for Tax Justice (GATJ), formed in 2013, as a spin-off from the UK Tax Justice Network (formed in 2003) is a coalition of civil society organizations and activists (e.g. Action Aid, Christian Aid, Oxfam) with five regional networks in Africa, Latin America, Asia–Australia, North America, and Europe. Core activities include 'campaigning for greater transparency, democratic oversight and redistribution of wealth in national and global tax systems' (Global Alliance for Tax Justice, n.d.). Global Witness was formed in 1999 to achieve 'full transparency in the mining, logging, oil and gas sectors, so that citizens who own those resources can benefit fairly from them, now and in the future' (Global Witness, n.d.). It is funded by donations from trusts, foundations, and governments to investigate, research, and campaign to draw attention to 'the hidden links between demand for natural resources, corruption, armed conflict and environmental destruction' (Global Witness, n.d). These civil society organizations have succeeded in addressing international transparency issues, particularly in the extractives sector, with a high degree of expert knowledge and a keen eye for presentation and publicity (e.g. using celebrity supporters for media purposes). Their arguments have had impacts among governments and have also been advanced in scholarly (e.g. Christensen, Kapoor, and Murphy, 2004) and professional forums (SustainAbility, 2006). PWYP summed up the transparency revenue problem in the extractives sector in written evidence to a UK House of Commons Select Committee:

Developing countries have widely failed to mobilize natural resources revenues for development, through both under-collection and poor revenue management. The extractive industries are a key source of developing country income, but weak contractual terms, secrecy, corruption and lack of accountability are common, and there is evidence of tax non-compliance. (UK Parliament, 2012)

In conclusion, this lack of transparency and accountability in revenues from oil, gas, and mining exacerbates poor governance and leads to corruption, conflict, and poverty. A 2012 survey by Ernst and Young concluded that the oil and gas industry was subject to the most prosecutions for bribery and corruption in the UK of any sector over the past four years (Chazan, 2012). Jenkins and Newell (2014) note that companies rarely address tax issues, whether in their CSR reports or in their corporate codes of conduct. They cite an OECD (2000) study in which only one of the 233 codes published by individual companies, industry, and trade associations, and partnerships of stakeholders and intergovernmental organizations made any mention of taxation. Where taxation is mentioned in a CSR context, it is usually only to confirm that laws will be abided by. Jenkins and Newell's own analysis of FTSE4Good listed firms did find a somewhat higher likelihood of reference to tax in CSR reports, but they concluded that this was generally couched in terms of legal compliance and responsibilities to shareholders (2014: 390).

Despite their overall skepticism, Jenkins and Newell (2014: 386–88) note, first, the growth of companies referring to their 'corporate citizenship' and suggest that this should lead to CSR companies being ready to pay their fair share. Second, they contend that from a stakeholder perspective, companies should be expected to pay taxes, as the state provides services to companies in the form of the educational, legal, and communications infrastructure. Third, they argue that if CSR is about 'going beyond compliance' then companies should not use the argument that they are legally compliant to justify gross tax minimization – now a major issue facing the more developed countries. Finally, mimicking the 'business case' literature for CSR, Jenkins and Newell (2014) point to threats of reputational damage, litigation, losing contracts with government, losses to shareholder value, and risks of future regulation, as considerations, which should lead firms to adopt full tax compliance into their CSR policies.

Notwithstanding the relative reluctance of corporations to say much about tax issues in their CSR reporting, the issue has acquired a place on CSR agendas. This is evidenced in the addition of the 'Anti-Corruption' principle to the United National Global Compact

(UNGC), which states that: 'Businesses should work against corruption in all its forms, including extortion and bribery' (UN Global Compact, n.d.; see Muller and Kolk on the tax performance of companies claiming CSR credentials).

The Extractive Industries Transparency Initiative

Our analysis in this section is divided into three parts: an introduction to the EITI; an analysis of UK and Norwegian, and other governments', support for the EITI; and a summary.

The EITI emerged in 2003 as:

> a global Standard to promote open and accountable management of natural resources … (in which it is) supported by a coalition of governments, companies and civil society. (EITI, n.d.-a)

The EITI was born in the context of dual demands from, on the one hand, UK civil society groups (e.g. Publish What You Pay; Global Witness) in the late 1990s/early 2000s, for companies operating in countries with poor transparency and government accountability to develop 'a policy of full transparency'. On the other hand, oil companies solicited the UK government to drive reporting so as to reduce conflict with host governments and to establish a global baseline of disclosure requirements for companies. The UK government, through the Department for International Development (DfID), brought together civil society, company, and government representatives to establish a statement of principles to increase transparency of payments and revenues in the extractive sector, the EITI (EITI, 2009).

The EITI describes its objectives as:

> to strengthen government and company systems, inform public debate, and enhance trust. EITI implementation takes place in each member country supported by a multi-stakeholder forum or coalition of governments, companies and civil society working together. (EITI, n.d.-a)

Its seeks to promote economic growth and poverty reduction through greater transparency, because:

> natural resources, such as oil, gas, metals and minerals, belong to a country's citizens. Extraction of these resources can lead to economic growth and

social development. However, when poorly managed it has too often lead to corruption and even conflict. More openness around how a country manages its natural resource wealth is necessary to ensure that these resources can benefit all citizens. (EITI, n.d.-a)

The EITI values reflect 'the importance of collective approaches to governance' (EITI 2016a), including: business (it is supported by about 70 of the largest oil, gas and mining companies); civil society (it is supported by more than 650 NGOs); as well as member and candidate governments and inter-governmental actors across the globe.

In brief, the EITI has developed from a CSR-inspired multi-stakeholder organization administered within a UK government department (2002–06) to a non-profit organization whose secretariat is located in Norway, and which is supported by the Norwegian government. The focus for the operationalization of the initiative has shifted from the UK government and motivated companies to the national governments of the candidate and compliant countries, and this was facilitated by financial support from the Multi-Donor Trust Fund of the World Bank. It has developed from a relatively 'vague initiative' in 2002, in the EITI's own words, to the agreement of twelve principles (2003), to adopt indicators of these principles with an agreed validation methodology (2009), and to become a standard (2013, updated in 2016) with requirements for implementing these principles.

The EITI is designed to include home and host governments of natural resource corporations, public and private business organizations, business associations, civil society, and international agencies (e.g. the World Bank, IMF, UN, OECD). If the national government of a country decides to implement the EITI standard, then all companies operating in the country, including state-owned companies, are required to publish what they have paid to the government, wherever they are registered. The EITI requires an independent reconciliation of what government discloses that it has received, and what the companies say they have paid. This is to uncover and act upon any discrepancies and inaccuracies. The EITI is built around twelve principles summarized in Table 6.2.

The EITI establishes a mechanism for debate about the resources inside the member countries, particularly through the national multi-stakeholder platforms for dialogue about the use of their country's natural resources that the EITI initiated. In short, the EITI represents an international standard, but it is implemented nationally. This means

Table 6.2 *Twelve Principles of the EITI*

1. Belief in the prudent use of natural resource wealth for sustainable economic growth
2. Sovereign governments to manage natural resource wealth for national development
3. Long-run benefits of resource extraction
4. Public understanding of government revenues and expenditure help public debate and inform choice about sustainable development
5. Transparency by governments and extractive industries companies to enhance public financial management and accountability
6. Transparency must be set in the context of respect for contracts and laws
7. Domestic and foreign direct investment may be increased with financial transparency
8. Government accountability to all citizens for revenue streams and public expenditure
9. High standards of transparency and accountability in public life, government, and business
10. A consistent, workable, and simple approach to the disclosure of payments and revenues
11. Payments' disclosure should involve all extractive industry companies operating therein
12. All stakeholders have important and relevant contributions to make

Note: For principles in full, see EITI (2016b).

that each national multi-stakeholder group determines how to adapt the EITI implementation process to reflect local circumstances, needs, or preferences including, for example, a specific legal environment or the details of the payments to be published.

National government membership of the EITI is achieved through distinct phases. The first concerns the application to become a candidate country through a public statement of intent; a commitment to work with companies and civil society organizations on implementing the initiative; the appointment of a senior official to lead the EITI implementation and of a multi-stakeholder group to oversee the implementation; and the multi-stakeholder group agreement of a work plan. The second phase, the preparation for candidacy, requires the member governments to: ensure that civil society organizations are operating freely; to engage the companies to implement the EITI

Table 6.3 *Seven Requirements of the EITI Standard*

1. Effective oversight by the multi-stakeholder group
2. Timely publication of EITI Reports
3. EITI Reports that include contextual information about the extractive industries
4. The production of comprehensive EITI Reports that include full government disclosure of extractive industry revenues, and disclosure of all material payments to government by oil, gas, and mining companies
5. A credible assurance process applying international standards
6. EITI Reports that are comprehensible, actively promoted, publicly accessible, and contribute to public debate
7. The multi-stakeholder group to take steps to act on lessons learned and review the outcomes and impact of EITI implementation

Source: EITI (2016c).

and the multi-stakeholder group to agree on issues of materiality and the reporting templates; to appoint an organization to reconcile the governmental and company reports; and to provide an assurance of the probity of the company and government reports. The third phase consists of disclosure requirements for the companies and the government reports, whose reconciliation is to be confirmed by the multi-stakeholder group. It also confirms that the work of the reconciler body was properly carried out; that the reports are accessible and that companies to support the reports and the government and multi-stakeholder group act on the lessons learned. Compliant countries are required to maintain adherence to the EITI standard in order to retain this status (Sovacool and Andrews, 2015: 185).

Member countries must adhere to the EITI standard for reporting activity in the oil, gas, and mining sectors ranging from the awarding of licenses and contracts; through monitoring production and collecting taxes; to allocating the revenues. The seven requirements of the EITI standard are presented in Table 6.3.

Turning to its own governance, we find that the EITI participants are representatives from: governments and their agencies; oil, gas, and mining companies; asset management companies and pension funds; international NGOs; and local civil society groups. The EITI arranges a Global Conference at least every three years in order to provide an international forum for its stakeholders and to appoint the Board, which oversees the EITI. The Board consists of: an independent Chair (currently Fredrik Reinfeldt, a former Swedish prime minister), and country, company, institutional investor and civil society representatives. Invited observers to EITI Board meetings include representatives of such international organizations as the World Bank and the IMF.

One way of assessing the EITI's significance is simply to consider its growth of membership and of formal association by countries, companies, and civil society actors. Progress was initially slow with only half-a-dozen countries showing interest, and it took nine years for the first country, Azerbaijan, to become compliant. Subsequently interest in EITI membership has mushroomed in terms of national government memberships, business associates and investor supporters, making it the most comprehensive normative and practical mechanism for the governance of natural resource extraction (Lehmann, 2015). As of September 2016, fifty-one countries implement the EITI (2016c) standard; thirty-one countries are deemed EITI compliant; and forty-one countries have published revenue reports (even if not all are fully compliant). Eighteen countries, described as 'EITI Candidates', are at earlier stages of implementing the initiative (EITI, n.d.-c). A significant development is the growth of membership of more developed countries with significant extractive sectors (e.g. Norway, Australia, the United States, the UK, France). This has significantly increased the legitimacy of the EITI (authors' interview with Clare Short, November 2015), and addressed the criticism that remaining outside the standard could be seen as 'hypocritical and even somewhat colonialist' (Moody-Stuart, 2014: 46).

The EITI has also grown in terms of 'supporters', specifically more than 90 companies involved in oil, gas and mining, and more than eighty global investment institutions (Sovacool and Andrews, 2015). In addition, several key business associations in the sector are numbered among the EITI's Partner Organizations (the Australia–Africa Mining Industry Group; the International Council on Mining and Metals; and the International Organisation of Oil and Gas Producers). Their motivations are anchored in the benefits participating companies enjoy such as increased legitimacy; more secure and informed investments; and operation on a 'level playing field' with other companies (EITI, 2016c). Companies are thought to reap both reputational and commercial rewards by engaging in and shaping the policy debate with government, civil society, and producers (EITI, 2015a).

In turn, companies benefit financially from a more secure investment climate and the reputation gained from showing their commitment to governments (ibid). This can provide both a 'license to operate' in host countries (Department for Business, Innovation & Skills, 2014) and confidence of a greater levelling of the respective host country playing fields.

Another indicator of EITI growth is the increased support of civil society organizations, now numbering more than 400 NGOs (e.g. the Catholic Agency for Overseas Aid, Global Witness, Natural Resource Governance Institute, Open Society Institute, Oxfam, Publish What you Pay Coalition, Caritas, Transparency International). Some of these are represented on the EITI Advisory Board along with some county-specific NGOs (e.g. the Economic Research Center, Azerbaijan; Publish What You Pay, Nigeria; Association Africaine de Défense des Droits de l'Homme; Institute for Essential Services Reform, Indonesia; Cordaid, the Netherlands).

An indicator of the increasing institutional strength of the EITI is the growth of its membership. This has been a gradual process as the initial principles have been successively complemented by greater specification of compliance criteria and provision of assistance with meeting these. First, a Validation Guide was published in 2005 to assist participants on how to produce reports. Subsequently new EITI rules were published after the 2009 and 2011 conferences, which were complemented with Policy Notes to provide further clarification and guidance. Following criticism of the lack of societal impact of the EITI, in 2013 a commissioned report (Scanteam, 2011) on the the EITI standard was issued in 2013. This entailed a shift from 'indicators' of compliance to 'requirements' for compliance. In order to enable better disclosure, the standard offered a clearer set of rules and required reports to be more easily understandable at the respective national levels. It also required state-owned 'National Oil Companies' of the member countries (accounting for 80 per cent of world's oil production) to report (EITI, 2016b).

A second form of regulatory change requires EITI member governments to report disaggregated payments *by each company* rather than simply aggregated payment data (EITI International Secretariat, January 2015). This change was partly in response to the long-standing civil society pressure for such an approach but also to complement US and EU decisions to adopt regulations that included similar requirements (interview with Clare Short November 2014). This important interaction between the pioneering soft mandate of the EITI and the subsequent more coercive transparency initiatives will be discussed in further sections.

A third form of regulatory change enables the EITI to downgrade the status of member countries from 'compliant' to 'candidate' countries in circumstances of unacceptable government behaviour. For example, the Azerbaijan government's restrictions on civil society in 2015 prompted the EITI to downgrade the country's status.

A fourth regulatory development in the 2016 standard was the requirement (from 2020) for full disclosure of the ownership of companies making or receiving payments in extractive industries. This has arisen following the fear that 'shell companies' can be used to divert oil (*The Economist*, 24 October 2015: 61). This addresses the long-standing criticism that the EITI had excluded the complex stages in industry value chain (Mouan, 2010). Other changes were designed, first, to enable member governments to use existing reporting systems to make their results transparent thereby lightening the administrative burden and complexity. Second, however, there were increased requirements for member governments and their respective multi-stakeholder groups, to learn from the reports in order to effect appropriate reforms (EITI, 2016b).

Another sign of the regulatory significance of the EITI is that it has been integrated into international institutions. For example the Global Reporting Initiative (GRI) has included the EITI in its framework and the World Bank has incorporated the EITI's extractives sector guidance (Lehmann, 2015; Mouan, 2010).

A final indicator of the significance of the EITI is in its substantive impact. As of 2016, USD 2.09 trillion in revenues have been disclosed and 305 fiscal years have been captured in EITI reports (EITI, 2016d). There are also reports of substantial revenues identified and made available to the public purse. For example, in Nigeria, missing payments of close to USD 10 billion have been reported, mainly from the Nigerian National Petroleum Corporation (NNPC) (Lehmann, 2015). This resulted in the return of USD 2 billion to the government and the modification of the 2012 Executive Draft of the Petroleum Industry Bill because it was thought to be inadequate in its initial form to reorganize the NNPC (Gillies, 2014, cited in Lehmann, 2015).

The EITI has not been without criticisms. Some of these have been directly addressed as the EITI has evolved whereas other criticisms may still be seen to apply. While it is not our purpose to give a detailed analysis of these issues, we note the main points of contention. At the most general level, there is the criticism that transparency does not deliver accountability. This argument is a very common and broad one and in this context is made on the assumption that corrupt governments and corporations are quite able to cover their tracks while also appearing transparent. So a particular criticism in this context goes that we know little about the operations and anti-corruption programmes of EITI countries, and this is what really matters (Transparency International, 2008: 24). Second, there is the argument that transparency of government revenues is simply an inappropriate, or at least incomplete, tool for establishing fiscal responsibility (Frynas, 2009a, 2009b). The argument is that to achieve accountability, government expenditures need to be transparent. Moreover, Frynas, in making this criticism, also adds that the link between revenue transparency and benefits for host countries is unproven – and he cites a wider literature regarding country transparency and notes its focus on expenditures and not revenues (Frynas, 2009a, 2009b).

Third, a criticism goes that the EITI provides transparency only in those countries whose governments are willing to be held accountable: others can continue to benefit from opaque payments from the extractives sector with impunity. Moreover, it is also possible for governments to sign up for the EITI but benefit from the relative weakness of the media and the civil society in developing countries (Frynas, 2009b: 147). Aaronson (2011) argues that some EITI member governments have not allowed civil society actors sufficient opportunities to participate, nor provided them with sufficient information about EITI processes to be effective partners. One study reported that the EITI had adverse impacts on the improvement of government–citizen relations with increased detention and trials of anti-corruption activists (Lehmann, 2015). Thus in many member countries, the public and legislators are not sufficiently aware of the EITI systems to affect its ostensible objective, improved public accountability. Perversely, when the EITI suspends a member country for its questionable practices (e.g. Equatorial Guinea), its extractive industries payments are totally removed from the transparency and scrutiny that the EITI would have intended, thereby compounding the original problem.

Fourth, some experts question the model of using company transparency as a means of holding governments accountable. Frynas, for
example, cites the reluctance of many companies to take on advanced
roles in governance (Frynas, 2009b: 138) and adds that companies
often exacerbate the very governance problems in question through
lobbying to secure corporate objectives such as tax minimization and
avoidance (Frynas, 2009b: 157). This is an area that the EITI will pay
more attention to in in the coming years (EITI, 2015b).

Finally, the EITI has been criticized for its slow progress, for example, in terms of securing successful compliance (Aaronson, 2011). It is
in the nature of multi-stakeholder organizations that progress is usually as fast as the slowest member allows. Aaronson (2011) argues that
the EITI is weakened by its multi-stakeholder design as the main partners – government, business, and civil society – have different visions
for its mission and hence are slow to make agreements.

Having established how and why the EITI has become a leading
international CSR multi-stakeholder initiative, we now turn to the role
of national governments in its origins and development.

National Governments and the EITI

We explore the roles of national home and host governments in regulating the transparency of business to government payments through
the EITI. We focus on the role of the UK government in shaping this
new regulatory initiative to promote tax transparency and the role of
the Norwegian government in maintaining and developing it.

In its formative stages, particularly, the EITI was regarded as a form
of private regulation established to make up for missing or inadequate
governmental regulation. The EITI is usually classed among CSR's
multi-stakeholder initiatives (MSIs) both by practitioner organizations (e.g. CSR Weltweit) and by academics (e.g. Grayson and Nelson,
2013). MSIs are a collaborative form of CSR governance that involves
stakeholders on a voluntary basis and that crosses state/non-state and
profit/non-profit boundaries (Fransen, 2012; Rasche, 2012; Utting,
2002). In order for companies to demonstrate their willingness to
meet growing demands for social responsibility, many have joined
MSIs (Anner, 2014; Fung et al., 2001, 2007). Although, by virtue of
its core membership of national governments the EITI has also been
termed an inter-governmental organization, it has the characteristics

of a CSR-oriented MSI and it is therefore included in our study as a CSR initiative. First, the EITI describes itself as a:

multi-stakeholder coalition of governments, companies, investors, civil society organisations, and partner organisations (and states that) (a) multi-stakeholder group oversees the EITI process in implementing countries and internationally through the EITI Board. (EITI, n.d.-d)

Second, the EITI was created to enable MNCs to address accusations of irresponsibility in their tax and other payments to host governments on the basis of a level playing field. Third, as noted earlier, the EITI numbers many of the world's leading oil, gas, and mining companies, investor institutions, and extractives business associations among its 'supporters' and 'partners'. Fourth, the supporter companies make financial contributions to the EITI either directly or through their industry bodies. For individual companies, these currently range from USD 20,000 to USD 60,000 depending on the company size. Fifth, there are six companies on the EITI Board (one of which is an investor representative), accounting for 30 per cent of the members (the remainder being divided between country representatives (9), civil society representatives (50) and a Chair). Sixth, these companies use their 'supporter status' to signal their CSR credentials. For example, in the section of its corporate website, Shell states that as 'a founder and board member of the Extractive Industries Transparency Initiative (EITI) … we continue to advocate mandatory country-by-country global reporting, as most tax payments are made at the corporate level to national governments' (2016). It describes its EITI membership as in line with its ethical policy (2016). In its 2015 Corporate Responsibility Report, Chevron refers to its membership of, and participation in, the EITI as integral to its efforts to promote global transparency (2015). Finally, academic authorities on CSR include the EITI in their discussion of the phenomenon. Grayson and Nelson (2013) describe the EITI as a multi-stakeholder initiative 'promoting CSR'. Haufler describes the origins of the EITI in terms of the intersection of three overlapping transnational networks: 'corruption, conflict and *corporate social responsibility*' (2001: 54, emphasis added; see also Mena and Palazzo, 2012).

In this context of a CSR-oriented MSI, we consider the role of government for the EITI. The UK government played critical roles on the inception of the EITI, first in negotiation of its multi-stakeholder approach, and second in formally launching the initiative.

In 1999 the NGO Global Witness published a report *A Crude Awakening* on the lack of transparency and government accountability in the oil industry, highlighting how the Angolan civil war was financed by oil money. This led to the 'Publish What You Pay' campaign for transparency over the taxes paid by each local mine as a way to empowering local communities, particularly in their demands for public services. In 2001 John Browne, chief executive officer of BP, responded to the campaign by publishing payments that BP had made to the government of Angola – USD 111 million for the off-shore license alone (Browne, 2010). This sparked threats to the company from the Angolan government, which led Browne to conclude that 'Clearly a unilateral approach, where one company or one country was under pressure to publish what you pay was not workable' (Browne, 2010 cited at EITI, 2016a).

The UK government determined to address the collective action problem that John Browne had identified regarding transparency in the extractives sector (i.e. the disincentives for a single MNC to be transparent). Prime Minister Tony Blair prepared to announce the EITI at the Johannesburg World Summit for Sustainable Development (2002) and although the speech was never made, it was published (EITI, 2016a). In 2003 the UK government hosted the first EITI Plenary Conference at which DfID brokered an initial partnership of companies (notably BP), NGOs (notably Global Witness), and governments to form a transparency standard. The EITI was duly launched in 2003 with its twelve core principles. The UK government provided initial operational facilitation in the form of organizational resources and financial subsidy, and including through its network of embassies and consulates.

The UK government also played an important role in providing *continuing* support to the operations of the EITI in its early years, through further endorsement and facilitation, in terms of physical and fiscal resources, as well as in brokerage activities. It contributed £1 million at the outset to develop the Initiative, and from 2002 to 2006 it provided a small EITI secretariat based in DfID. This role proved to be crucial in the formative years in persuading the first developing country members to join up and engage with the process. As a result, following the 2003 meeting, four countries (Azerbaijan, Ghana, the Kyrgyz

Republic, and Nigeria) pledged to apply the EITI principles and, shortly after, Peru, the Republic of Congo, Sao Tome e Principe, Timor Leste, and Trinidad and Tobago (EITI, 2016a) agreed to apply the principles as well. More broadly the UK government used its position in intergovernmental organizations both to endorse the EITI and – through international facilitation – to win its endorsement by these other governments. Thus the Initiative was endorsed by the 2004 G8 Summit at Sea Island and by the 2005 Commission for Africa Report at the G8 Gleneagles Summit. This contributed to the decisions by governments to sign up to the Initiative in the early stages (see further sections).

From 2006, the EITI established greater independence from the UK government, signaled in its non-profit status, and the appointment of its own Advisory Board at the two yearly members' conference. DfID was 'happy that the EITI had developed and "left home"' (authors' interview, Clare Short, November 2014). But this did not mean that from this point the EITI became independent of government. Rather, various forms of government facilitation of the EITI in the form of physical and fiscal contributions continue. In 2007, the Norwegian government offered continuing support for the EITI's operations in the form of an International Secretariat in Oslo. There are also various forms of periodic support for the EITI's operations, mainly through funding from such governments as the UK, Denmark, Norway, and Sweden.

The fifty or so governments engaged with the EITI, whether as compliant or candidate countries, also directly support the EITI through endorsement and facilitation by implementing its principles and standards. They establish the national-level procedures and committees to ensure the reconciliation of company reports on payments made and government reports on payments received, and to publish these. At the national level governments also form partnerships with national NGOs, and they mandate to require those extractives companies operating within their borders to report. Other forms of governmental support include membership of the EITI Advisory Board of representatives of the implementing governments (currently Togo, Republic of Congo, Liberia, Ghana, Peru, Timor-Leste, Azerbaijan, and Kazakhstan) and the supporting country governments (currently Canada, United States, Belgium, Sweden, and France).

Turning to the question as to why governments acted to support the EITI, we start with the UK case. First, a key contextual factor is that the extractive industry is a sector of major importance to the British economy. For example, the UK is home to some of the world's largest extractive firms such as BP, Shell, and Rio Tinto. The UK is also a major source of finance to the extractive sector. Thus, the argument for a level playing field motivated the UK government to find a means of ensuring that its home companies were not disadvantaged by their responsiveness to home society expectations of responsibility. The UK identified an interest in the international reputation of its business as articulated more broadly by CSR minister Margaret Hodge: 'underpinning our approach is our belief that economic prosperity and social justice are interlinked and not competing objectives … it makes sense for business to act in a responsible way which ensures their longer term sustainability' (2006). For the government of Norway, continuing support to the EITI, fits with the country's long-term internationalist agenda and it has been able to act as an exemplar member having joined the Initiative in 2007.

Many governments are motivated to join the EITI by increasing tax transparency as a way to strengthen their legitimacy, accountability, good governance, and economic and political stability which overall creates a more fertile investment climate (Lehmann, 2015; Mouan, 2010). In addition, conflicts around the extractives sector are likely to be reduced, which signals a more secure investment atmosphere (ibid). For example, a study of the country benefits associated with joining the EITI confirms that participation results in both increased access to aid (corresponding to a country's level of implementation) as well as a reduction in corruption (measured by the Transparency International Corruption Perceptions Index) (Dávid-Barrett and Okamura, 2013). Short (2014) has also confirmed the link between the EITI and an increase in the ratio of FDI (Foreign Direct Investment) amount to GDP (Growth Domestic Products).

It appears that transparent countries have lower debt levels and lower budget deficits (Alt and Lassen, 2006a, 2006b). The EITI itself contends that the implementation of the standard results in more effective government systems, which facilitate better tax collection and budgetary planning (EITI, 2016c.) This certainly must be of interest to representatives of host country governments. Of equal significance is, of course, the fact that a transparent government engenders citizens' trust (Ibid.).

Government and Direct Regulation of the EITI: Summary

A number of key conclusions about national government and the regulation of international CSR can be drawn. Notwithstanding the criticisms noted of the EITI, it has quickly assumed the status, first, of an international CSR MSI and subsequently of a standard reflecting a membership of national governments, companies, NGOs, investors, and other international organizations. It 'improves informational flows between the rulers and the ruled' (Frynas, 2009b: 145) and creates opportunities for civil society roles to expand.

The very fact that so many companies are supporting the initiative indicates its value to them in obviating the collective action problems that BP faced in Angola, in the legitimacy and respectability that it endows upon them, and the opportunities to learn more about accountable business in some of the most challenging circumstances (Frynas, 2009a, 2009b). That this is complemented by the involvement of auditors and civil social organizations in the EITI which can only strengthen these advantages to the supporting companies.

The role of the UK, Norway, and other national governments has been critically important in its initiation and development through their regulatory resources of endorsement, facilitation, and partnership. These regulatory resources have been deployed interactively with civil society and business actors, and indeed with other governments, which, like companies are both regulators by virtue of their EITI membership and are regulated through the transparency mechanisms. The UK government proved critical by acting as a 'deal maker' in an atmosphere of mutual suspicion between the key companies and NGOs, particularly Global Witness. This is reflected in its unique resource of governing authority, which underpinned the continuing legitimacy with which it was able to endow the EITI (authors' interview with Clare Short, November 2014). This resource was supplemented by its inimitable organizational assets including its network of consuls and embassies. While the fiscal resources that the UK government initially provided were limited, in the initiation and early stages of the EITI, this gave confidence to companies to sign up and make financial commitments.

We have seen how 'home' national governments can initiate multistakeholder regulation of corporations in the form of an organization, the EITI, which other national governments, 'home' and 'host', can join. By virtue of their collective action, these governments can improve regulation of transparency of the resources sector by mandating compliance of companies at the respective national levels. While some companies might themselves be motivated to be transparent, as illustrated by the case of BP, there may be others who do so reluctantly, and only because of the EITI. This is because the EITI has now created an effective international standard, by virtue of the multiplication of national government members; the number and significance of the associated companies and investor organizations; the support of significant international governmental organizations; and the legitimacy that it conveys by virtue of the key civil society supporters. The fact that it operates in so many countries means that companies cannot so easily adopt 'exit' strategies when threatened with mandates for transparency (although many significant resource-rich countries, such as China and Russia, are still not associated with the EITI).

In contrast to expectations from the business and society literature concerning the obsolescence of national government for the regulation of international business, our analysis tells a different story. National governments have been the vital actors in the EITI, in its initiation and operationalization. The significance of these developments will be examined more closely, first, in relation to wider governmental activities to increase transparency in the extractives sector (at the end of the chapter) and, more generally, in our broader consideration of national government and CSR interactions in the closing Chapter.

Government Policies for Transparency of Payments in the Extractives Sector Indirectly

We now assess national government policy, which supported CSR for transparency in the extractives sector – specifically the EITI – indirectly. We examine two regulatory initiatives which impose demands on the international responsibilities of companies either listed on domestic stock exchanges, in the case of the United States, or registered in the domestic territory, in the case of the EU. These are, respectively, the United States' 2010 Dodd–Frank Wall Street Reform and Consumer Protection Act (particularly Section 1504) and the 2013 amendments to the European Union's Accounting Directive. We examine the interactions of these more traditional, coercive forms of government regulation with the softer forms of regulation that we examined in the case of the EITI.

We shall see that although there is no formal relationship between these forms of government mandate and the EITI, they are related in a number of key respects. First, national governments responsible for the regulations are also engaged with the EITI: they do not see their mandates as rendering the softer EITI obsolete. The US government, although not responsible for the initiation of the Dodd–Frank Act, which was the result of a Congressional initiative, nonetheless adopted it. The UK government, which had played a pioneering role in the EITI, while not solely responsible for the amendment to the EU Accounting Directive, was its main advocate (authors' interview with representative of DG Internal Market Directorate General, European Commission, November 2014). Second, the US (2011) and UK (2014) governments' applications for EITI membership in 2014 have been regarded as a major fillip to the EITI's own momentum (*The Economist*, 2014). Third, we will see how assessments of the EITI directly informed the Dodd–Frank Act which, in turn, led to a strengthening of the EITI regulations. Fourth, the initiation and operationalization of the US and the EU regulations took a very different course from that of the UK in launching the EITI, reminding us of the importance not only of national governments but also of 'home' national and regional political systems in the shaping of regulation of international responsible business.

The US Approach: The Dodd–Frank Act Section 1504

In response to the banking sector shortcomings which led to the 2008 financial crisis, the US government (in the form of the Congress and the Presidency) adopted the Dodd–Frank Wall Street Reform and Consumer Protection Act[1] in 2010 (the Dodd–Frank Act). Its core elements are to bring increased transparency of derivatives, to establish a new oversight council to evaluate systemic risk, to bring consumer protection reforms and measures to improve accounting, and to increase regulation of credit rating agencies, all in order to better regulate US financial markets.

However, as we shall see in the later sections, the Act also focuses on Conflict Minerals (Section 1502), Mine Safety Disclosures (Section

1503), and, our particular interest, Payments to Governments by
Resource Extraction Issuers (Section 1504). In passing these sections
into law, the US Congress aimed to improve transparency and provide
investors and citizens with tools to hold companies and governments
more accountable.

Section 1504 requires stock-exchange-listed oil, natural gas, and minerals companies to file reports to the Securities Exchange Commission
(SEC) on project-level payments to reigning governments.[2] It specifies that 'extractive industries firms listed in the US must declare all
government spending on a country and project basis'. It amends the
1934 Securities Exchange Act to direct the SEC to promulgate rules
requiring resource extraction companies[3] to include in their annual
reports (in an interactive data format) details of payments made to a
foreign government or the federal government for the purpose of the
commercial development of oil, natural gas, or minerals. This reflects
the aims of the EITI, to increase transparency and accountability of
payments between resource extracting companies and governments, to
enable local communities in resource-rich countries to expose corruption and to hold governments accountable so that tax revenues could
be allocated to economic and social development, as well as making
the extractives corporations more transparent.

The Dodd–Frank Act Sections 1502 and 1504 followed public
outcry in the United States over conflict minerals in the Democratic
Republic of Congo. They mandate company transparency whereas the
EITI does not do so, though it does require its member governments
to do so. But by virtue of being an Act of Congress, the Dodd–Frank
Act was only passed following a drawn-out legislative process, and
a subsequent judicial process. This is because the United States' separation of powers between the executive branch of government (the
President), the legislative branch (Congress, consisting of the House
of Representatives and the Senate) yields much greater powers to its
legislators, relative to the executive, than does the UK and other parliamentary systems (Knudsen, 2017). As a result, US-organized interests focus their lobbying activity on the legislature in the process of
lawmaking.

This explains why, first, a US financial services regulation bill came
to include 'riders' concerning the responsibilities of US companies
abroad. Several Congress members saw an opportunity to exploit a
shifting political climate opposed to conflict diamonds[4] and favouring

greater tax transparency in the extractive sector (Kaufmann and Penciakova, 2011). Thus, Section 1504 emerged in an environment where a number of international initiatives clamoured for increased accountability and transparency including the Group of Eight's (G8) 'Muskova Declaration: Recovery and New Beginnings' which called on countries in the extractives sector to engender greater governance and accountability (Lynn, 2011). As in the UK there had been a decade or so of high-profile 'Publish What You Pay' PWYP (US) campaign by a coalition of NGOs including Revenue Watch, Oxfam, Global Witness, Earthrights, the ONE Campaign, and many other groups (Lissakers, 2012). PWYP (US) had long argued that the EITI offered insufficient regulation of tax payments in extractives, particularly as it only regulated those extractive companies which volunteered to comply (Factor, 2014). Moreover, at that time it only provided national aggregate-level, not company-level, data. PWYP (US) met with Congressman Barney Frank to 'educate' him about the 'resource curse in 2004 and 2005' (interview with authors, Oxfam, October 2014 and September 2015). His initial response was that the lack of transparency of company tax payments should be dealt with under the *Foreign Corrupt Practices Act* (FCPA), a coercive regulation against corruption. The PWYP (US) response was that the FCPA only deals with illegitimate payments, which are outside the reach of the EITI, thus justifying the proposed bill (PWYP, interview with authors, 22 October 2014).

The PWYP (US) view was supported by several key business actors including institutional investors (e.g. Calvert Investments) who argued that transparent companies will attract more investors because disclosure clarifies investment risks (Kaufmann and Penciakova, 2011). Some large extractive companies (e.g. Rio Tinto) pointed out that tax transparency can be a competitive advantage as firms can provide host governments with clear evidence of how they contribute to government revenues and to communities. Yet others (e.g. the Electronic Industry Citizenship Coalition; the Global Electronic Sustainability Initiative; the Conflict-Free Smelter Program; the OECD Due Diligence Guidance for Responsible Supply Chains of Minerals from Conflict-Affected and High-Risk Areas) judged that business simply had to respond to the societal demands for transparency. Thus, the law was not only a monitoring mechanism but emblematic of the social pressure on corporations that pervaded the public sphere (Reinecke and Ansari, 2015)

Accordingly, the promoters of Sections 1502 and 1504 exploited Dodd–Frank's focus on the SEC's requirement that extractive firms engage in additional non-financial disclosures and in so doing promote certain humanitarian and diplomatic goals. Issues such as due diligence, accountability, and transparency are established themes in the SEC's duties which could be built upon. For example, the 2009 'Energy Security through Transparency Act'[5] (S. 1700) requires all listed extractive companies to publish their payments in all the countries where they operate and this was used as a justification for Section 1504, also known as the Cardin–Lugar amendment, named after the two Senators who submitted it. According to Senator Cardin, US security concerns played a role in regulating tax payments in the oil industry: 'We know the value of oil, but it goes well beyond oil resources. For all those reasons, this is part of our security dimension of this country, and that's why we got so involved on this issue' (Kaufmann and Penciakova, 2011).

Some large companies (e.g. Shell) and industry associations (e.g. the American Petroleum Institute (API)) opposed the disclosure rule in Section 1504 and lobbied heavily against rules that would require project-level disclosure. They lobbied for various exemptions, including the so-called tyrant veto, which would exempt companies from disclosing payments in countries where payment disclosure was prohibited by local law. The API argued that project-level disclosure would be costly and would position publicly traded firms at a competitive disadvantage; furthermore, companies might face in-country discrimination against companies from countries with no disclosure requirements. The API and several companies argued that the disclosure provisions constituted a violation of their ability to compete internationally (Kaufmann and Penciakova, 2011).

However, the Bill was duly passed by Congress and was signed by President Obama in July 2010. Responsibility for designing the final rules on the implementation of Section 1504 was passed to the SEC, which led to yet further rounds of lobbying. Indeed, even before the SEC announced the rules, it was subject to a suit by the PWYP (US) for the delay in finalizing the framework. The final rules were announced in August 2012 following a 2–1 vote in favour by the commissioners (SEC, 2012).[6]

Once the Act came into effect in 2010, many companies changed their posture of 'least resistance' to one of 'active engagement' in the two-year multi-stakeholder consultation process spearheaded by the SEC (Reinecke and Ansari, 2015). Through this public dialogue, a number of companies were now purportedly motivated to engage in dialogue with NGOs and other stakeholders on the issue with the possibility of contributing to the detailed design of the regulation. Committed companies such as Dell, GE, Microsoft, and Philips disassociated themselves from the industry lawsuits (see further sections) against the ruling being persuaded that there was a 'moral imperative' to end violence and human rights abuses (Reinecke and Ansari, 2015).

While Section 1504 is now operative, as is often the case with US legislation, the issue entered the arena of judicial politics. The API, the US Chamber of Commerce, and two other trade associations filed suit in the federal court in the District of Columbia, seeking to strike down Section 1504 of the Dodd–Frank Act and overturn its regulations requiring oil, gas, and mining companies to disclose the payments that they make to governments for all extractive projects. The API argued that mandatory disclosures are unconstitutional violations of companies' First Amendment ('Freedom of Speech') rights, and that the SEC conducted inadequate economic analysis and failed to minimize competitive burdens. The API also requested a stay of the rule pending the outcome of its lawsuit which was opposed by the PWYP (US) on the grounds that oil companies were not likely to win their lawsuit, that there was no danger of 'irreparable injury' to oil companies, and that delaying compliance was not in the public interest. The SEC rejected the request for a stay and the matter proceeded to court.

After several stages of judicial maneuvering,[7] in June 2016 the SEC announced its rules confirming that firms in the sector are required to report payments to the US and foreign governments and to the SEC itself. This included reporting of transactions of subsidiaries and of entities that the respective company controls (SEC Press Release 35 78147).

The US endeavours to secure transparency regulation were much more adversarial and drawn-own than the UK process, reflecting both the United States' extended legislative process (giving opportunities for 'riders' to be added to Dodd–Frank, and for congressional decisions to be challenged in the courts) as well as the substantive context of what was perceived by the opponents to Dodd–Frank as an unwelcome threat of coercion. This is a reminder that the regulation of international responsible business by national governments reflects features of specific political systems (Matten and Moon, 2008) rather than solely the political will of governments.

Research on the effects of Dodd–Frank Section 1504 is still in its infancy. However, the impact is expected to be large given the scope, nature, and complementarity of the law with other transparency initiatives. First, more than a thousand companies and half of the globe's extractive industry market can be found under the SEC's jurisdiction, including many of the wealthiest global oil and mining companies (e.g. Exxon, BP, Shell, Total, Chevron, Rio Tinto, Vale, BHP Billiton) and state-owned enterprises (e.g. Petrobras, Sinpec, and Petrochina) which are also set to be subject to the information disclosure requirements (Natural Resource Governance Institute, 2016). Second, there are no exemptions for foreign or small companies. Third, as already mentioned, Section 1504 was developed to supplement the EITI by requiring companies to provide additional details which might be used by citizens and investors in areas that lack political capacity or will to ensure implementation of the EITI (ibid).

Let us turn to the question of motivation: why did US government policy take this distinctive course? First, it bears stressing that, as in congressional politics generally, there was much that was circumstantial regarding the openness of Dodd and Frank to the civil society lobbyists who pressed for the inclusion of Section 1504. Second, although some business organizations opposed the section, there were others which were prepared to engage in the Dodd–Frank processes once legislation looked likely. It remains to be seen if Section 1504 will ever be implemented since on 3 February 2017 President Trump signed an executive order to roll back the Dodd–Frank Act (Protess and Davis 3 February 2017).

EU Accounting Directive Disclosure Requirements for the Extractive Industry

In 2013 the EU Commission reached an agreement with the European Parliament on new disclosure requirements for the extractive and forestry industries.[8] These requirements were incorporated into revisions to the Accountancy Directives (78/660/EEC and 83/349/EEC) and the Transparency Directive (2004/109/EC) (the EU Directives). Member countries were given until July 2015 to incorporate these rules.[9]

Although the EU had already set goals for 'trade, taxation and transparency' (authors' interviews, 19 November 2014 with the EU Commission, Directorate General Internal Market and Services, and Directorate General International Cooperation and Development), the main push for the EU Directives came from the UK, especially when it held the presidency of the EU and of the Group of 8, an inter-governmental association of leading economies (France, Germany, Italy, Japan, Italy, the UK, the United States, the EU – Russia's membership was suspended).

The EU Directives generally are in alignment with the EITI guidelines and resemble the US Dodd–Frank Act Section 1504, although the EU legislation also includes companies in the primary logging industry (Barnier, 2014). Most significantly from our perspective, they extend the requirement for the tax transparency of EU companies operating outside of the EU. In other words, they reflect the reach of governments to regulate this aspect of responsible business beyond the borders of their core jurisdictions. The EU Directive Amendments introduce a new obligation for listed and large non-listed extractive companies to report all material payments to governments broken down by country and, when appropriate, by project. The EU Directives define a large company as one which exceeds two of the three following criteria: turnover €40 million; total assets €20 million; and 250 or more employees. The EU Directives require the following types of information to be reported: taxes levied on the income, production, or profits of companies; royalties; dividends; signature, discovery, and production bonuses; license fees, rental fees, entry fees, and other considerations for licenses and/or concessions; payments for infrastructure improvements (EU Commission, 2 June 2013).

Again, it is a little early to judge the impact of the EU Directives: the leader of Global Witness's oil campaign has noted that 'the new EU laws show that momentum towards a global transparency standard for the extractive industries is virtually unstoppable' (*The Guardian*, 2013).

To turn to the question of motivation for the EU, a key factor appears to be that it was keen to establish a level playing field for European firms vis-à-vis US firms. This was because European firms are much more likely to be listed both on a European stock exchange as well as in the United States. In contrast, most US firms are more likely to be listed only in the United States. Hence European firms often have to manage both US and European regulatory requirements whereas US firms have to meet only US requirements (authors' interview, civil servant, Directorate General Internal Market and Services, 19 November 2014).

Government Policies of the United States and the EU for Transparency in the Extractives Sector: Summary

The Dodd–Frank and EU Accounting Directive amendments show how, as in national non-financial reporting policies, governments can use their domestic power to require transparency over financial matters to reshape the international regulatory context for MNCs. MNCs do retain some choice in the Dodd–Frank case that of de-listing from the US stock exchanges, as some European companies did in the wake of the Sarbanes–Oxley Act. However, this 'choice' is likely only to be effective for a very small number of extractives companies trading in the United States. This option is not available in the EU case as the Directive applies to companies based on size, not listing, and their only choice is whether to register outside the EU, which is very unlikely for most.

Public Policies for CSR in Transparency in Extractives Industry Payments: Discussion

This chapter addressed the relationship between public policies and CSR in the context of a long-standing issue in international development: transparency of payments in the resources sector. This reflects two other related issues: allegations of the misuse of public finances by developing country governments and public officials, and side payments to such governments and officials by international corporations to secure licenses, tax holidays, and other advantages. Both of these issues are problematic in themselves in terms, respectively of the probity of political systems and the distortions to markets that they represent. They are also deleterious to developing country populations, and hence unite international development and CSR agendas. We summarize our answers to the research questions posed (see Table 6.1) in Table 6.4 and Table 6.5.

Table 6.4 *Research Questions 1–3 on Government Policies for Transparency in the Extractives Sector, Directly and Indirectly*

Research questions	Types of policies		
	Policies to support transparency in the extractives sector directly	Policies to support transparency in the extractives sector indirectly
1. How do government policies support transparency in the extractives sector: through endorsement, facilitation, partnership, or mandate?	UK, Norway Belgium, Canada, Denmark, France, Sweden, and US governments endorse and facilitate the EITI Compliant EITI member governments partner with national NGOs and mandate compliance with the EITI standard in their jurisdiction	Mandate: United States enacts Dodd–Frank Section 1504 (2010) EU enacts Accounting Directive amendments (2013)
2. What roles do government policies play in supporting transparency in the extractives sector *directly*: as initiators or contributors to operations of CSR initiatives?	*Initiation:* UK of EITI (critical role in securing agreement and providing initial resources) Contributor to operations: ongoing – UK and Norway governments provide core funding and organizational support for the EITI *Contributor to operations:* ongoing – Belgium, Canada, Denmark, France, Sweden, and US government membership of EITI Advisory Board	N/A

(continued)

Table 6.4 (*cont.*)

Research questions	Types of policies	
	Policies to support transparency in the extractives sector directly	Policies to support transparency in the extractives sector indirectly
	Contributor to operations: periodic – Sweden and Denmark government project finance to EITI	
	Resource country governments join the EITI and mandate compliance with the standard in their jurisdiction	
3. Why do governments make policies for transparency in the extractives sector?	High social salience of transparency issues	NGO pressures on legislators; but also counter pressures (United States)
	Business pressure on UK government for a level playing field	
	Increased policy interest in multi-stakeholder approaches to governance	Perception of limitations of CSR initiatives
	Increased policy attention to international development	General focus on business transparency post-2008
	Corporate and civil society desire for agreement on ethical standards. Government allays mutual suspicions	EU firms seeking level playing field

First, with respect to the question of how governments support transparency in the extractives industry (Research Question 1) we find the full range of forms of the policy deployed. Critically, the UK government brought its public policy resources of endorsement and facilitation to support CSR directly in the shape of the EITI. This was both prior to its formation (through brokerage between business and civil society organizations) and at its inception, as well as in the form of continuing support for the EITI's ongoing operations. Norway took over the role of providing core continuing support for the EITI's operations, also deploying endorsement and facilitation thereby continuing the support for EITI directly. This has attracted the support of other governments for the EITI's operations directly whether on a continuing or periodic basis.

As the model of the EITI unfolded, a different sort of governmental role emerged – and one that was agreed to by business as well as civil society EITI board members. 'Host' governments which adopt the EITI principles are required to mandate compliance with the EITI standard in their own jurisdiction. Like the accounting regulation we noted in Denmark (Chapter 4), we see how companies' own motivation and initiative for CSR solutions were supported directly by government. As the EITI regulations developed, they acquired a stronger sense of mandate within host countries though they are nonetheless used by companies for their CSR learning, practices, and legitimization.

Another approach to the issue of transparency in the resources sector has been that of mandate by 'home' governments to require transparency of companies registered in their jurisdictions concerning their international operations. We therefore described the Dodd–Frank Act and the EU Accounting Directive Amendments as government policy to support CSR indirectly. This is because the policies impact on the same regulatory environment in which the CSR initiative, in this case the EITI, and associated companies operate (see the discussion of their interactions in further pages).

Concerning the question about the roles that government policies directed to the EITI played (Research Question 2), we found that the UK was critical to the initiation of the EITI – and even was involved at the pre-inception stages of the initiative in bringing parties together. Subsequently, the UK and Norway provided substantial continuing organizational support for the initiative, and numerous other governments have done so on a periodic basis. With the development of the

EITI's own governance system, 'compliant' and 'candidate' governments have taken an increasingly supportive role of the operations on a continuing basis, most obviously by implementing the EITI principles (Table 6.2) and standard requirements (Table 6.3), and by serving on the EITI Advisory Committee.

Turning to the question of why governments support CSR directly (Research Question 3), we find that all the forms of public policy we identified were motivated by similar considerations of societal pressures. These were reinforced by a sense for all four of the main governments concerned – the UK, Norway, the United States, and the EU – that public policy in this field, whether by supporting CSR directly or indirectly by influencing the wider regulatory environment, was consistent with their own wider international development policy commitments. Moreover, the Dodd–Frank Act Section 1504 and EU Accounting Directive Amendments were also both motivated by a view that while the EITI was a positive initiative, a stronger regulation was required to increase effective transparency.

However, government motivations reflected different responses to domestic business pressure. In the UK case, the government's policies were broadly reflective of shared sentiment among business and civil society that the absence of transparency in the extractives industry was problematic. It was therefore able to negotiate with key extractive firms and to broker the initial agreement with them and civil society groups to overcome their mutual suspicions. In the US case, there was a more adversarial environment in which certain extractive industry firms have attempted to resist the initial Dodd–Frank Act Section 1504 in its legislative stages and then through judicial review. Other governments, which support the EITI directly, have been motivated by combinations of international development policy commitments and concern for the reputations of their companies. They are also motivated by a sense that the EITI was proving effective in this policy area to which they also had wider policy commitments.

The motivation of host governments both to join the EITI and then to agree to mandate its principles and standard in their own jurisdictions reflects the beliefs of host governments that this represented a substantive improvement in governance and that leading companies might be less likely to invest in their countries in the absence of the operationalization of the EITI. In other words, the collective action logic originally articulated from a company perspective now extended to governments. Thus governments, particularly for some of the smaller members, perceive that there are risks to them of remaining outside the EITI.

We now turn to the question of the interactions between different sorts of government policy support for CSR, domestically and internationally, and directly and indirectly (Research Question 4 – see summary in Table 6.5).

Concerning the domestic–international interactions, we found that a unilateral initiative of the UK government at the inception of the EITI started an incremental process of internationalization. It attracted MNCs and international civil society organizations concerned with the respective international agendas as its first members and attracted, initially a few, small host country governments and then a much larger number. Crucially it attracted other home country 'supporter' governments, initially and most notably Norway. The effectiveness and capacity of the EITI is predicated on these developments.

Second, the internationally legitimized principles and the standard of the EITI, supported by government policies of the UK, Norway, and other governments, have been translated voluntarily into domestic-level effectiveness via the national government mandate of the EITI systems of transparency by 'compliant' country governments.

There have also been clear interactions between the types of government support for CSR directly and indirectly. The initiation and operationalization of the EITI were all critically reliant on initially the UK and subsequently the Norwegian governments. They have collectively led to the multiplication of other company supporters, and supporter and member governments and international governmental organizations. More profoundly, they have informed a voluntary process which has culminated in the mandate of the EITI standard for all extractive industry operators (including those that are state-owned) within the respective countries. Thus the voluntary EITI regulates governments in order to ensure transparency in extractive industry MNCs' payments. It is significant that the Obama administration committed to complying with, and joining, the EITI. This suggests that the US government believed that the voluntarism and partnership elements of the EITI, and particularly the buy-in of the host governments, is a complement to the 'hard rule' entailed in Dodd–Frank.

Although it would be an exaggeration to describe the EITI, the Dodd–Frank Act, and the EU Accounting Directive Amendments as coordinated with one another, they have developed in full cognizance of one another and with explicit reference to one another. Moreover they also complement one another. For example, the EITI requires the disclosure of payments made to each governmental department (e.g. national to local) and on a project (e.g. license and contract) level in the host country where it engages. The Dodd–Frank Act and the EU Accounting Directive Amendments require this transparency in the respective home country/jurisdiction. Some claim that these different forms of interaction can amount to normative regulatory pressure for raising standards as illustrated in the view that the UK's adoption of the EU Accounting Directive amendments put moral pressure on the US SEC to re-issue the implementation of the Dodd–Frank Act regarding project-level disclosure (Global Witness, 2013).

The US Act and the amended EU Directives mandate companies by virtue of their US and EU registration, and thereby may include companies which might be operating outside EITI member countries. Thus, these mandates indirectly support the EITI initiative by re-shaping the regulatory environment in which a wider range of companies operate – irrespective of whether or not they operate in countries whose governments have voluntarily joined the EITI or whether the companies have volunteered to support the EITI. Moreover, there is explicit reference to the EITI in Section 1504 which calls on the SEC to acknowledge EITI guidelines (Lynn, 2011). This is further illustrated by the way in which the prospect of Dodd–Frank was used as a basis to ratchet up the regulatory effect of the EITI, and the ways in which the EITI motivated EU policymakers and, by its limitations, it motivated civil society to press for Dodd–Frank. Significantly also, the US determination to join the EITI was described by the EITI Chair as 'a vital development for the EITI' (authors' interview with Clare Short, November 2014).

The EITI strengthened its standard in the light of Dodd–Frank. Moreover, when the regulations giving effect to Section 1504 were confirmed following the unsuccessful challenge, the EITI made an extensive commentary. It states that:

It is hoped that the SEC's rules will strengthen the efforts of the EITI community and others to improve natural resource governance globally and also spur more timely and detailed reporting in EITI countries. It will hopefully also be an encouragement to other major producing countries to join the process ... Hopefully, companies listed in the US will see the SEC's rules as an opportunity to use the EITI process to ensure a level playing field where they operate and to engage in the public debate to understand how best to manage the sector ... It is welcome that the SEC has recognised the importance of the US-EITI process. Further work is needed to recognise EITI Reporting in other countries so that there is no duplication of reporting and consistency in the data made available to the public ... Publishing data is necessary, but not enough. EITI implementation is most effective when it promotes and informs dialogue between government, industry and civil society, and encourages informed debate about the reforms that are needed to ensure that the extractive industries support national development priorities. (EITI, 2016e)

When the US Securities Commission announced the confirmation of its regulations to fulfill Section 1504, it commented that these would be consistent with the requirements of the United States' membership of the EITI (as well as the requirements of the governments of Canada and the EU) and that reports prepared for the US EITI purposes could be used for compliance with this section of Dodd–Frank (SEC, 2015). Both these statements neatly encapsulate the relationship and complementarity between the two forms of government support for CSR.

It is nonetheless worth stressing that the EITI retains its role in CSR in these interactions. For example, Anglo-American's Business Integrity Policy specifies a range of corruption issues including those which would be susceptible to prosecution as well as those which simply threaten to damage the company's reputation and accounts. Significantly, Anglo-American signals its commitment to good governance with explicit reference to 'international frameworks such as the Extractive Industries Transparency Initiative' and a commitment to act as 'advocates for the EITI in the countries where we operate'. It adds that 'where our host government has decided to implement the EITI we will fully support the process' and disclose 'our tax and royalty payments for our most significant countries of operation in our annual Report to Society' (Anglo-American, 2014). Equally, there is evidence that the EITI international standard is being employed domestically in wider transparency issues than those to which it is ostensibly addressed. For example, the US government has adapted and mainstreamed the EITI disclosures system in the management of natural resource revenues from US Federal Lands (EITI, 2015a).

Table 6.5 *Interactions between Different Forms of Policy for Transparency in the Extractives Sector*

Research questions	Types of policies
	Policies to support for transparency in the extractives sector *directly* and *indirectly*
4. **What are the interactions between different sorts of public policies for transparency in the extractives sector?** a. **Between domestic and international policies** b. **Between direct and indirect policies**	EITI initiated by one national government in order to establish international standard to be applied by other (host) national governments to regulate MNC's payments. Dodd–Frank Act and EU Accounting amendments use transparency to regulate 'home'-based companies internationally. UK government is key advocate of EU amendments to Accounting Directive for 'level playing field' for EU member MNCs. EITI informs framing of Dodd–Frank and EU Amendments EITI standard strengthened in light of Dodd–Frank EITI standard deployed in domestic regulation

This suggests that there is not such a clear dichotomy between hard and soft mandate, rather there is extensive interaction between these forms of regulation of responsible business. Table 6.5 highlights interactions between public policies that support transparency directly and indirectly.

So, national governments were crucial in establishing what began as a CSR initiative. They initiated and operationalized the EITI through interactions with the business and civil society sectors, and deployed their resources of endorsement and facilitation. Moreover, as a result of its design, geographical multiplication, and regulatory intensification, the EITI is now effectively a mandate in the host countries whose governments have joined the Initiative. But this has been achieved on a consensual basis. The EITI became a reference point for campaigners and legislators in the United States who wanted to ensure compliance with the transparency principle and was a motivator for the EU Directives. Non-coercive regulation for CSR and coercive regulation

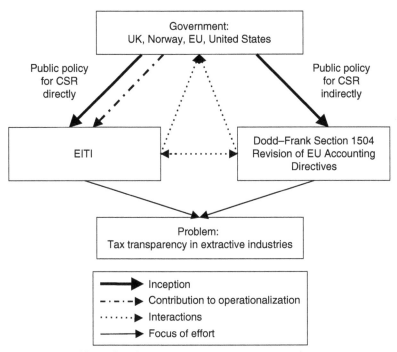

Figure 6.1 Public policy for transparency in extractive industries

by national governments are not necessarily in conflict: rather they interact with and feed off one another. Figure 6.1 shows public policy for transparency in extractive industries.

Notes

1 The Dodd–Frank Act is named after Representative Barney Frank, a Democrat from Massachusetts, and Senator Christopher John Dodd, a Democrat from Connecticut (Frank and Dodd both retired in January 2013 at the end of the 111th Congress). Between 2007 and 2013, Frank served as chairman of the Financial Services Committee in the House of Representatives and thus was one the most influential politicians in the United States. Dodd served as a senator from Connecticut for a thirty-year period and was thus also a senior politician by dint of long service.

2 Regarding the potential impact of Section 1504 on international oil companies, one estimate suggests (focusing on Iraq as a case study) that between a half and two-thirds of international oil company activity

measured by both oil production and revenue could be subject to the new law (*Ethical Corporation*, 27 September 2010).

3 Eligible companies are those which file periodic reports under the Securities and Exchange Act of 1934 and engage in the commercial development of oil, natural gas, and minerals (PwC, 'Another Side of Dodd Frank: Understanding Section 1504': 2).

4 Woody, 2013, footnote 51: See Press Release, Russ Feingold, US Senator, Feingold Statement on Congo Conflict Minerals and Transparency Amendments to Financial Regulatory Reform Bill (19 May 2010): cited in http://www.arlpi.org/august-2-2010, 'This amendment specifically responds to the continued crisis in the eastern region of the (DRC). Despite efforts to curb the violence, mass atrocities and widespread sexual violence and rape continue at an alarming rate. Some have justifiably labeled eastern Congo as "the worst place in the world to be female". Several of us in this body, including senators Brownback and Durbin and I, have travelled to this region and seen first-hand the tragedy of this relentless crisis'.

5 Senator Lugar from the Foreign Affairs Committee became interested in tax transparency in extractives from an energy and security perspective (Purdue University, 2006). Lugar visited a number of extractives countries and wrote a report on the resource curse. Subsequently, Senators Cardin and Lugar wrote the Energy Securities and Transparency Act (*The Huffington Post*, 2012).

6 This section rests largely on an account from Earth Rights about the legal process pertaining to Section 1504 (Earth Rights International, n.d.).

7 First, the Washington DC Circuit Court judge dismissed the case on the grounds that the Court had no jurisdiction. In July 2013, the Washington DC District Court Judge Bates issued an opinion making the rule void, concluding that the SEC needed to reconsider two aspects of the rule: (1) the requirement that all company payment reports be made public, and (2) the decision not to grant any exemptions for foreign-law prohibitions (US District Court, District of Columbia 2013). The PWYP (US) sued the SEC for failure to issue new transparency rules required by Dodd–Frank 1504.

8 Although the EU is manifestly not a national government, we include it in our analysis, first because, as noted in Chapter 3, it more closely resembles a national political system (with a legislature, an executive, and a judiciary) than an inter-governmental organization. Moreover, the EU Directives in question apply to corporations outside the EU's own sphere of territorial authority. Directive 2013/50/EU of the European Parliament and of the Council of 22 October 2013 amending Directive 2004/109/EC of the European Parliament and of the Council on the harmonization of

transparency requirements in relation to information about issuers whose securities are admitted to trading on a regulated market, Directive 2003/71/EC of the European Parliament and of the Council on the prospectus to be published when securities are offered to the public or admitted to trading and Commission Directive 2007/14/EC laying down detailed rules for the implementation of certain provisions of Directive 2004/109/EC Text with EEA relevance. *OJ L 294, 6.11.2013*, pp. 13–27.

9 As in the comparison of the EITI and the Dodd–Frank Act, the circumstances of the initiation of revisions of the *1978 EU Accounting Directive* and the *2004 EU Transparency Directive* reflect distinctive features of the European Union legislative processes. The European Parliament and the Council of Ministers (which are together the equivalent of the legislature) review proposals put forward by the Commission (the executive branch of government) and propose amendments. If the Council and the Parliament cannot agree upon amendments, a second reading takes place. In the second reading, the Parliament and Council can again propose amendments. If the two institutions agree on amendments, the proposed legislation can be adopted. If they cannot agree, a conciliation process is instituted to find a solution. Both the Council and the Parliament can block the legislative proposal at this final reading.

7 | Conclusion: Visible Hands for Responsible International Business

Our starting point for this book was our puzzlement that so much of the literature on the origins of CSR did not assign a significant role to the state as a driver of CSR and, more generally, that there were conflicting views about the nature of this relationship. In this book we offer a re-interpretation of the role of government policies for driving international CSR, specifically non-financial reporting, ethical trade, and tax transparency in the extractives industry. With reference to the title of our book, *Visible Hands: Government Regulation and International Business Responsibility*, we contend that rather than CSR being driven solely by the invisible hands of the market and the actors therein – the assumption of much of the literature on CSR – the visible hands of governments can contribute significantly to shaping CSR initiatives and their operationalization. The relationships between government and CSR reflect both embedded effects of the way CSR has been institutionalized in national public policy legacies and agential decisions of governments that adopt international CSR policies as part of managing their own policy agendas.

As a result of our analysis we, first, extend the literature on CSR and national government. This theme is either ignored in much CSR literature or, when it is addressed, it is dominated by attention to government policies for *home* country responsibility (Albareda et al., 2008; Campbell, 2007; Midttun et al., 2006; Steurer, 2010). We focus on the seemingly paradoxical case of public policies that directly regulate responsible business behaviour *abroad*. In doing so we explore how domestic forms of public policy shape international CSR. In contrast to much recent scholarship on CSR and global governance we identify a continued role for the state. Our argument thus contrasts with scholars such as Scherer and Palazzo (2011) and Scherer et al. (2016), who focus on the inability of states to regulate business activity through coercive means and who thus propose the concept of 'Political CSR' in which MNCs assume governmental roles.

182

Second, whereas some scholars such as Bartley (2007), Bernstein and Cashore (2012), and Ruggie (2003) have noted the role of government in shaping international CSR initiatives such as the Forest Stewardship Council or the UN Global Compact, our analysis extends their work by focusing in more detail on how governments make policy for CSR in terms of the different forms of policy deployed; on what effects these policies bring to CSR initiatives; on why governments are involved in shaping CSR; and on the interactions among different types of CSR policy. We argue that governments play a role in developing international CSR and have adopted a wide range of public policies to that end, typically soft in nature, for example, through endorsement, facilitation, and partnership, but also even through the mandate of varying strengths.

Third, we found that government policies for CSR *directly* interact with other government initiatives. These government initiatives support CSR *indirectly* as they are not CSR-specific but address the same problem to which the CSR initiatives are intended and are in cognizance of the respective CSR initiatives.

In this chapter we bring together our findings in order to address our contribution to the literature on CSR and government as well as limitations of our argument and suggestions for further research. But, first, we reprise the answers we pose to our four research questions.

Forms and Roles of Government Policies for CSR

In this section we address Research Questions 1 and 2:

1. How do government policies support CSR through endorsement, facilitation, partnership, or mandate?
2. What roles do government policies play in supporting CSR *directly*: as initiators or contributors to operations?

Looking first at the forms of government policies for international CSR directly, we see that they take all forms, as proposed in the findings of our analysis of European government policies (Chapter 3). These policies can be deployed at the inception of CSR initiatives or in the form of contributions to their operations, either on an ongoing basis or periodically.

We found that the category of *facilitation* is the cornerstone for government CSR policies. This includes 'brokering agreements' at the pre-inception stage of CSR initiatives reflecting the unique resources of government authority and legitimacy. It includes 'providing funding', be it at the inception of an initiative or on an ongoing basis. Although funding is not a unique resource of governments, nonetheless governments have extensive fiscal capacity which was deployed in ongoing and periodic funding of CSR initiatives. Governments also provide 'organizational resources' often through in-kind contributions of office space, secondments, and advisory positions, and sometimes through their more unique resources of knowledge founded on their embassy networks, for example. Finally, government facilitation of CSR initiatives was also achieved through their ability to 'shape markets' through public procurement policies.

Although our case studies did not reflect many formal *partnerships* of government with CSR initiatives, in the ETI and the EITI there was evidence of partnership-type language and culture not only among the CSR initiative members but also between them and the respective supporting governments. Thus we saw the UK minister for state for international development speak of the ETI as a 'central partner' in government policy for responsible supply chains (Chapter 5).

Governmental use of *mandate* was evident in our cases, although this tended to arise incrementally. The Danish regulation of non-financial reporting emerged following endorsement and facilitation of CSR initiatives (e.g. the UN Global Compact), was extended initially through a soft version of the law (i.e. reports were only required of those companies which claimed CSR) and, even in its present manifestation, it is 'soft' with respect to the forms of compliance. The EITI – which started as a voluntary initiative principally by companies, civil society organizations, and the UK government – now provides a framework for host governments to mandate transparency within their own borders. The ETI was never supported by mandate but, paradoxically perhaps, it was a source of specialist knowledge in the design of domestic-mandated regulation of labour in the UK.

One theme to emerge from our findings concerns the dynamism in the respective roles of governments in supporting the CSR cases we examined. It was not generally the case that any particular form of public policy for CSR was singular and stable, rather policies built upon one another both within and among governmental jurisdictions. This was evident in a variety of ways.

First, we saw this most obviously in the case of the Danish non-financial reporting law. This initially built upon endorsement and facilitation of CSR initiatives for non-financial reporting such as the GRI and the UN Global Compact. Furthermore, the lead government supporter of the EITI changed from the UK to Norway – seemingly without hitch or acrimony. A number of governments which initially only took a 'supporter' role of the EITI have subsequently also joined, meaning that they partake in responsibility for the development of the initiative and its rules, and that they are subject to those same rules. To turn to ethical trade, in the cases of the Scandinavian variants of the ETI, whereas they were initially only beneficiaries of government policies of facilitation through periodic funding of their operationalization, they are now engaged in a partnership-type relationship with the Nordic Council of Ministers. These forms of policy for CSR can build upon one another and can develop and strengthen as witnessed in all our cases.

Turning to policies to support CSR indirectly, we have identified *mandate* as the main form, through the use of trade regulation for ethical trade and legislated requirements for transparency in the extractives industry. Whereas mandates are conventionally associated with problem-focused regulation (as depicted in Figure 2.2), in the post–Rana Plaza case, mandate was used to address the problem by re-configuring the regulatory environment for MNCs sourcing from the Bangladesh RMG industry. This was done by the utilization of US executive trade policy powers via the intermediary of the Bangladesh government. In the case of the Dodd–Frank Act Section 1504, the transparency requirement is operated through the administration of stock exchange rules and thus falls outside the most coercive forms of regulation at governments' disposal. The attendant rules still allow an element of discretion on a company's part as it can withdraw from listing on US stock exchanges. Moreover, mechanisms for securing compliance fall short of those that could be at the immediate disposal of government. The EU transparency regulation, however, applies irrespective of stock exchange listing, though this applies to a narrower range of companies. Our findings are summarized in Table 7.1.

The Motivation for Governments to Make Policy for CSR

We now address Research Question 3:

Why do governments make policies for CSR?

Table 7.1 *How Do Governments Make Policies to Support CSR and What Roles Do These Play?*

Research questions	Types of policies for CSR	
	Policies for CSR directly	Policies for CSR indirectly
1. How do government policies support CSR: through endorsement, facilitation, partnership, or mandate?	Endorsement, facilitation, partnership, mandate (often simultaneously or sequentially) Facilitation is the cornerstone: deal-making; financial and organizational support; market shaping	Governments use mandates in the form of: 1. trade policies to secure change in regulatory environment 2. transparency/ reporting requirements 'at home' for MNCs abroad
2. What roles do government policies play in supporting CSR *directly*: as initiators or contributors to operations?	Facilitation at pre-inception stage of CSR initiative Facilitation at the inception of CSR initiatives Contributions to their operations: ongoing or periodically	N/A

Our analysis enabled insights into government motivations to develop policies to support CSR directly and indirectly. We found a range of motivations which applied both to direct and indirect policy-making for CSR.

As we indicated in Chapters 4–6, the substantive social challenges on which the CSR issues emerged – accountability for non-financial activities; ethical trade; and transparency of tax payments in the extractive industries – acquired a salience greater than that simply associated with business agenda items such as managing business risk and establishing a level playing field. Rather they were seen and presented as of broad societal concern.

Regarding the ETI and the EITI, we found that the issues of ethical trade and transparency had achieved high levels of salience in civil society. As a result, the UK government perceived this pressure to be acting upon it, particularly given that it had made distinctive commitments to international development agendas. CSR solutions underpinned the UK government's broader policy ambitions, so much so that the government worked to facilitate an agreement between the mutually suspicious business and civil society organizations. Overall business and civil society organizations agreed that 'something had to be done' and thus shared an interest in agreeing on standards and developing a multi-stakeholder-based solution.

This brings us to the motivation of governments to develop policies to support CSR directly because of its potential alignment with wider government policy settings. The UK and the Scandinavian governments are known for aiming to align the international reputation of their MNCs with their international industrial, trade, and development policies. Support for CSR initiatives which address these issues is a tangible way to invest in this reputation. Although our evidence illustrates this with regard to policies to support CSR directly, this may also apply to those governments, which support CSR indirectly.

Conversely, governments are also aware of some of the limitations of CSR organizations and regulations. This was clear, for example, for the UK and US governments, which pursued financial transparency policies to support CSR indirectly though Dodd–Frank and the EU Accounting Directive Amendments notwithstanding their support for the EITI.

For some governments, policies to support CSR directly are an adjunct to a broader commitment to a preferred policymaking style of social partnership or consensus-seeking among key actors. The Scandinavian governments have long been associated with an approach to policymaking based on consensus seeking and collaboration among key actors. The Blair government in the UK also stressed how it brought different approaches to policymaking described in such terms as 'stakeholder democracy' and the 'third way'. These themes were evident in the roles of the UK, Danish and Norwegian governments in the cases we have presented.

These roles contrast with those of government in the United States where support for CSR initiatives directly is more rare (cf. the Clinton administration's support for the Fair Labor Association and the

Obama administration's support for the post–Rana Plaza Alliance). Reflecting their more collaborative business-government traditions, European firms are more willing to join international CSR multi-stakeholder initiatives with business-critical actors such as unions and civil society actors. The United States has a more top-down regulatory approach, which promotes hard law for international CSR or encourages business-driven voluntary CSR initiatives (Knudsen, 2017). However, despite these different regulatory traditions in December 2016, the US government also developed the US National Action Plan for Responsible Business Conduct to promote and incentivize responsible business.

In this institutional context we witnessed a more adversarial relationship between some business organizations on the one hand, and the government and civil society organizations on the other in the judicial challenges to Dodd–Frank Section 1504. Despite this context, the US government was also motivated by a desire for a level playing field for US MNCs sourcing from Bangladesh and for US textile workers competing with Bangladesh imports which reflected lower labour standards and remuneration. Hence the US government's support for the Alliance, directly, and for ethical trade, indirectly, in its recourse to the threat of trade sanctions to press the Bangladesh government to introduce and administer generally higher labour standards.

Our conclusions about government motivation to support CSR are summarized in Table 7.2.

Interactions of Public Policies in Support of CSR

We now turn to address Research Question 4:

What are the interactions between different sorts of public policy to support CSR?

1. Between domestic and international policies for CSR?
2. Between direct and indirect public policies for CSR?

We first examine interactions between domestic and international public policies to support CSR in our three cases. Second, we investigate interactions between direct and indirect public policies to support CSR through our case studies of ethical trade and of transparent tax payments in the extractives industry.

We find interactions between a domestic and an international focus of public policies for CSR in all cases. We also find that CSR

Table 7.2 *Why Do Governments Make Policy for CSR?*

Research question 3	Types of policies	
	Policies to support CSR *directly*	Policies to support CSR *indirectly*
Why do governments make policies for CSR?	High social salience of issues	High social salience of issues
	Perception of limitations of CSR initiatives without government as facilitator.	Perception of some business interest in 'level playing field' abroad and of government capacity to secure this
	Perception of some business interest in agreeing upon standards	
	Public policy interest in MSI/partnership approaches – agreement among stakeholders to collaborate, i.e. opportunities of CSR	Mandatory regulation reflecting policy tradition in light of expected limitations of CSR

initiatives expanded from their country of origin to other countries whose governments then developed the initiatives further. Concerning the Danish government's non-financial reporting requirements, a shift took place from a focus on domestic social and employment initiatives to a focus on the international activities of Danish firms and their suppliers.

In the case of ethical trade we see that government policy for CSR shifts from having a domestic to an international focus in a number of different ways. For example, the ETI was first established in the UK and provided ethical trade guidance to UK firms only. However, the ETI then expanded its reach from the UK to other countries such as Norway and Denmark, and many Norwegian and Danish firms have subsequently adopted the ETI principles. We also see that both the EU and the US government promote better working conditions in Bangladesh by directly supporting the CSR initiatives, the Alliance and the Accord, but also by indirectly supporting CSR by pressuring the Bangladeshi government to adopt legislation to improve labour rights and working conditions.

In the case of tax transparency in extractives, the EITI originated in the UK and now regulates host country governments and the multinational extractive firms operating in these countries. This initiative has expanded its geographical reach significantly to nearly fifty countries. Public policies for indirect CSR such as Dodd–Frank's Section 1504 and the EU Accounting Directive amendments mandate tax transparency in large US and EU extractive firms as they operate internationally. Finally, in the case of non-financial reporting we see that the Danish government's reporting requirements (as well as similar requirements in several other EU member states) have been adopted and further developed by the EU Commission's directive on non-financial reporting.

In Chapters 5 and 6 we examined government policies that support CSR directly and how these policies interact with government policies that address the same social problem as the CSR initiatives target and, in so doing, how they support CSR indirectly. In both cases we saw that CSR initiatives supported by governments directly can shape the development of wider mandated government policies for CSR indirectly at home and/or abroad. In short, CSR initiatives supported by governments directly can contribute to the adoption of mandatory policies for CSR indirectly.

In the case of ethical trade, the ETI's focus on improving labour standards in global supply chains informed the UK government's adoption of mandated policies (e.g. the 2004 UK Gangmasters and the 2015 Modern Slavery Acts). Furthermore, the Norwegian government adopted public procurement criteria that include IEH principles. Following the Rana Plaza factory collapse, the EU and the United States have indirectly supported CSR policies abroad by encouraging the Bangladeshi government's adoption of legislation that reflects the safety requirements inherent in the Accord and Alliance. In the case of tax transparency in the extractives industry, the EITI contributed to shaping mandatory legislation in the United States (the Dodd–Frank's Section 1504) and in the EU (the revision of the EU Accounting Directive).

In the cases of ethical trade and tax transparency in the extractives sector we also saw that public policies can support CSR indirectly by shaping the institutional context or by supporting the CSR initiatives. In short, public policies that were not specifically adopted to address CSR initiatives can nonetheless contribute to these CSR initiatives by changing the wider regulatory context for CSR or by providing government financial and/or administrative support for the CSR initiatives. For example, the US decision to withhold preferential trade status from Bangladeshi products after the Rana Plaza disaster is an example of a government policy that indirectly contributed to supporting CSR initiatives such as the Accord and Alliance. As access to the United States, and potentially also to the EU, markets was threatened, the Bangladeshi government has been obliged to adopt new legislation that addresses the same problem as the Accord and Alliance. Thus the regulatory context for these CSR initiatives has been strengthened. Furthermore, the US and European governments have offered substantial financial and technical support to the Alliance and the Accord. Focusing on extractives, the US government has supported the EITI by choosing to become an EITI member. The EITI was also indirectly supported by a stronger regulatory context in the form of the Dodd–Frank Act's Section 1504 and by the EU Accounting Directive Amendments which both explicitly stated that the EITI complemented these legal requirements.

In the case of extractives (and to some extent also in ethical trade), governments have sought to ensure consistency across direct and indirect public policy initiatives for CSR in order to level the playing field as companies compete across borders. Table 7.3 provides an overview of interactions between different forms of government support for CSR.

Conclusions: CSR and Government, Domestic Governance, and Global Governance

Our conclusions refer back to the literatures with which we framed our analysis in Chapter 2: Government and CSR; CSR and domestic governance; and CSR and global governance.

Government and CSR

We take issue with the literature that perceives CSR solely as private initiatives by firms that go beyond legal and governmental requirements. We identified two dominant views within this dichotomous perspective. The 'express' view, which contends that by definition CSR excludes those policies and actions by corporations that reflect a

Table 7.3 *Interactions between Different Forms of Policy for CSR*

Research question 4	Types of CSR policies
What are the interactions between government policies that support CSR initiatives?	
1. Between domestic and international public policies for CSR?	Domestic CSR choices entail international obligations Domestic CSR initiatives supported by government policy directly attract MNCs from other countries CSR initiatives expanded from their country of origin to other countries whose governments then developed the initiatives further
2. Between direct and indirect public policies for CSR	CSR initiatives that are supported by governments directly can be extended and supplemented by wider government policies for CSR indirectly Public policies can support CSR indirectly by shaping the institutional context or by supporting the CSR initiatives Governments seek to ensure consistency across direct and indirect public policy initiatives

direct relationship with government policy. But we also noted the 'implied' view in which conceptions of CSR say little or nothing about the relationship with government. In contrast, we favour the related perspective that sees government and CSR as linked. We examine two views: a structural view sees CSR as 'embedded' in domestic political and economic institutions while an 'agential' view sees government as having agency in shaping CSR. In contrast to much of the government and CSR literature, we systematically address the 'how', the 'what' effect, and the 'why' questions about these relationships in our analysis of aggregate data and case studies. As detailed earlier, we find that governments use a range of CSR policy forms and these can build upon one another as well as interact with other public policies.

Second, we find that government policies for CSR can be effective at the inception of CSR initiatives and in support of the initiatives' operations, whether on a continuing or one-off basis. Third, we find that governments are motivated to support CSR by a combination of considerations, principally, because CSR agendas are also salient for governments; governments identify opportunities and limits to CSR; governments can recognize CSR as a means to meeting their own substantive policy objectives and preferred policy approaches.

We explore these contributions to the government and CSR literature more closely in the following sections on CSR and domestic governance, and CSR and global governance.

CSR and Domestic Governance

We highlight government agency and explore how it is embedded in particular domestic and political economic institutions. The domestic governance literature has primarily focused on developing new ways of governing within national boundaries and particularly on new forms of governance such as innovative regulatory approaches of government and public–private partnerships. This literature interprets CSR primarily as domestically oriented initiatives that are shaped – if not determined – by domestic political and economic institutions. Although we highlight the importance and capacity of new forms of governance for bringing to light new social solutions, we take issue with the tendency of this literature to see CSR as primarily embedded in or structured by these domestic institutions. Our contention is that governments also use CSR for policy innovation and change to a greater extent than this literature acknowledges.

While the indirect public policies entail the more traditional forms of policies – mandatory and legally enforced – such as trade policies or company reporting, these policies interact with CSR initiatives that are more explorative and collaborative in the way they function. Our book shows that CSR's role in domestic governance is not simply to create arms' length governance by which government delegates responsibility for the respective problems. Rather, CSR's role in our cases is also linked to the core capacities of and purposes of government as illustrated in the extent of facilitation policy and the instances of mandate which are prevalent in our case studies.

CSR and Global Governance

The literature on CSR and global governance emphasizes how governments have become less able to regulate effectively as business activities increasingly transcend national borders. This literature argues that the weakening of the regulatory capacity of governments results in the rise of private regulation to address social problems that transcend borders. Many scholars have identified new governance roles for CSR in the context of globalization. The political CSR literature is a key example. Although this literature includes the state as a main political actor with civil society actors and business, scholars such as Scherer and Palazzo (2007, 2011) emphasize global and multi-level governance as their key focus. However, this literature does not have much to say about the political processes that lead to government involvement in CSR initiatives or programmes or how governments can influence such programs (e.g. Scherer et al., 2016).

Other scholars highlight how globalization shapes variation in the degrees and forms of legalization (Abbott and Snidal, 2000; Abbott et al., 2015; McBarnet, 2007). Rather than attempt coercive mandate as alternatives to private regulation, governments have adopted CSR regulation in order to enhance international competitiveness or to promote certain economic and political development goals. This trend prompted socio-legal scholars to coin the term 'the new accountability' to conceptualize government 'soft' regulation of CSR (McBarnet, 2007). Accordingly, the law is primarily used to encourage business responsibility so the stress is not so much on the voluntariness or coercion as on the business responsibility itself. Although governments are using strong mandates to regulate some aspects of international business (e.g., the US and UK anti-corruption regulation), strong mandate is merely one end of a regulatory spectrum rather than the totality of regulation.

The type of government policies of particular interest to us are better described as softer forms of mandate, which do not stress detailed conformance requirements or punishments for failure to comply – although over time as these policies interact with 'indirect' government policies we see in some of our cases a trend towards more specific CSR requirements. Hence, we are primarily interested in government CSR policies where corporations are able to exercise choice as to whether to, and how to, conform. We have explored the interactions of what we refer to as policies that provide support for CSR directly, with public policies that address the same problem and thus offer support for CSR indirectly. We have demonstrated that direct and indirect initiatives co-develop in cognizance of each other and in the case of tax transparency, they directly inform each other. Thus we focus on government as a driver of international CSR through mainly softer forms of government initiatives in direct support of CSR that contribute to and are informed by more traditional forms of government initiatives (trade or accounting provisions) that ultimately support the CSR initiatives albeit indirectly.

Discussion: Contributions, Implications, Limitations, and Further Research

Our book title and the closing section of Chapter 1 engaged the metaphors of invisible and visible hands. We now turn to their implications for our understanding of government in CSR. We note that Smith's coinage of 'invisible hands' was in the context of his argued superiority of market logics, rather than the ethical and organizational character of company decisions to engage in CSR. Our point here is that the visibility of government policies for CSR, directly or indirectly, should be considered a complement to the discretionary behaviour of business organizations that engage in CSR.

Our research is interdisciplinary and bridges management scholarship with a focus on business in society, as well as political science with a focus on government. We contribute to both literatures by addressing how governments through public policies (the focus of political science) can shape the social strategies of corporations (the focus of business in society scholarship) particularly as they operate abroad.

The political science research that we are inspired by has traditionally explored the role of domestic political and economic institutions. While it would not be correct to say that this literature views policy outcomes simply as determined by institutional structure, we highlight government agency – a focus that is emerging significantly in the historical institutionalist tradition (Martin, 2015; Thelen, 2015).

The management scholarship on CSR tends to downplay the role of government, and it is significant that the CSR literature that we identified as broadly sympathetic with our project to bring government back into exploring CSR comes from political and other social science including international relations (Ruggie, 2003), regulation (Bernstein and Cashore, 2002), and socio-legal studies (McBarnet, 2007). On the basis of our analysis in this book, the idea that CSR is a government-free zone is not tenable other than by denying that the cases we have examined constitute CSR – despite the fact that the corporations and the governments affirm that these initiatives are CSR. Our analysis therefore suggests that Bowen's (1953) inclusion of policies that meet the 'objectives and values of our society' (6) in his definition of CSR may warrant inclusion of government relationships with CSR, as suggested by Preston and Post's (1975) support for business involvement in, and accountability for, public policy. We have therefore given substance to Gond et al.'s (2011) idea that the self-regulation of CSR is governed, and to the ways in which this reflects both the legacies of inherited government policies and in the contemporary acts of government agency. Thus we support the wider view (e.g. Bartley, 2007; Wood and Wright, 2015) that management scholarship, more broadly than that on CSR alone, needs to attend more closely to the role of government.

Contributions

We make four contributions which we now elaborate upon: the relatedness of the 'embedded' and 'agential' views on government and CSR; the developments between different forms of CSR policy; the relationships between domestic and international CSR policies; and the framework of direct and indirect policies for CSR.

Our first main contribution is that CSR reflects both the embeddedness of governmental institutions and the agency of a variety of governmental actors in their specific issue and institutional contexts. This clearly challenges the dichotomous perspective of government and CSR but it also extends the 'related' perspective of government and CSR by stressing the relationships between the two variant views therein: the embedded and the agential views. The role of agency reflects the fact that governments have choices about how to regulate, in this case, domestic and international social problems, whether to do so in an unmediated fashion (Figure 2.2) or to do so either by supporting CSR initiatives directly or indirectly through the regulatory environment in which corporations operate (Figure 2.1).

Our second contribution is to show how different forms of public policy for CSR (detailed earlier) interact and develop from one another. Our analysis revealed clear instances of policy learning in the dynamics and adaptation of forms of policy for CSR. In the case of the Danish regulation for non-financial reporting and of the transparency of payments in the extractives industry we saw how endorsement and facilitation paved the way for government mandate, and in the former case we identified different strengths of mandate. Whereas the mode of facilitation has remained a constant in the case of governmental policies for the ETI and its Scandinavian variants, it is striking that these CSR organizations also reflected partnership-type relationships. Further, they have played a role in wider governmental regulation contributing to: the use of mandate in the UK employment Acts; facilitation of CSR in the Norwegian public procurement legislation; and the coordination of inter-governmentalism in the case of the Norwegian and Danish ETIs and the Nordic Council of Ministers. Although Gond et al. (2011) hypothesize such a development in West European CSR they do not substantiate it. And although Auld et al. (2008) anticipate that government will have different relationships with different types of CSR, they do not anticipate such dynamism. So our contribution here has two key features. The first is that governments and CSR organizations take an adaptive approach to the forms of regulation that shape their relationships. Second, the government–CSR relationship is not uni-directional, but two-way as government policy shapes the institutionalization of CSR, and as CSR institutions contribute to government policymaking. Neither of these points is adequately addressed in the CSR and government literature to date.

Our third contribution is to highlight the domestic–international relationship between government policies for CSR and the international reach of these policies. In order to do this we take our starting point in the literature on domestic governance and CSR and apply it to the problem of global CSR governance. Whereas scholars such as Campbell (2007) noted the embedded relationship and those such as Albareda et al. (2007) and Steurer (2010) have recognized the agential relationship between government and domestic CSR, we have explored how the combined embedded and agential roles of government for CSR can extend from the domestic to international spheres. Furthermore, while scholars such as Scherer and Palazzo (2011) recognize the significance of corporations and CSR for global governance issues, they do not sufficiently account for the government roles therein, which our study underlines.

The fourth contribution is the framework of 'direct' and 'indirect' public policies for CSR, which is a novel approach for analysing different ways that governments engage in CSR policies and the interaction of these policies. This arises from our combining the CSR and domestic governance literature, which stresses the policies for CSR directly, with the global governance and CSR literature, which drew our attention to the issues of ethical trade and transparency in payments in extractives in which we found our evidence of government agency. Although other authors have recognized different ways in which governments regulate some of the CSR-type problems (e.g. Auld et al., 2008 who relate this to the different types of CSR; Schneider and Scherer, 2016; Ueberbacher et al., 2016 who apply the Abbot and Snidal approach of hard and soft law to CSR issues), our approach is distinct. Most importantly our approach to identifying policies for CSR directly and indirectly does not isolate CSR and government policies for CSR from other key developments in their respective issue areas. We find that this is vital for a proper appreciation of the place of CSR in wider domestic and global governance. Otherwise the questions of CSR and governance are assessed in ignorance of key developments in the areas to which CSR is directed. It is perfectly possible that governments could simultaneously make policies for CSR directly and indirectly as a means of addressing a problem, without any cognizance of, or relationship between, these two approaches. However, our examples suggest that governmental actors making policies for CSR indirectly are all too aware of, indeed are motivated by, the operation of CSR initiatives that they or other governments have supported. Moreover, we also find that CSR initiatives are also aware of, and responsive to, such changes in their regulatory environments.

Our contribution concerning policies for CSR directly and indirectly further confirms the significance of CSR for wider governance as well as the significance of government for CSR. The cases of CSR that we have explored offer evidence of CSR as a factor in wider contemporary governance. It is not only a further refutation of the dichotomous perspective. It is also a substantive contribution in that we have also shown *how* CSR is related to wider governance by virtue of being directly related to national governments and a consideration in the calculation of governments' wider regulatory initiatives in the respective policy areas, which we call policies for CSR indirectly.

In this respect our analysis substantiates Braithwaite and Drahos' contention that:

The state is constituted by and helps constitute a web of regulatory controls that is continually rewoven to remake the regulatory state. States act as agents for other actors such as business corporations and other actors act as agents for states. (2000: 479)

But our analysis also enables us to invert Braithwaite and Drahos's contention and suggest that CSR is constituted by and helps constitute a web of regulatory controls that is continually rewoven to remake the regulatory state. CSR initiatives act as agents for other actors such as *states* and other actors (e.g. states) act as agents for CSR.

This is not so say that CSR initiatives, or the corporations that are their principal actors, are just like states. As noted throughout our analysis, they possess very different resources and relational powers, but we have given a comprehensive picture of CSR's involvement in forms of blended governance as a result of governments' policies to support it directly and indirectly.

Our analysis also enables further reflection on governance as defined by Mayntz:

the entirety of co-existing forms of collective regulation of societal issues: ranging from the institutionalized self-organization of civil society and the different forms of cooperation between public and private actors to the sovereign acts of states. (2004: 6)

In our analysis we have shown that the place of government and CSR initiatives in governance is less about being on a spectrum or 'range' but more about being involved in networked interactions. We have seen how the cooperation of different actor types precedes, engages in parallel with, and succeeds the sovereign acts of states. Although in some cases, parallel governance involving government and CSR initiatives may be entirely coincidental and even contradictory, in our analysis, we have found evidence of mutual cognisance, anticipation, and adaptation. But these interactions between government and CSR, whether reflecting policies to support CSR directly or indirectly, are not uncoordinated or 'orchestrated' as Abbot and Snidal argue for the role of International Governance Organizations in global governance through intermediaries that participate in the governance systems voluntarily (Abbott et al., 2015). Rather they appear to better reflect the metaphor of 'improvisation' – or jazz (Hatch, 1999) – in which no single player orchestrates but the collective actions (or music) reflect the mutually aware interactions of private and public actors (or players) who echo and build on one another's contributions. Although the hands of government are visible, they are not solely orchestrating international CSR; rather they are part of an ensemble of improvisation.

Hatch noted how conventional jazz elements (1997: 75) re-describe organizational structures. Of particular relevance to our analysis are the elements of:

'soloing' or taking the lead; 'comping' or supporting others lead; 'trading fours' or switching between leading and supporting; 'listening' or opening the space for others' lead; 'responding' or responding to or accommodating others ideas. (81)

So government has agency and that has proved crucial in the cases we have examined. However, the agency is in the context of other agents not only playing the same music but also leading, supporting, switching, opening space, and responding and accommodating.

The government–CSR relations that we explore not only reflect the context for improvisation in which orchestration is absent, but also prompt the revisiting of the conventional structural distinctions between government policy and CSR. This is partly because there is no single set of governmental interactions with international CSR initiatives: rather there are multiple governmental engagements either sequential or simultaneous. But more importantly yet, each CSR initiative has its own organizational character reflecting the respective business and civil society actors involved.

Implications

A number of key implications arise from our analysis: that CSR and public policy are closely intertwined; that the role of corporations in public policy raises further questions about corporate power; and that accordingly, corporations would do well to identify the ways in which they retain their independence in the context of their governance roles.

We find that CSR has become more explicitly integrated in public policy as a result of its combined contributions to governance. CSR is informed by public policy as well as contributes to it and, arguably in our cases, can strengthen it. Nonetheless, it is clearly important for corporations and CSR initiatives to distinguish what their roles are in relation to public policy and together in domestic and global governance.

Second, although our analysis has not directly addressed the question of corporate power in the relationships between government and CSR that we have explored (but see Moon et al., 2005), this is definitely important. It is important from a legitimacy perspective that, through the government–CSR relationships that we have explored, corporations are not seen to have unduly influenced public policymakers to bring inappropriate advantage to them collectively and individually (Reich, 2008; see also Davis, 2015). On the basis of our findings, corporations are seen to be powerful. This is evident in the motivation for CSR initiatives which came about precisely because of: the social salience of the shortcomings on corporate reporting of non-financial activities; the impact of Western MNCs on the working conditions in their international RMG supply chains; and the fiscal significance of extractive MNCs payments to host country governments. We also see that through government involvement in the CSR initiatives which we have detailed, corporate power can be constrained.

Third, and relatedly, it is equally important for corporations and CSR initiatives not to be regarded as mere pawns of government in the sorts of developments that we have outlined. Here, as in the earlier point, the metaphor of jazz may be helpful, but nonetheless careful articulation of distinctive and independent roles of governments, corporations, and CSR initiatives in their interactions will be useful for all round legitimacy. Thus in government relations with CSR, the actors retain choice about what and how to 'play' (Hatch, 1999: 82). This is not only crucial to the art of improvisation but also to the integrity of the players.

Limitations

Notwithstanding the significance of our contributions, a number of limitations should be noted: the limited number of cases; the omission of government motivation in our original research design; and our selection of cases which may lead to an under-estimation of hostile relations between government and CSR.

First, and most obviously, our conclusions are based on a small number of cases, albeit closely studied over time. Moreover, they were selected to enable us to highlight the 'how', the 'to what' effect, and the 'why' of governmental support for CSR. Our analysis presented in Chapter 3 on CSR polices in Europe is representative at least for that continent and for that period. However, we selected the cases of non-financial reporting, ethical trade, and tax transparency in extractives because they represent three major areas of CSR, which reveal direct and indirect public policies for CSR. The cases are intended to open up conceptual lenses and research frameworks for further research. Our focus here is not to explain the causes of indirect and direct public policies of CSR because to do so would require us to compare our cases to other cases where the indirect and direct linkages did not emerge. Our findings raise questions for research that might enable wider generalization.

Second, in hindsight we might have more purposefully explored the question of government motivation for making policies in support of CSR directly and indirectly. Our insights emerged in the course of the analysis, rather than as a result of the application of a specific analytical framework. Likewise, within the cases selected, the issue of 'cognizance' between government policymakers of direct and indirect policies for CSR and with CSR initiatives in themselves emerged. But our analysis was not designed to identify and evaluate this factor. Therefore, in hindsight, this factor in our account of government–CSR relations could have been specified more closely in our design and pursued more purposefully thereafter.

Third, although our analysis suggests generally propitious relationships between government, corporations, and CSR initiatives, it is possible that our analysis has downplayed points of 'behind the scenes' tension, incompatibility, and even mutual hostility (which we did evidence in the United States in the very public differences in reaction to Dodd–Frank Section 1504). Relatedly, our cases did not reveal unintended and deleterious effects of the government policies for CSR on CSR initiatives. In theory, such lacks of synergy are entirely possible, as they are even among more unmediated cases of public policy.

Most of these limitations in our own approach open up opportunities for further research to which we now turn.

Further Research

Despite its limitations, our analysis, findings, and contributions raise a number of questions for further research concerning: the conceptualization of forms of policy for CSR and the relationships between embedded and agential government policy for CSR; the role of CSR/policy learning in the relationships we have studied; the extent and nature of isomorphic tendencies in CSR and global governance; and the implementation processes and outcomes of the sorts of policies that we have explored.

First, we expect that further research can be conducted in the conceptualization of government policies for CSR beyond our formulation of forms of policy (i.e. endorsement, facilitation, partnership, and mandate – from soft to hard) and the distinction of policies that support CSR directly. An area of further research is reviewing the ways these forms of regulation are conceptualized and how the policies themselves adapt to one another and to changing circumstances and balances of interest (see also Cashore et al., 2004). This looks especially appropriate as our public policy form 'facilitation' covers such a range of governmental modes and resources (see the earlier sections).

Relatedly, while our analysis has been innovative in detailing the interactions of embeddedness and agency, further research could be conducted on the relationships between types of embeddedness and agency choices. This could include reference to the national business systems – or varieties of capitalism – in which CSR is embedded as well as the types of agency deployed by governments whether in terms of CSR issues addressed or the forms of policy support provided.

A second area of future research that emerged from our analysis is to examine *how* policy learning takes place among all actors in CSR organizations and particularly, from our perspective, in government. Our study has detailed interactions, but a closer analysis of how the respective actors gain insights into the roles of other players and their potential for institutional strengthening will be highly valuable.

Whilst we have identified a key motivation for government policy for CSR to be the perception that their own policy approaches and priorities can be supported by policies for CSR, closer analyses can be conducted of what advantages CSR policies actually bring to governmental policy agendas. It could also explore in greater detail the interactions within and among organizations and policymakers involved in

CSR initiatives and wider government policies to shape the regulatory context for CSR. The area of anti-corruption policies is an obvious case in point here, where governments have both mandated requisite behaviour but have also supported private initiatives (Hansen, 2017). This sort of research could include closer attention to the types of formal and informal exchanges between actors from these different types of organizations as well as to their circulation among the actor types through employment, secondments consultancies, and partnerships. Together our insights into the interactions of policies for CSR directly and indirectly, and the dynamism among the forms that these policies can take, reveal a rich array of policy resources and opportunities for government. But can these resources and opportunities be deployed more generally? Whilst our findings clearly revealed mutual cognizance and understanding among actors of their respective counterparts – whether in government or in CSR initiatives – as noted earlier, we would hesitate to conclude that the interactions and dynamics were coordinated or 'orchestrated' (Abbot and Snidal, 2015).

A third issue for further research concerns whether in the context of CSR, globalization, and global governance, there is an underlying isomorphic tendency in the issue focus, modes, and rationalizations of CSR as suggested in Matten and Moon (2008). Our research was not expressly designed to address this question but two inferences can be reasonably drawn. First, the cases we have investigated all have the effect of developing international solutions to CSR issues. Second, there is no single 'international' pattern to these initiatives in terms of their membership, regulatory balance, and scope. They appear to be issue specific and this provides scope for further research.

Finally, although our analysis has had a lot to say about regulatory inputs, processes, and organizational interactions we have said little about outcomes both of direct and indirect forms of policy, as well as their combined effects. This remains a challenge in CSR research in general even though since Pressman and Wildavsky (1973), political scientists have sought to grapple with the question of how implementation processes fulfil or frustrate the intentions of policymakers. But in our case, the question remains as to whether government-related CSR policies have led to: improved societal trust in corporations as a result of direct policies for non-financial reporting; better working conditions and remuneration in the Bangladesh and wider RMG supply chains as a result of direct and indirect policies for ethical trade; more accountable and better deployed public finances in developing countries as a result of direct and indirect policies for transparency of MNC payments to those governments. We trust at least that our framing of government policies for international CSR can assist in such important endeavours.

Bibliography

Aaronson, S. A. 2002. 'How The Europeans Got a Head Start on Policies to Promote Global Corporate Responsibility.' *Corporate Environmental Strategy*, 9(4): 356–367.

Aaronson, S. A., 2011. 'Limited partnership: Business, government, civil society, and the public in the Extractive Industries Transparency Initiative (EITI).' *Public Administration and Development*, 31(1), 50–63.

Abbott, K. W., Genschel, P., Snidal, D., and Zangl, B. 2015. *International Organisations as Orchestrators*. Cambridge University Press.

Abbott, K. W., and Snidal, D. 2000. 'Hard and Soft Law in International Governance.' *International Organization*, 54(3): 421–456.

Accord on Fire and Building Safety. n.d. 'Accord.' Retrieved from http://bangladeshaccord.org [accessed 4 January 2017].

2013. 'Bangladesh Accord Appoints Its Leadership Team.' 17 October. Retrieved from http://bangladeshaccord.org/2013/10/bangladesh-accord-appoints-leadership-team [accessed 12 May 2015].

Action Aid. 2008. *Hole in the Pocket: Why Unpaid Taxes are the Missing Link in Development Finance*. Briefing Paper, November, London.

Africa Focus, 2010. 'USA/Congo (Kinshasa): Conflict Minerals Law' *Africa Focus*. Retrieved from http://www.africafocus.org/docs10/cgk1007a.php [accessed 6 November 2015].

Aglietta, M. 1980. *A Theory of Capitalist Regulation: The US Experience*, London: New Left Books.

Aguilera, R. V., and Jackson, G. 2003. 'The Cross-National Diversity of Corporate Governance: Dimensions and Determinants.' *Academy of Management Review*, 28(3): 447–465.

Aguilera, R.V., Rupp, D. E., Williams, C. A., and Ganapathi, J. 2007. 'Putting The S Back In Corporate Social Responsibility: A Multilevel Theory Of Social Change In Organizations.' *Academy of Management Review*, 32(3): 836–863.

Aguinis, H., and Glavas, A., 2012. 'What We Know and Don't Know About Corporate Social Responsibility: A Review and Research Agenda.' *Journal of Management* 38: 932–968.

Albareda, L., Lozano, J. M., Tencati, A., Midttun, A., and Perrini, F. 2008. 'The Changing Role of Governments in Corporate Social Responsibility: Drivers and Responses.' *Business Ethics: A European Review*, 17(4): 347–363.

Albareda, L., Lozano, J. M., and Ysa, T. 2007. 'Public Policies on Corporate Social Responsibility: The Role of Governments in Europe', *Journal of Business Ethics*, 74(4): 391–407.

Albareda, L., Lozano, J. M., Tencati, A., Midttun, A., and Perrini, F. 2008. 'The Changing Role of Governments in Corporate Social Responsibility: Drivers and Responses.' *Business Ethics: A European Review*, 17(4): 347–363.

Alliance for Bangladesh Worker Safety. n.d.-a. 'About the Alliance for Bangladesh Worker Safety.' Retrieved from http://www.bangladeshworker safety.org/who-we-are/about-the-alliance [accessed 7 January 2017].

n.d-b. 'Remediation.' Retrieved from http://www.bangladeshworker safety.org/what-we-do/remediation [accessed 7 January 2017].

n.d.-c. 'Factory list and inspections reports.' Retrieved from http://www .bangladeshworkersafety.org/factory/factory-list-inspection-reports [accessed 7 January 2017].

Alt, J., and Lassen, D. 2006a. 'Fiscal transparency, political parties and debt in OECD countries.' *European Economic Review*, 50(6): 1403–39.

2006b. 'Transparency, Political Polarization, and Political Budget Cycles in OECD countries.' *American Journal of Political Science*, 50(3): 530–550.

Amable, B. 2003. *The Diversity of Modern Capitalism*. Oxford: Oxford University Press.

Amengual, M. and Chirot, L., 2016. 'Reinforcing the State Transnational and State Labor Regulation in Indonesia.' *ILR Review* 69 (5): 1056–1080.

Amin, A. 2004. 'Regulating Economic Globalization.' *Transactions of the Institute of British Geographies*, 29(2): 217–33.

Anglo-American. 2014. *Business Intergrity Policy*. London: Anglo American.

Anner, M. S. 2014. 'Wildcat Strikes and Social Dialogue in Vietnam's Apparel Export Sector.' *Paper presented at Labor and Employment Relations Association (LERA) Annual Meeting*. Portland, OR.

Antal, A. B., and Sobczak, A., 2007. 'Corporate Social Responsibility in France A Mix of National Traditions and International Influences'. *Business & Society*, 46(1): 9–32.

Auld, G., Bernstein, S., and Cashore, B. 2008. 'The New Corporate Social Responsibility.' *Annual Review of Environment and Resources*, 33(1): 413–435.

Auty, R. M. 1993. *Sustaining Development in Mine & Economies: The Resource Curse Thesis*. London: Routledge.

Avi-Yonah, Reuven S. 2005 'The Cyclical Transformations of the Corporate Form: A Historical Perspective on Corporate Social Responsibility.' *Delaware Journal of Corporate Law*, 30(3): 767–818.

Ayres, I., and Braithwaite, J. 1992. *Responsive Regulation. Transcending the Deregulation Debate*. Oxford: Oxford University Press.

Baldwin, R., Cave, M., and Lodge, M. 2011. *Understanding Regulation: Theory, Strategy, and Practice Business & Management*. Oxford: Oxford University Press.

Bansal, P., and Roth, K. 2000. 'Why Companies Go Green: A Model of Ecological Responsiveness.' *The Academy of Management Journal*, 43(4): 717–736.

Barnier, M. 2014. 'The EU Transparency and Accounting Directives.' *The Journal of World Energy Law & Business*, 7(1), 16–19.

Barrientos, S., and Smith, S. 2005. 'Fair trade and ethical trade: are there moves towards convergence?' *Sustainable Development* 13: 190–98.

   2006. *The ETI Code of Labour Practice: Do Workers Really Benefit?* Brighton: Institute of Development Studies, University of Sussex.

   2007. 'Do Workers Benefit from Ethical Trade? Assessing Codes of Labour Practice in Global Production Systems.' *Third World Quarterly*, 28(4): 713–729.

Bartley, T. 2007. 'Institutional Emergence in an Era of Globalization: The Rise of Transnational Private Regulation of Labor and Environmental Conditions.' *American Journal of Sociology*, 113(2), 297–351.

bbs.gov.bd (Bangladesh National Portal), n.d. 'Bangladesh Bureau of Statistics-Government of the People's Republic of Bangladesh.' Retrieved from http://bbs.gov.bd/ [accessed 7 January 2017].

Beer, S. H. 1965. *Modern British Politics: Parties and Pressure Groups in the Collectivist Age*. New York: Random House.

Berle, A., and Means., G. 1932. *The Modern Corporation and Private Property*. New York: Commerce Clearing House Inc.

Bernstein, S., and Cashore, B. 2002. 'The International-Domestic Nexus: The Effects of International Trade and Environmental Politics on the Canadian Forest Sector.' In Howlett (ed.) *Canadian Forest Policy: Regimes, Policy Dynamics and Institutional Adaptations*. Toronto: University of Toronto Press, 2002: 65–93.

Bernstein, S., and Cashore, B. 2007. 'Can Non-state Global Governance Be Legitimate? An Analytical Framework.' *Regulation & Governance* 1 (4): 347–371.

   2012. 'Complex Global Governance and Domestic Policies: Four Pathways of Influence.' *International Affairs*, 88(3): 585–604.

Blair, T. 1997. 'Leader's Speech, Brighton 1997.' *British Political Speech*, May 1. Retrived from http://www.britishpoliticalspeech.org/speech -archive.htm?speech=203#banner [accessed 1 June 2016].

Blowfield, M. 2005. 'Corporate Social Responsibility Reinventing the Meaning of Development.' *International Affairs*, 81(3): 515–524.

——— 2010. 'Business and Poverty Reduction.' In P. Utting ans J. C. Marques (eds) *Corporate Social Responsibility and Regulatory Governance: Towards Inclusive Development?* New York: Palgrave Macmillan: 124–150.

——— 1999. 'Ethical Trade: A Review of Developments and Issues.' *Third World Quarterly*, 20(4): 753–770.

Blowfield, M., and Murray, A. 2008. *Corporate Responsibility: A Critical Introduction.* New York, NY: Oxford University Press.

Börzel, T. A., Hönke, J., and Thauer, C., 2012. 'Multinational Corporations, Corporate Responsibility and the Nation State: Does it really take the State?' *Business and Politics* 14 (3): 1–34.

Börzel, T. A. Heritier, A., Kranz, N., and Thauer, Christian R. 2011. 'Racing to the Top? Regulatory Competition among Firms in Areas of Limited Statehood.' In T. Risse and U. Lehmkuhl (eds) *Governance without a State? Policies and Politics in Areas of Limited Statehood.* New York: Colombia University Press: 144–170.

Börzel, T. A., and Risse, T. 2010. 'Governance without a State: Can it work?' *Regulation & Governance*, 4(2): 113–134.

Boswell, J. 1983. 'The Informal Social Control of Business in Britain: 1880–1939.' *Business History Review*, 57(2): 237–257.

Bowen, H. R. 1953. *Social Responsibilities of the Businessman.* New York: Harper & Row.

Boyer, R. 2004. *Une Théorie du Capitalisme est-elle Possible?* Paris: Odile Jacob.

Braendle, U. C., and Noll, J. 2006. 'Enlarged EU: Enlarged Corporate Governance? Why Directives Might Be More Appropriate for Transition Economies.' *Corporate Governance: The International Journal of Business in Society*, 6(3): 296–304.

Braithwaite, J., Coglianese, C., and Levi-Faur, D. 2008. 'Change and Challenge in Regulation and Governance.' *Regulation & Governance*, 2(4): 381–382.

Braithwaite, J., and Drahos, P. 2000. *Global Business Regulation.* New York: Cambridge University Press.

Brammer, S., Jackson, G., and Matten, D. 2012. 'Corporate Social Responsibility and Institutional Theory: New Perspectives on Private Governance.' *Socio-Economic Review*, 10(1): 3–28.

Bredgaard, T. 2004. '*Virksomhedernes sociale ansvar – Fra offentlig politik til virksomhedspolitik.*' Ph.d.-afhandling. Institut for Økonomi: Institut for Økonomi, Politik og Forvaltning.

Brown, D. 2012. 'Labour Standards and Human Rights.' In A. Narlikar, M. Dauton, and R. M. Stern (eds) *The Oxford Handbook on The World Trade Organization*, Oxford University Press: 697–718.

Brown, D., and Knudsen, J. S. 2012. 'Managing corporate responsibility globally and locally: Lessons from a CR leader.' *Business and Politics*, 14(3): 29.

Brown, M. 2013 'Digging into SEC Mineral Disclosure Policies.' Retrieved from https://www.mayerbrown.com/pt/publications/detailprint.aspx?publication=9687 [accessed 9 October 2016].

Brown, T. A., and Knudsen, J. S. 2015. 'The Role of Domestic Institutions and Market Pressures as Drivers of Corporate Social Responsibility (CSR): An Examination of Company CSR Initiatives in Denmark and the UK.' *Political Studies*, 63(1): 181–201.

Browne, J. 2010. *Beyond Business: An Inspirational Memoir Form a Visionary Leader*. Weindenfeld & Nicolson.

Buhmann, K. 2010. 'CSR-rapportering som refleksiv ret: Årsregnskabslovens CSR-redegørelseskrav som typeeksempel.' *Juristen*, 92 (4): 104–13.

Burgoon, B. 2001. 'Globalization and Welfare Compensation: Disentangling the Ties that Bind.' *International Organization* 55(3): 509–51.

Butler, S. 2010. 'Primark ramps up ethical efforts after expose on working practices,' *The Telegraph*, January 21. Retrieved from http://www.telegraph.co.uk/finance/newsbysector/retailandconsumer/7037887/Primarkramps-up-ethical-efforts-after-expose-on-working-practices.html [accessed 11 June 2015].

Campbell, J. L. 2007. 'Why would corporations behave in socially responsible ways? An Institutional Theory of Corporate Social Responsibility.' *Academy of Management Review*, 32(3): 946–967.

Carroll, A. B. 1979. 'A Three-Dimensional Model of Corporate Performance.' *Academy of Management Review*, 4(4): 497–505.

Cashore, B., Auld, G., and Newsom, D. 2004. *Governing Through Markets: Forest Certification and the Emergence of Non-State Authority*. New Haven; London: Yale University Press.

Castelló, I., Etter, M., and Årup Nielsen, F. 2016. 'Strategies of Legitimacy Through Social Media: The Networked Strategy: Strategies of Legitimacy Through Social Media.' *Journal of Management Studies*, 53(3): 402–432.

Chambers, E., Chapple, W., Moon, J., and Sullivan, M., 2003. 'CSR in Asia: A Seven Country study of CSR Website Reporting'. *ResearchGate*.

Chapple, W., and Moon, J. 2005. 'Corporate social responsibility (CSR) in Asia: A seven-country study of CSR web site reporting'. *Business and Society* 44(4): 415–441.

Chazan, G. 2012. 'Oil and Gas has the Highest Bribery Rate', *The Financial Times*, 15 July. Retrieved from: https://www.ft.com/content/c84ead24 -ce7e-11e1-bc0c-00144feabdc0 [accessed 17 June 2015].

Chevron, 2015. 'Corporate Responsibility Reporting.' *chevron.com*. Retrieved from https://www.chevron.com/corporate-responsibility/ reporting [accessed 8 January 2017].

Christensen, J., Kapoor, S., and Murphy, R. 2004 'The Social Irresponsibility of Corporate Tax Avoidance: Taking CSR to the Bottom Line.' *Development*, 47(3): 37–44.

Clapham, A. 2006. *Human Rights Obligations of Non-State Actors.* New York: Oxford University Press.

Clark, J. M. 1916. 'The Changing Basis of Economic Responsibility.' *The Journal of Political Economy*, 24(3): 209–229.

Clean Clothes Campaign, 2014. 'Still waiting. Victims of workplace tragedies including Ali Enterprises fire and the collapsed Rana Plaza still waiting for compensation.' Retrieved from https://cleanclothes.org/news/press -releases/2014/09/11/still-waiting [accessed 11 June 2015].

CNN, 2013. 'Prime minister says Bangladesh is reforming its garment industry'. by T. Watkins, *CNN.com*. Retrieved from http://www.cnn .com/2013/05/02/world/asia/bangladesh-building-collapse/index.html [accessed 7 January 2017].

Collier, P., and Hoeffler, A. 1998 'On the Economic Causes of Civil War.' *Oxford Economic Papers*, 50(4): 563–73.

Cooper, B. 2009. 'Non-financial reporting – Learning from Denmark', *Ethical Corporation*, March 10.

Coslovsky, S. V. and Locke, R., 2013. 'Parallel Paths to Enforcement Private Compliance, Public Regulation, and Labor Standards in the Brazilian Sugar Sector.' *Politics & Society* 41: 497–526.

COWI (for the Danish Business Authority), 2014. 'Kortlaegning af danske virksomheders redegoerelse for samfundsansvar.' Retrieved from https:// samfundsansvar.dk/undersoegelser-af-lovkravets-effekt [accessed 8 January 2017].

CSR Weltweit, n.d. 'CSR WeltWeit. Deutsche Unternehmen – Global engagiert.' Retrieved from http://www.csrgermany.de/www/csr_cms_ relaunch.nsf/id/8F6GR9-csr-weltweit-deutsche-unternehmen–global-engagiert-de [accessed 8 January 2017].

Dahl, R., and Lindblom, C. E. 1953. *Politics, Economics, and Welfare: Planning and Politico-Economic Systems Resolved into Basic Social Processes.* New York: Harper.

 1992. *Politics, Economics and Welfare.* New Brunswick: Transaction Publishers.

Daily Star, 2015. 'Accord, Alliance a noose around the neck: Muhith'. June 16. Retrieved from http://www.thedailystar.net/business/accord-alliance -noose-around-the-neck-muhith-97669 [accessed 5 December 2015].

Daly, H. 1996. *Beyond Growth*. Boston: Beacon Press.

Danida. 2013. 'About Danida.' Retrieved from at http://um.dk/en/danida -en/about-danida/ [accessed 4 June 2013].

Danish Business Authority. n.d. 'Legislation.' *CSRgov – Legislation*, Retrieved from http://csrgov.dk/legislation [accessed 27 May 2016].

2010. 'Corporate Social Responsibility and Reporting in Denmark: Impact of the Legal Requirements for Reporting on CSR in the Danish Financial Statements Act.' *Danish Commerce and Companies Agency*, August. Retrieved from http://CSRgov.dk [accessed 27 May, 2016].

Danish Government, 2008. 'Proposal for an Act Amending the Danish Financial Statements Act. (Report on Social Responsibility for Large Businesses).' *GlobalDenmark Translations*. Retrieved from http:// csrgov.dk/file/319999/proposal_report_on_social_resp_december_ 2008.pdf [accessed 15 December 2012].

2012. 'Responsible Growth: Action Plan for Corporate Social Responsibility 2012–2015.' Retrieved from http://csrgov.dk/danish_ action_plan_2012. [accessed 29 May 2016].

David-Barrett, L., and Okamura, K. 2013. 'Why do Corrupt Countries Join EITI.' Working Paper 38. *European Research Center for Anticorruption and State-Building* (ERCAS).

Davis, G. F. 2015. 'Corporate Power in the Twenty-First Century.' In S. Rangan (ed.) *Performance and Progress: Essays on Capitalism, Business and Society*. Oxford: Oxford University Press: 395–414.

Davis, K. 1973. 'The Case for and Against Business Assumption of Social Responsibilities.' *Academy of Management Journal*, 16(2): 312–322.

de Bakker, F. G. A., and den Hond, F., 2008. 'Introducing the Politics of Stakeholder Influence: A Review Essay.' *Business & Society*, 47(1): 8–20.

de Búrca, G., Keohane, R., and Sabel, C. 2014. 'Global Experimentalist Governance.' *New York University Public Law and Legal Theory Working Papers*. Retrieved from http://lsr.nellco.org/nyu_plltwp/485 [accessed 20 July 2016].

Dearlove, J. 1973. *The Politics of Policy in Local Government: The Making and Maintenance of Public Policy in the Royal Borough of Kensington and Chelsea*. Cambridge: Cambridge University Press.

Department for Business Innovation and Skills. 2014. 'UK Implementation of the EU Accounting Directive: Chapter 10: Extractive industries reporting – Government response to consultation.' Retrieved from

https://www.gov.uk/government/uploads/system/uploads/attachment_
data/file/343599/bis-14-1006-eu-accounting-directive-implementation
-extractive-industries-reporting-response.pdf [accessed 8 January
2017].

Detomasi, D. A. 2007 'The Multinational Corporation and Global
Governance: Modelling Global Publicd Policy Networks' *Journal of
Business Ethics* 71 (3): 321–34.

DIEH. n.d.-a. 'Members.' Retrieved from www.dieh.dk/in-english/members
[accessed 11 June 2015].

n.d.-b. 'DIEH Guidelines.' Retrieved from www.dieh.dk/etisk-handel/
hvordan-etisk-handel/dieh-retningslinjer-for-etisk-handel/dieh-guide
lines [accessed 11 June 2015].

Diller, J. 1999. 'A Social Conscience in the Global Marketplace? Labour
Dimensions of Codes of Conduct, Social Labelling and Investor
Initiatives.' *International Labour Review*, 138(2): 99–129.

Distelhorst, G., Locke, R. M., Pal, T., Samel, H., 2015. 'Production goes
Global, Compliance stays Local: Private Regulation in the Global
Electronics Industry.' *Regulation & Governance* 9(3): 224–242.

Doh, J. P. 2005. 'Offshore Outsourcing: Implications for International
Business and Strategic Management Theory and Practice.' *Journal of
Management Studies*, 42(3): 695–704.

Domberger, S. 1999. *The Contracting Organization: A Strategic Guide to
Outsourcing*. New York: Oxford University Press.

Drezner, D. W., 2001. 'Globalization and Policy Convergence.' *International
Studies Review* 3(1): 53–78.

Duina, F. 2015. 'Beyond Free Trade: Accounting for Labor and
Environmental Governance Standards in NAFTA.' In T. A. Börzel and
V. Van Hüllen (eds.) *Governance Transfer by Regional Organizations,
Governance and Limited Statehood Series*. UK: Palgrave Macmillan:
177–191.

Dyck, A., Ling, K. V., Roth, L., and Wagner, H. 2015. 'Do Institutional
Investors Drive Corporate Social Responsibility? International
Evidence', Working Paper, November 18, Rothman School of Business,
University of Toronto.

Earth Rights International, n.d. 'American Petroleum Institute v. SEC:
Revenue Transparency Litigation'. Retrieved from https://www.earth
rights.org/legal/american-petroleum-institute-v-sec-revenue-trans
parency-litigation [accessed 8 January 2017].

Elkington, J. 1997. *Cannibals with Forks: The Triple Bottom Line of 21st
Century Business*. London: Capstone.

Esping-Andersen, G. 1990. *The Three Worlds of Welfare Capitalism*.
Princeton: Princeton University Press.

Ethical Corporation, 2010. *Oil and Gas Revenues: Iraq's Transparency Surge*. Ethical Corporation.

Ethical Trading Initiative (ETI). n.d.-a. 'Training'. Retrieved from http://www.ethicaltrade.org/training [accessed 7 January 2017].

n.d.-b. 'Funding.' Retrieved from http://www.ethicaltrade.org/about-eti/funding [acessed 27 July 2013].

2013. 'Cross-party support for collaboration on Bangladesh.' Retrieved from http://www.ethicaltrade.org/news-and-events/news/cross-party-support-for-collaboration-on-Bangladesh [accessed 12 September 2015].

2015. 'Respect for workers worldwide'. Retrieved from http://www.ethicaltrade.org/ [accessed 11 June 2015].

2016. 'ETI Base Code'. Retrieved from http://www.ethicaltrade.org/eti-base-code [accessed 12 December 2016].

Ethical Trading Initiative Norway (IEH). n.d.-a 'Public Procurement'. Retrieved from http://etiskhandel.no/English/Public_procurement/index.html [accessed 17 June 2015].

European Commission. 2001. 'COM(2001) 366 Final Green Paper: Promoting a European Framework for Corporate Social Responsibility.' *Commission of the European Communities*, July 18. Retrieved from: http://eur-lex.europa.eu/legal-content/EN/TXT/?uri=CELEX:52001DC0366 [accessed 10 October 2015].

2011. 'Communication from the Commission to the European Parliament, the Council, the European Economic and Social Committee and the Committee of the Regions: A renewed EU strategy 2011–14 for Corporate Social Responsibility'. Retrieved from: http://eur-lex.europa.eu/legal-content/EN/TXT/PDF/?uri=CELEX:52011DC0681&from=EN [accessed 11 June 2015].

2011. 'More Responsible Businesses Can Foster More Growth in Europe.' October 25. Retrieved from http://europa.eu/rapid/press-release_IP-11-1238_en.htm [accessed 27 May 2016].

2012. 'Commission Plans to Modernise European Company Law and Corporate Governance.' December 12. Retrieved from http://europa.eu/rapid/press-release_IP-12-1340_en.htm [accessed 27 May 2016].

2013. 'Commission Moves to Enhance Business Transparency on Social and Environmental Matters.' April 16. Retrieved from http://europa.eu/rapid/press-release_IP-13-330_en.htm [accessed 27 May 2016].

2013. 'EU Trade Commissioner De Gucht Launches Global Sustainability Compact in Response to Bangladesh Tragedy.' July 8, 2013. Retrieved from http://trade.ec.europa.eu/doclib/press/index.cfm?id=935 [accessed 8 June 2016].

2014. 'Disclosure of non-financial information: Europe's largest companies to be more transparent on social and environmental issues.'

September 29. Retrieved from http://europa.eu/rapid/press-release_
STATEMENT-14-291_en.htm [accessed 7 January 2017].

2014. 'Corporate Social Responsibility National Public Policies in the
European Union – Compendium 2014.' November 2014. Retrieved
from https://ec.europa.eu/digital-single-market/news/corporate-social
-responsibility-national-public-policies-european-union-compendium
-2014 [accessed 15 April 2014].

2016. 'Non-Financial Reporting. Banking and Finance: Company
Reporting.' Retrieved from http://ec.europa.eu/finance/company
-reporting/non-financial_reporting/index_en.htm [accessed 12 October
2016].

2016. 'Bangladesh – Trade.' 28 September 2016. Retrieved from http://
ec.europa.eu/trade/policy/countries-and-regions/countries/bangladesh/
[accessed 9 December 2016].

European Parliament and the Council. 2004. 'DIRECTIVE 2004/17/EC.'
Official Journal of the European Union, March 31. Retrieved from
http://eur-lex.europa.eu/LexUriServ/LexUriServ.do?uri=OJ:L:2004:134:
0001:0113:en:PDF [accessed 9 December 2015].

2004. 'DIRECTIVE 2004/18/EC.' March 31. Retrieved from http://
eur-lex.europa.eu/legal-content/EN/TXT/PDF/?uri=CELEX:
32004L0018&from=en [accessed 9 December 2015].

2013. 'DIRECTIVE 2013/34/EU.' Retrieved from: http://eur-lex.europa
.eu/LexUriServ/LexUriServ.do?uri=OJ:L:2013:182:0019:0076:EN:
PDF [accessed 17 June 2015].

2014. 'DIRECTIVE 2014/95/EU' Retrieved from http://eur-lex.europa
.eu/legal-content/EN/ALL/?uri=CELEX%3A32014L0095 [accessed 6
January 2017].

Executive Office of the President, Office of the US Trade Representative.
2016. *Public Hearing for US Generalized System of Preferences (GSP)
Review of Country Parctices*, 28 March 2016.

Extractive Industries Transparency Initiative (EITI), n.d.-a 'What is the
EITI?' Retrieved from https://eiti.org/eiti [accessed 26 June 2015].

n.d.-b. 'EITI Countries.' Retrieved from https://eiti.org/countries [accessed
4 November 2015].

n.d.-c. 'Stakeholders.' Retrieved from https://eiti.org/supporters [accessed
8 June 2016].

2012. 'How to become a supporting country.' Retrieved from: https://
eiti.org/sites/default/files/documents/2012-03-28_how_to_support_-_
countries.pdf [accessed 8 October 2016].

2013. 'The EITI Principles'. Retrieved from https://eiti.org/standard/
principles [accessed 8 June 2016].

2014. 'Promoting public awareness about how countries manage their oil gas and mineral resources – The Extractive Industries Transparency Initiative.' Retrieved from https://eiti.org [accessed 8 June 2015].

2015a. 'The EITI, NOCs & the first trade the extractive industries transparency initiative as a tool for improving the trading climate with national oil companies (NOCs).' Retrieved from: https://eiti.org/sites/default/files/documents/EITI_Brief_NOC_FirstTrade_March2015.pdf. [accessed 12 December 2016].

2015b. 'Review of recommendations arising from EITI reporting.' Retrieved from https://eiti.org/sites/default/files/documents/eiti-report-recommendations_final.pdf [accessed 12 December 2016].

2016a. 'History of the EITI.' Retrieved from https://eiti.org/es/node/3391 [accessed 8 October 2016].

2016b. 'The EITI Standard 2016.' Retrieved from https://eiti.org/node/4487 [accessed 11 June 2015].

2016c. 'EITI fact sheet 2016.' Retrieved from: https://eiti.org/sites/default/files/documents/eiti_factsheet_en.pdf. [Accessed June 17, 2016].

2016d. 'Homepage: Extractive Industries Transparency Initiative.' Retrieved from: https://eiti.org/ [accessed 17 June 2016].

2016e. 'EITI Statement on the SEC's regulation on mandatory company disclosure.' Retrieved from https://eiti.org/node/7266 [accessed 8 October 2016].

Factor, A. 2014. 'Dodd-Frank's Specialized Disclosure Provisions 1502 and 1504: Small Business, Big Impact.' *Ohio State Entrepreneurial Business Law Journal*, 9(5).

Fair Labor Association, 2012. 'History | Fair Labor Association.' Retrieved from http://www.fairlabor.org/about-us/history [accessed 5 January 2017].

Fairbrass, J. 2011. 'Exploring Corporate Social Responsibility Policy in the European Union: A Discursive Institutionalist Analysis.' *Journal of Common Market Studies*, 49(5): 949–70.

Fernández, J. L., and Melé, D. 2005. 'Spain: From a Paternalistic Path to Sustainable Companies.' In W. Habisch, M. Wegner, R. Schmidpeter, and J. Jonker (eds) *Corporate Social Responsibility Across Europe*. Berlin: Springer: 289–302.

Fortanier, F., and Kolk, A. 2007. 'On the Economic Dimensions of Corporate Social Responsibility: Exploring Fortune Global 250 Reports.' *Business and Society*, 46(4): 457–478.

Fox, T., Ward, H., and Howard, B. 2002. '*Public Sector Roles in Strengthening Corporate Social Responsibility: A Baseline Study.*' *The World Bank Group*. Retrieved from: http://pubs.iied.org/pdfs/16017IIED.pdf [accessed 11 June 2015].

Fransen, L. 2012. 'Multi-Stakeholder Governance and Voluntary Programme Interactions: Legitimization Politics in the Institutional Design of Corporate Social Responsibility.' *Socio-Economic Review*, 10(1): 163–192.

Fransen, L., and Burgoon, B. 2014. 'Privatizing or Socializing Corporate Responsibility Business Participation in Voluntary Programs.' *Business Society*, 53(4): 583–619.

   2012. 'A Market for Worker Rights: Explaining Business Support for International Private Labour Regulation.' *Review of International Political Economy*, 19(2): 236–266.

Freeman, R. E. 1984. *Strategic Management: A Stakeholder Approach*. Boston: Harper Collins College Div.

Friedman, M. 1958. 'Introduction.' In L. E. Read (ed.) *I, Pencil: My Family Tree as Told to Leonard E. Read*. New York: The Foundation for Economic Education. Oline Library of Liberty version (Liberty Fund): 5–6. http://lf-oll.s3.amazonaws.com/titles/112/Read_0202_EBk_v6.0.pdf [accessed 20 June 2017].

Friedman, T. L. 2005. *The World is Flat: A Brief History of the Twenty-first Century*. New York: Farrar, Straus and Giroux.

Frynas, J. G. 2009a. *Beyond Corporate Social Responsibility: Oil Multinationals and Social Challenges*. Cambridge: Cambridge University Press.

   2009b. 'Corporate Social Responsibility or Government Regulation? Evidence on Oil Spill Prevention.' *Ecology and Society*, 17(4): 4.

Fukuyama, F. 2004. *State Building: Governance and World Order in the 21st Century*. Ithaca: Cornell University Press.

Fung, A., Graham, M., and Weil, D. 2007. *Full Disclosure: The Perils and Promise of Transparency*. New York: Cambridge University Press.

Fung, A., O'Rourke, D., and Sabel, C. 2001. 'Realizing Labor Standards.' *Boston Review*, February-March, Retrieved from: http://new.boston review.net/BR26.1/fung.html [accessed 8 January 2017].

Garcia-Johnson, R. 2000. *Exporting Environmentalism: U.S. Multinational Chemical Corporations in Brazil and Mexico*. Cambridge: MIT Press Cambridge.

Giddens, A. 1998. *The Third Way: The Renewal of Social Democracy*. Cambridge: Polity Press.

Gjølberg, M. 2009. 'The Origin of Corporate Social Responsibility: Global Forces or National Legacies?' *Socio-Economic Review*, 7(4): 605–637.

Global Alliance for Tax Justice. n.d. 'About Us.' Retrieved from http://www .globaltaxjustice.org/en/about [accessed 8 June 2015].

Global Reporting Initiative. 2013. 'GRI is the global standard as sustainability reporting goes mainstream, says KPMG survey.' Retrieved from

https://www.globalreporting.org/information/news-and-press-center/
Pages/GRI-is-the-global-standard-as-sustainability-reporting-goes
-mainstream-says-KPMG-survey.aspx [accessed 7 January 2017].

2016a. 'Enabling Positive Change. Frequently Asked Questions – G4 FAQ'S.' Retrieved from https://www.globalreporting.org/information/FAQs/G4FAQ/Pages/default.aspx [accessed 7 January 2017].

2016b. 'An introduction to G4 – The next generation of sustainability reporting.' Retrieved from https://www.globalreporting.org/resourcelibrary/GRI-An-introduction-to-G4.pdf [accessed 7 January 2017].

Global Witness. n.d. 'About Us – Global Witness exposes the hidden links between demand for natural resources, corruption, armed conflict and environmental destruction.' Retrieved from https://www.globalwitness.org/en/about-us/ [accessed 26 June 2016].

2013. 'UK lead on oil and mining transparency law sends strong signal to U.S.' Press Release. 31 October 2013. Retrieved from https://www.globalwitness.org/en/archive/uk-lead-oil-and-mining-transparency-law-sends-strong-signal-us/ [accessed 26 June 2016].

Gond, J. P., Kang, N., and Moon, J. 2011. 'The Government of Self-regulation: on the Comparative Dynamics of Corporate Social Responsibility.' *Economy and Society*, 40(4): 640–671.

Granovetter, M. 1985. 'Economic Action and Social Structure: The Problem of Embeddedness.' *American Journal of Sociology*, 91(3): 481–510.

Grayson, D. and Nelson, J. 2013. *Corporate Social Responsibility: The Past, Present, and Future of Alliances for Sustainable Capitalism*. Standord, CA: Stanford University Press.

Hale, A. 2000. 'What Hope for 'Ethical' Trade in the Globalized Garment Industry?' *Antipode*, 32(4): 349–356.

Hall, P. 2015. 'How Growth Strategies Develop in the Developed Democracies.' SciencesPo presentation, December 2015 (unpublished).

Hall, P., and Soskice, D. 2001. *Varieties of Capitalism: The Institutional Foundations of Comparative Advantage*. New York: Oxford University Press.

Hansen, H. K. 2017. 'Anti-corruption Governance and Global Business' in A. Rasche, M. Morsing and J. Moon (eds) *CSR: Strategy, Governance and Communication*. Cambridge University Press.

Hassel, A., Knudsen, J. S., & Wagner, B., 2016. 'Winning the Battle or losing the War: The Impact of European Integration on Labour Market Institutions in Germany and Denmark.' *Journal of European Public Policy*, 23(8): 1218–1239.

Hatch, M. J. 1997. 'Jazzing up the Theory of Organizational Improvisation.' *Advances in Strategic Management*, 14: 181–191.

1999. 'Exploring the Empty Spaces of Organizing: How improvisational Jazz helps redescribe Organizational Structure.' *Organization Studies*, 20(1): 75–100.

Haufler, V. 2001. *A Public Role for the Private Sector: Industry Self-regulation in a Global Economy*. Washington DC: Carnegie Endowment for International Peace.

Hériter, A., and Eckert, S. 2008. 'New Modes of Governance in the Shadow of Hierarchy: Self-regulation by Industry in Europe.' *Journal of Public Policy*, 28(1):113–138.

Herzig, C., and Kühn, A.-L. 2017. 'Corporate Responsibility Reporting,' In J. Moon, M. Morsing, and Rasche, A. (eds) *Corporate Social Responsibility. Strategy, Communication and Governance*. London: Cambridge University Press.

HMG. 1997. *Eliminating World Poverty: A Challenge for the 21st Century November*, Cm 3789.

Hodge, M. 2006. 'The British CSR Strategy: How a Government Supports the Good Work.' In J. Hennigfeld, M. Pohl, and N. Tolhurst (eds) *The ICCA Handbook on Corporate Social Responsibility*. London: John Wiley and Sons: 99–112.

Hogwood, B. and Peters, B. G. 1982. 'The dynamics of Policy Change: Policy Succession.' *Policy Sciences* 14 (3): 225–245.

Hollingsworth, J. R., and Boyer, R. 1997. *Contemporary Capitalism: The Embeddedness of Institutions*. Cambridge: Cambridge University Press.

Hood, C. 1986. *The Tools of Government*. London: Chatham House Publishers.

House of Commons. 1999. 'Trade and Industry, Sixth Report'. *Hansard*, March 8. Retrieved from http://www.publications.parliament.uk/pa/cm199899/cmhansrd/vo990308/text/90308w08.htm [accessed 7 January 2017].

Huffington Post. 2013. 'Bangladesh's Labor Reform Puts Profits Before Workers.' Retrieved from http://www.huffingtonpost.com/2013/07/25/bangladesh-labor-reform_n_3653850.html [accessed 22 October 2015].

Hughes, A. 2001. 'Multi-Stakeholder Approaches to Ethical Trade: Towards a Reorganisation of UK Retailers' Global Supply Chains?' *Journal of Economic Geography* 1 (4): 421–37.

Hughes, A., Buttle, M., and Wrigley, N. 2007. 'Organizational Geographies of Corporate Responsibility: A UK-US Comparison of Retailers' Ethical Trading Initiatives.' *Journal of Economic Geography* 1(4): 491–513.

Human Rights Watch. 2013. 'Bangladesh: Tradegy Shows Urgency of Worker Protection.' April 25. Retrieved from https://www.hrw.org/news/2013/04/25/bangladesh-tragedy-shows-urgency-worker-protections [accessed 8 June 2016].

Humphreys, M., Sachs, J. D., and Stiglitz, J. E. 2007. *Escaping the Resource Curse*. New York: Columbia University Press.

Institute for Global and Human Rights, n.d. 'Factory Collapse in Bangladesh.' Retrieved from http://www.globallabourrights.org/campaigns/factory-collapse-in-bangladesh [accessed 13 March 2016].

International Labour Organization (ILO) 2013. 'Support the Implementation of the Sustainability Compact.' Retrieved from http://www.ilo.org/dhaka/Whatwedo/Projects/WCMS_396191/lang–en/index.htm [accessed 7 January 2017].

2016. 'Improving Working Conditions in the Ready Made Garment Industry: Progress and Achievements.' Retrieved from http://www.ilo.org/dhaka/Whatwedo/Projects/WCMS_240343/lang–en/index.htm [accessed 11 January 2017].

Ioannou, I., and Serafeim, G. 2014. 'The Consequences of Mandatory Corporate Sustainability Reporting: Evidence from Four Countries.' *Harvard Business School Research Working Paper*, no. 11–100.

IOD PARC. 2015. 'Ethical Trading Initiative – External Evaluation: Executive Summary.' April 16. Retrieved from http://www.ethicaltrade.org/resources/eti-external-evaluation [accessed 7 January 2017].

Irish Department of the Environment, Heritage and Local Government, 2010. *The Climate Change Response Act*.

Iversen, T., and Soskice, D. 2006. 'Electoral Institutions and the Politics of Coalitions: Why Some Democracies Redistribute More Than Others.' *American Political Science Review*, 100(2): 165–181.

Jackson, C., and Apostolakou, A. 2010. 'Corporate Social Responsibility in Western Europe: An Institutional Mirror or Substitute?' *Journal of Business Ethics*, 94(3): 371–394.

Jackson, G., and Bartosch, J. 2016. *Corporate Responsibility in Different Varieties of Capitalism: Exploring the Role of National Institutions*. Germany: Bertelsmann Foundation.

Jenkins, R. O., Pearson, R., and Seyfang, G. 2002. *Corporate Responsibility and Labour Rights: Codes of Conduct in the Global Economy*. London: Earthscan.

Jenkins, R., and Newell, P. 2014. 'CSR, Tax and Development.' *Third World Quarterly*, 34(3): 378–396.

Jones, T. M. 1980. 'Corporate Social Responsibility Revisited, Redefined.' *California Management Review*, 22(3): 59–67.

Kang, N., and Moon, J. 2012. 'Institutional Complementarity between Corporate Governance and Corporate Social Responsibility: A Comparative Institutional Analysis of Three Capitalisms.' *Socio-Economic Review*, 10(1): 85–108.

Kaplan, R. 2015. 'Who has been Regulating Whom, Business or Society? The Mid-20th-century Institutionalization of 'Corporate Responsibility' in the USA.' *Socio-economic Review*, 13(1): 125–155.

Karl, T. L. 2005. 'Understanding the Resource Curse.' In A. Schiffrin and S. Tsalik (eds) *Covering Oil*. New York: Open Society Institute: 211–20.

Kaufmann, D., and Penciakova, V. 2011. 'Transparancy, Conflict Minerals and Natural Resources: Debating Sections 1502 and 1504 of the Dodd-Frank Act', *Brookings*, December 20. Retrieved from https://www.brookings.edu/opinions/transparency-conflict-minerals-and-natural-resources-debating-sections-1502-and-1504-of-the-dodd-frank-act [accessed 11 June 2015].

Kell, G. 2012. '12 Years Later Reflections on the Growth of the UN Global Compact.' *Business & Society*, 52(1): 31–52.

Keohane, R. 1984. *Corporate Social Responsibility Revisited, Redefined*. Princeton: Princeton University Press.

Khan, M. R. I., and Wichterich, C. 2015. 'After Rana Plaza: Multi-Stakeholder Governance of the RMG Industry in Bangladesh.' *Global Labour Column*. Retrieved from http://column.global-labour-university.org/2015/09/after-rana-plaza-multi-stakeholder.html [accessed 7 June 2017].

Khanna, P. 2011. 'Making Labour Voices Heard During an Industrial Crisis: Workers' Struggles in the Bangladesh Garment Industry.' *Labour, Capital and Society / Travail, Capital et Société*, 44(2): 106–129.

Kim, R. C., and Moon, J. 2015. 'Dynamics of Corporate Social Responsibility in Asia: Knowledge and Norms.' *Asian Business & Management*, 14(5): 349–382.

Kinderman, D. 2013. 'Corporate Social Responsibility in the EU, 1993–2013: Institutional Ambiguity, Economic Crises, Business Legitimacy and Bureaucratic Politics.' *Journal of Common Market Studies*, 51(4): 701–720.

2016. 'Mandatory Non-Financial Reporting in the UK.' Unpublished research note.

2012. 'Free Us up so We Can Be Responsible!' The Co-Evolution of Corporate Social Responsibility and Neo-Liberalism in the UK, 1977–2010.' *Socio-Economic Review*, 10(1): 29–57.

Knopf, J., Kahlenborn, W., Hajduk, T. et al. 2010. *Corporate Social Responsibility: National Public Policies in the European Union*. Directorate-General for Employment, Social Affairs and Equal Opportunities. Berlin: Adelphi.

Knudsen, J. S. 2002. 'Breaking with Tradition: Liberalization of Services Trade in the European Union.' Unpublished PhD thesis. Department of Political Science, MIT.

2011. 'Company Delistings from the UN Global Compact: Limited Business Demand or Domestic Governance Failure?' *Journal of Business Ethics* 103: 331–49.

2017. 'Government Regulation of International Corporate Social Responsibility in the US and the UK: How Domestic Institutions Shape Mandatory and Supportive Initiatives'. Forthcoming in *British Journal of Industrial Relations*.

2017. 'How Do Domestic Regulatory Traditions Shape CSR in Large International US and UK firms?' *Global Policy*, 8(S3): 29–41.

Knudsen, J. S. and Brown, D. 2015. 'Why Governments Intervene: Exploring Mixed Motives for Public Policies on Corporate Social Responsibility.' *Public Policy and Administration*, 30(1): 51–72.

Knudsen, J. S., Moon, J., and Slager, R. 2015. 'Government Policies for Corporate Social Responsibility in Europe: A Comparative Analysis of Institutionalisation.' *Policy & Politics*, 43(1): 81–99.

Kolk, A. 2014. 'Partnerships as a Panacea for Addressing Global Problems? On Rational, Contexts, Actors, Impact and Limitations.' In M. M. Seitanidi and A. Crane (eds) *Social Partnerships and Responsible Business: a Research Handbook*, New York: Routledge, Taylor & Francis Group: 15–41.

Kooiman, J. 2000. 'Societal Governance: Levels, Models and Orders of Social-Political Interaction.' In J. Pierre (ed.) *Debating Governance: Authority, Steering and Democracy*, New York: Oxford University Press.

Kostova, T., and Zaheer, S. 1999. 'Organizational Legitimacy under Conditions of Complexity: The Case of the Multinational Enterprise.' *The Academy of Management Review*, 24(1): 64–81.

KPMG, Global Reporting Initiative, United Nations Environment Programme, and Centre for Corporate Governance in Africa. 2013. 'Carrots and Sticks: Sustainability Reporting Policies Worldwide – Today's Best Practice, Tomorrow's Trend.' Retrieved from https://www .globalreporting.org/resourcelibrary/Carrots-and-Sticks.pdf [accessed 31 May 2016].

Krasner, S. 1983. *International Regimes*. Ithaca, NY: Cornell University Press.

Krichewsky, D. 2014. 'The Socially Responsible Company as a Strategy Second-Order Observer. An Indian Case'. *Max Planck Institut für Gesellschaftsforschung*, July 2014, Köln, MPIfG Discussion Paper 14/10: 26.

LeBaron, G., and Rümpkopf, A, 2017. 'Steering CSR Through Public Regulation: A Comparison of the Impact of the UK Bribery Act and Modern Slavery Act on Supply Chain Governance'. *Global Policy*, 8(53): 15–28.

legislation.gov.uk, 2004. 'Gangmasters (Licensing) Act 2004' Retrieved from http://www.legislation.gov.uk/ukpga/2004/11/contents [accessed 7 January 2017].

2015. 'Modern Slavery Act 2015.' Retrieved from http://www.legislation .gov.uk/ukpga/2015/30/contents/enacted [accessed 7 January 2017].

Lehmann, V. 2015. 'Natural Resources, the Extractive Industries Transparency Initiative, and Global Governance.' *The Hague Institute for Global Justice and the Stimson Center*: 1–18.

Lim, A., and Tsutsui, K. 2012. 'Globalization and Commitment in Corporate Social Responsibility: Cross-National Analyses of Institutional and Political-Economy Effects.' *American Sociological Review*, 77(1): 69–98.

Lissakers, K., 2012. 'SEC Oil and Mining Rule an End to Secrecy, an Advance for.' *The Huffington Post*. Retrieved from http://www .huffingtonpost.com/karin-lissakers/sec-oil-and-mining-rule-a_b_ 1828514.html [accessed 11 June 2015].

Locke, R. 2013. *The Promise and Limits of Private Power: Promoting Labor Standards in a Global Economy*. Cambridge: Cambridge University Press.

Locke, R. M. 2013. *The Promise and Limits of Private Power: Promoting Labor Standards in a Global Economy*. Cambridge: Cambridge University Press.

Lynn, D. M. 2011. 'Dodd-Frank Act's Specialized Corporate Disclosure: Using the Securities Laws to Address Public Policy Issues.' *Journal of Business & Technology Law*, 6(2): 327.

MacDonald, L., 2013. 'How to Avoid Another Bangladesh Factory Disaster – Kimberly Elliott.' *Center For Global Development*. Retrieved from http:// www.cgdev.org/blog/how-avoid-another-bangladesh-factory-disaster -kimberly-elliott [accessed 7 May 2015].

Mahoney, J., and Thelen, K., 2009. *Explaining Institutional Change – Ambiguity, Agency, and Power*. Cambridge: Cambridge University Press: 252.

Manzur, S. 2016. 'The Rana Plaza Tragedy: A Game Changer or Business as Usual for Bangladesh? An Analysis of Manufacturer Perception of Labor Regulations.' Unpublished Bachelors Thesis. Tufts University, Massachusetts, USA.

Mares, I. 2003. *The Politics of Social Risk: Business and Welfare State Development*. Cambridge: Cambridge University Press.

Margolis, J. D., and Walsh, J. P. 2003. 'Misery Loves Companies: Rethinking Social Initiatives by Business.' *Administrative Science Quarterly*, 48(2): 268–305.

Marshall, R. 1981. 'The Labor Department in the Carter Administration: A summary Report.' *Bureau of International Labor Affairs*, January 14.

Retrieved from https://www.dol.gov/general/aboutdol/history/carter-ilab [accessed 9 December 2015].

Martin, C. J., and Swank, D. 2012. *The Political Construction of Business Interests: Coordination, Growth and Equality.* Cambridge: Cambridge University Press.

Matten, D., and Crane, A. 2005. 'Corporate Citizenship: Toward an Extended Theoretical Conceptualization.' *Academy of Management Review*, 30(1): 166–179.

Matten, D., and Moon, J. 2008. ''Implicit' and 'Explicit' CSR: A Conceptual Framework for a Comparative Understanding of Corporate Social Responsibility.' *Academy of Management Review* 33(2): 404–424.

Mayntz, R. 2004. 'Governance im Modernen Staat.' In A. Benz (ed.) *Governance – Regierenin Komplexen Regelsystemen: Eine Einführung*, Wiesbaden: Verlag für Sozialwissenschaften.

McBarnet, D. 2007. 'Corporate Social Responsibility Beyond Law, through Law, for Law: The New Corporate Accountability.' In D. McBarnet, A. Voiculescu, and T. Campbell (eds) *The New Accountability. Corporate Social Responsibility and the Law*, Cambridge: Cambridge University Press: 9–58.

McCrudden, C. 2007. 'Corporate Social Responsibility and Public Procurement.' In D. McBarnet, A. Voiculescu, and T. Campbell (eds) *The New Corporate Accountability: Corporate Social Responsibility and the Law.* Cambridge: Cambridge University Press: 93–118.

McGuire, J. W. 1963. *Business and Society.* New York: McGraw-Hill.

McWilliams, A., and Siegel, D. 2001. 'Corporate Social Responsibility: A Theory of the Firm Perspective.' *The Academy of Management Review*, 26(1): 117–127.

Mena, S., and Palazzo, G. 2012. 'Input and Output Legitimacy of Multi-Stakeholder Initiatives.' *Business Ethics Quarterly*, 22(3): 527–556.

Midttun, A., Gautesen, K., and Gjølberg, M. 2006. 'The Political Economy of CSR in Western Europe.' *Corporate Governance: The International Journal of Business in Society*, 6(4): 369–385.

Midttun, A., Gjølberg, M., Korula, A., Sweet, S., and Vallentin, S. 2015. 'Public Policies for Corporate Social Responsibility in Four Nordic Countries: Harmony of Goals and Conflict of Means.' *Business and Society*, 54(4): 464–500.

Midttun, A., Gjolberg, M., Kourula, A., Sweet, S., and Vallentin. S. 2012. 'Public Policies for Corporate Social Responsibility in Four Nordic Countries: Harmony of Goals and Conflict of Means,' *Business & Society*, 54(4): 464–500.

Ministry for Economics and Business Affairs (Økonomi- og Erhvervsministeriet). 2008. Høringsnotat. Forslag til ændring af Årsregnskabsloven. Redegørelse for samfundsansvar i større virksomheder. October 7.

Ministry of the Environment of the Czech Republic, 2008. 'Environmental Policy and Instruments: Integrated Pollution Register of the Environment: Environmental Policy and Instruments.' Retrieved from http://www.mzp .cz/en/environmental_policy_and_instruments [accessed 1 June 2016].

Ministry of Social Affairs. 2001. 'Botilbud Og Andre Sociale Tilbud Til Yngre Fysisk Handikappende.' *Beretning Om Den Handicappolitiske Udvikling*, February. Retrieved from http://www.statensnet.dk/ pligtarkiv/fremvis.pl?vaerkid=12764&reprid=0&filid=22&iarkiv=1) [accessed 27 May 2016].

Montgomery, S. L., and Chirot, D. 2015. *The Shape of the New: Four Big Ideas and How They Made the Modern World*. Princeton: Princeton University Press.

Moody-Stuart, Sir M. 2014. *Responsible Leadership: Lessons from the front line of sustainability and ethics* Greenleaf: Sheffield.

Moon, J. 2002. 'The Social Responsibility of Business and New Governance.' *Government and Opposition*, 37(3): 385–408.

2005. 'CSR in the UK – An Explicit Model of Business-Society Relations.' In A. Habisch, J. Jonker, M. Wegner, and R. Schmidpeter (eds.) *Corporate Social Responsibility Across Europe*. Berlin; New York: Springer: 51–65.

2014. '*Corporate Social Responsibility: A Very Short Introduction*'. Oxford: Oxford University Press.

Moon, J., Bondy, K., and Matten, D. 2012. 'An Institution of Corporate Social Responsibility (CSR): in Multi-National Corporations (MNCs): Form and Implications.' *Journal of Business Ethics*, 111(2): 281–299.

Moon, J., Crane, A., and Matten, D., 2005. 'Can Corporations Be Citizens?' *Business Ethics Quarterly*, 15(3): 429–453.

Moon, J., Gond, J.-P., and Murphy, L. 2017. 'Historical perspectives on CSR' in A. Rasche, M. Morsing and J. Moon (eds) *Corporate Social Responsibility: Strategy, Communication and Governance*. Cambridge: Cambridge University Press.

Moon, J., Slager, R., Brunn, C., Hardi, P., and Knudsen, J. S. 2012. 'Analysis of the National and EU Policies Supporting Corporate Social Responsibility and Impact, IMPACT Working Paper 2, 'IMPACT Project', European Commission (Framework 7 Program).' Retrieved from https://odpowiedzialnybiznes.pl/wp-content/uploads/attachments/ news/Analysis_of_national_and_EU_Policies_supporting_CSR_and_ Impact_CSRIMPACT_2012.pdf [accessed 12 December 2015].

Moon, J., and Vogel, D. 2008. 'Corporate Social Responsibility, Government, and Civil Society.' In A. Crane, A. McWilliams, D. Matten, J. Moon, and D. Siegel (eds) *The Oxford Handbook of Corporate Social Responsibility*. Oxford: Oxford University Press: 303–323.

Moon, J., and Willoughby, K. 1990. 'Local Enterprise Initiatives: Between State and Market in Esperance.' *Australian Journal of Public Administration*, 49(1): 23–37.

Moore, C., Richardson, J. J., and Moon, J., 1985. 'New Partnerships in Local Economic Development.' *Local Government Studies* 11(1): 19–33.

Moran, M. 1986. 'Theories of Regulation and Changes in Regulation: the Case of Financial Markets', *Political Studies*, 34(2): 185–201.

Morsing, M. 2005. 'Denmark: Inclusive Labour Market Strategies.' In A. Habisch, J. Jonker, M. Wegner, and R. Schmidpeter (eds) *Corporate Social Responsibility Across Europe*, Berlin: Springer-Verlag: 23–35.

Morsing, M., Midttun, A., and Plamas, K. 2007. 'Corporate Social Responsibility in Scandinavia: A Turn Towards the Business Case?' in S. Mart, G. Cheney, and J. Roper (eds), *The Debate Over Corporate Social Responsibility*, Oxford University Press: 87–104.

Mouan, L. C. 2010. 'Exploring the Potential Benefits of Asian Participation in the Extractive Industries Transparency Initiative: The Case of China.' *Business Strategy and the Environment*, 19(6): 367–76.

Muller, A., and Kolk, A. 2009. 'CSR Performance in Emerging Markets Evidence from Mexico.' *Journal of Business Ethics*, 85(2): 325–337.

2012. 'Responsible Tax as Corporate Social Responsibility: The Case of Multinational Enterprises and Effective Tax in India.' *Business & Society*, 54(4): 435–63.

Murphy, D. F., and Bendell, J. 1999. *Partners in Time? Business, NGOs and Sustainable Development*, UNRISD Discussion Paper No. 109.

Muthuri, J., Chapple, W., and Moon, J. 2009. 'An Integrated Approach to Implementing ‹Community Participation' in Corporate Community Involvement: Lessons from Magadi Soda Company in Kenya.' *Journal of Business Ethics* 85(2): 431–444.

Muthuri, J., Moon, J., and Idemudia, U. 2012. 'Corporate Innovation and Sustainable Community Development in Developing Countries.' *Business and Society*, 51(3): 355–381.

National Resource Governance Institute, 2016. 'Q&A: Company Disclosures Under Dodd-Frank Section 1504.' *Natural Resource Governance Institute*. Retrieved from http://www.resourcegovernance.org/blog/qa-company-disclosures-under-dodd-frank-section-1504 [accessed 12 December 2016].

O'Rourke, D. 2006. 'Multi-Stakeholder Regulation: Privatizing or Socializing Global Labor Standards?' *World Development*, 34(5): 899–918.

OECD, 2000. (Cited in Jenkins and Newell, 2013) *Codes of Corporate Conduct – An Expanded Review of their Contents.* OECD Working Party of the Trade Committee, Paris.

2005. *Modernizing Government. The Way Forward.* Retrieved from: http://www.oecd.org/gov/modernisinggovernmentthewayforward.htm [accessed 16 June 2015].

Offe, C. 2009. 'Governance: An 'Empty Signifier'?' *Constellations,* 16(4): 550–562.

Osborne, S. P. 2010. *The New Public Governance? Emerging Perspectives on the Theory and Practice of Public Governance,* London: Routledge.

Ostry, S. 1999. 'The Future of the WTO.' In S. M. Collins and R. Z. Lawrence (eds) *Brookings Trade Forum,* Washington DC: Brooking Press.

Owen, D. L., and O'Dwyer, B., 2008. 'Corporate Social Responsibility. The Reporting and Assurance Dimension'. in A. Crane, A. McWilliams, D. Matten, J. Moon and D. Siegel (eds) *The Oxford Handbook of Corporate Social Responsibility.* Oxford: Oxford University Press.

Oxfam, 2004. 'Trading away our Rights – Women working in Global Supply Chains.' Retrieved from https://www.oxfam.org/sites/www.oxfam.org/files/rights.pdf [accessed 7 January 2017].

2000. 'Tax Havens – Releasing the Hidden Billions for poverty alleviation Oxfam GM Policy Paper; Riggs, RA 1972.' Retrieved from http://policy-practice.oxfam.org.uk/publications/tax-havens-releasing-the-hidden-billions-for-poverty-eradication-114611 [accessed 8 June 2016].

Palan, R. 2003. *The Offshore World. Sovereign Markets, Virtual Places, and Nomad Millionaires.* Ithaca: Cornell University Press.

Palier, B., and Thelen, K. 2010. 'Institutionalizing Dualism: Complementarities and Change in France and Germany.' *Politics & Society,* 38(1): 119–148.

Parker, D. 2009. *The Official History of Privatisation.* New York: Routledge.

Pedersen, E. R. G., Neergaard, P., Pedersen, J. T., and Gwozdz, W. 2013. 'Conformance and Deviance: Company Responses to Institutional Pressures for Corporate Social Responsibility Reporting.' *Business Strategy and the Environment,* 22(6): 357–373.

Peters, B. G. 1996. *The Future of Governing: Four Emerging Models.* Lawrence: University Press of Kansas.

Pierre, J. 2000. 'Introduction: Understanding Governance.' In J. Pierre (ed.) *Debating Governance: Authority, Steering and Democracy,* Oxford: Oxford University Press.

Pierson, P. 2000. 'Increasing Returns, Path Dependence, and the Study of Politics.' *American Political Science Review,* 94(2): 251–267.

Piore, M. J., and Schrank, A., 2008. 'Toward Managed Flexibility: The Revival of Labour Inspection in the Latin World.' *International Labour Review* 147(1): 1–23.

Polanyi, K. 1944. *The Great Transformation: The Political and Economic Originis of Our Time.* New York: Farrar & Rinehart.

Porter, M., and Kramer, M. 2006. 'Strategy and Society. The Link between Competitive Advantage and Corporate Social Responsibility.' *Harvard Business Review* 84(12): 78–92.

Prakash, A., and Potoski, M., 2007. 'Collective Action through Voluntary Environmental Programs: A Club Theory Perspective.' *Policy Studies Journal* 35(4): 773–792.

Pressman, J. L., and Wildavsky, A., 1973. *How Great Expectations in Washington are dashed in Oakland.* Berkley: University of California Press.

Preston, L., and Post, J. E. 1975. *Private Management and Public Policy: The Principle of Public Responsibility.* Englewood Cliffs: Prentice Hall.

Protess, B., and Davis, J. H. 2017. 'Trump Moves to Roll Back Obama-Era Financial Regulations.' *The New York Times*, 3 February. Retrieved from https://www.nytimes.com/2017/02/03/business/dealbook/trump-congress-financial-regulations.html [accessed 20 June 2017].

Publish What You Pay. n.d.-a. 'Objectives.' Retrieved from www.publish whatyoupay.org/about/objectives [accessed 26 June 2015].

n.d.-b. 'Where we work.' Retrieved from www.publishwhatyoupay.org/where-we-work [accessed 26 June 2015].

Quelch, J. A., and Rodriguez, M. L. 2014-a. *Rana Plaza: Work place safety in Bangladesh (A).* Cambridge, MA: Harvard Business School.

2014-b. *Rana Plaza: Work place safety in Bangladesh (B).* Cambridge, MA: Harvard Business School.

Rahman, S. 2004. 'Global Shift: Bangladesh Garment Industry in Perspective.' *Asian Affairs*, 26(1): 75–91.

Rasche, A. 2012. 'Global Policies and Local Practice: Loose and Tight Couplings in Multi-Stakeholder Initiatives.' *Business Ethics Quarterly*, 22(4): 679–708.

Reich, R. B. 2008. *Supercapitalism: The Transformation of Business, Democracy, and Everyday Life.* New York: Knopf Doubleday Publishing Group.

Rein, M. 1982. 'The Social Policy of the Firm.' *Policy Sciences*, 14(2): 117–135.

Reinecke, J., and Ansari, S. 2015. 'Taming wicked problems: The role of framing in the construction of corporate social responsibility.' *Journal of Management Studies*, 53(3): 299–329.

Reinecke, J., and Donaghey, J. 2015. 'After Rana Plaza: Building Coalitional Power for Labour Rights between Unions and (consumption-based) Social Movement Organisations.' *Organization* 22(3): 720–740.

Rhodes, R. A. W. 1996. 'The New Governance: Governing without Government.' *Political Studies*, 44(4): 652–667.

1997. *Understanding Governance*. Buckingham: Open University Press.

Richardson, J. J. 1983. 'The Development of Corporate Responsibility in the U.K.' *Strathclyde Papers on Government and Politics*, 1.

Risse, T. 2002. 'Transnational Actors and World Politics.' In W. Carlsnaes, T. Risse, and B. Simmon (eds) *Handbook of International Relations*. London: Sage Publications: 255–274.

Risse-Kappen, T. 1995. 'Bringing Transnational Relations Back In: Introduction.' In T. Risse-Kappen (ed.) *Bringing Transnational Relations Back In: Non-State Actors, Domestic Structures and International Institutions*, Cambridge: Cambridge University Press: 3–34.

2004. 'Global Governance and Communicative Action.' in D. Held and M. Koenig-Archibugi (eds) *Global Governance and Public Accountability*, Oxford: Blackwell Publishing: 288–313.

Rivera-Lirio, J. M., and Muñoz-Torres, M. J. 2010. 'The Effectiveness of the Public Support Policies for the European Industry Financing as a Contribution to Sustainable Development.' *Journal of Business Ethics*, 94(4): 489–515.

Robinson, P. K. 2009. 'Responsible Retailing: Regulating Fair and Ethical Trade.' *Journal of International Development*, 21(7): 1015–1026.

Rodriguez-Garavito, C. A. 2005. 'Global Governance and Labor Rights: Codes of Conduct and Anti-Sweatshop Struggles in Global Apparel Factories in Mexico and Guatemala.' *Politics & Society* 33 (2): 203–333.

Rodrik, D. 2001. *The Global Governance of Trade: As If Development Really Mattered*, UNDP.

Roger, C. 1999. 'M&S Performs About-Turn to Back Ethical Trade Drive.' *Guardian*, April 01.

Ronconi, L. 2010. 'Enforcement and Compliance with Labor Regulations in Argentina.' *Industrial & Labor Relations Review*, 63 (4): 719–736.

Rose, R. 1976. 'On the Priorities of Government: A Developmental Analysis of Public Policies.' *European Journal of Political Research*, 4(3): 247–289.

1984. *Understanding Big Government: The Programme Approach*. London: Sage Publications.

1990. 'Inheritance Before Choice in Public Policy.' *Journal of Theoretical Politics*, 2(3): 263–291.

Rosenau, J. N. 2000. 'Change, Complexity, and Governance in Globalizing Space.' In P. Jon (ed.) *Debating Governance: Authority, Steering, and Democracy*: 169–200.

2005. 'Globalisation and Governance: Sustainability between Fragmentation and Integration.' In U. Petschow, J. N. Rosenau, and

E. U. von Weizsäcker (eds) *Governance and Sustainability: New Challenges for States, Companies and Civil Society*. Sheffield, UK: Greenleaf Publishing: 20–38.

Ross, M. L. 1999. 'The Political Economy of the Resource Curse.' *World Politics*, 51(2): 297–322.

Rosser, A. 2006. 'Escaping the Resource Curse.' *New Political Economy*, 11(4): 557–570.

Ruggie, J. 2003. 'Taking Embedded Liberalism Global: The Corporate Connection.' In D. Held and M. Koenig-Archibug (eds) *Taming Globalization: Frontiers of Governance*. Cambridge, England: Polity Press: 93–129.

Ruggie, J. G. 2004. 'Reconstituting the Global Public Domain – Issues, Actors, and Practices.' *European Journal of International Relations*, 10(4): 499–531.

Ryan, T., 2016. 'Solidarity Center, Public Presentation.' *Harvard Law School*, 24 September 2016.

Sabel, C. O., Rourke, D., and Fung, A. 2000. 'Ratcheting Labor Standards: Regulation for Continuous Improvement in the Global Workplace.' *KSG Working Paper No. 00–010; Columbia Law and Economic Working Paper No. 185; Columbia Law School, Pub. Law Research Paper No. 01–21*. Retrieved from: http://ssrn.com/abstractp253833 [accessed 20 October 2015].

Sachs, J. D., and Warner, A. M. 2001. 'Natural Resources and Economic Development: The Curse of Natural Resources.' *European Economic Review*, 45(4–6): 827–838.

Sainsbury's Supermarkets LTD, 2013. 'Code of Conduct for Ethical Trade.' Retrieved from http://www.j-sainsbury.co.uk/suppliers/ethical-trading/ [accessed 7 January 2017].

Savas, E. S. 2000. *Privatization and Public Private Partnerships*. New York: Chatham House Publishers.

Scanteam. 2011. 'Achievements and Strategic Options: Evaluation of the Extractive Industries Transparency Initiative.' *Final Report Oslo*. Retrieved from: https://eiti.org/document/2011-evaluation-report [accessed 8 June 2016].

Schaller, S. 2007. *The Democratic Legitimacy of Private Governance: An Analysis of the Ethical Trading Initiative*. Essen: Institute for Development and Peace, University of Duisburg.

Scherer, A. G., Rasche, A., Palazzo, G., and Spicer, A. 2016. 'Managing for Political Corporate Social Responsibility: New Challenges and Directions for PCSR 2.0: New Challenges and Directions for PCSR 2.0.' *Journal of Management Studies*, 53(3): 273–298.

Scherer, A. G. and Palazzo, G. 2007. 'Toward a Political Conception of Corporate Responsibility: Business and Society Seen from a

Habermasian Perspective.' *Academy of Management Review*, 32(4): 1096–1120.

2008. 'Globalization and Corporate Social Responsibility.' In A. Crane, A. McWilliams, D. Matten, D. J. Moon and D. Siegel (eds) *The Oxford Handbook of Corporate Social Responsibility*, Oxford: Oxford University Press: 413–431.

2011. 'The New Political Role of Business in a Globalized World: A Review of a New Perspective on CSR and its Implications for the Firm, Governance, and Democracy.' *Journal of Management Studies*, 48(4): 899–931.

Scherer, A. G. Rasche, A., Palazzo, G., and Spicer, A. 2016. 'Managing for Political Corporate Social Responsibility: New Challenges and Directions for PCSR 2.0: New Challenges and Directions for PCSR 2.0.' *Journal of Management Studies*, 53(3): 273–98.

Schmitter, P. and Lehmbruch, G. 1979. *Trends Towards Corporatist Intermediation*. London: Sage.

Schneider, A. and Scherer, A. G. 2016. 'Government Beyond the Shadow of Hierarchy – Business Firms as Intermediate Governance Actors'. Paper submitted to the pre-submission workshop for the Organisation Studies special issue on *Government and the Governance of Business Conduct: Implications for Management and Organization*.

Scholte, J. A. 2005. *Globalization: A Critical Introduction*. New York: Palgrave Macmillan.

2002. 'What is Globalization? The Definitional Issue – Again.' CSGR Working Paper No. 109/02.

Scott, C. 2004. 'Regulation in the Age of Governance: The Rise of the Post Regulatory State.' In J. Jordana and D. Levi-Faur (eds) *The Politics of Regulation: Institutions and Regulatory Reforms for the Age of Governance*. Cheltenham: Edward Elgar Publishing: 145–174.

Securities and Exchange Commission (SEC). 2015. 'Enhancing the transparency of Resource Extraction Payments'. Retrieved from https://www.sec.gov/news/statement/disclosure-of-payments-by-resource-extraction-issuers.html [accessed 8 December 2015].

Self, P. 1993. *Government by the Market? The Politics of Public Choice*. Boulder: Westview Press.

Shell Global, 2016. 'Revenues for Governments.' Retrieved from http://www.shell.com/sustainability/transparency/revenues-for-governments.html [accessed 11 December 2016].

Short, C. 2014. 'The Development of the Extractive Industries Transparency Initiative.' *The Journal of World Energy Law & Business*, 7(1): 8–15.

Smith, A. 1776. *An Inquiry into the Nature and Causes of the Wealth of Nations*. London: W. Strahan and T. Cadell.

Smith, S., and Barrientos, S. 2005. 'Fair Trade and Ethical Trade: Are There Moves Towards Convergence?' *Sustainable Development* 13(3): 190–98.

Socialministeriet, 2001. 'Beretning om Den handicappolitiske udvikling. Botilbud og andre sociale tilbud til yngre fysisk handicappede.' Retrieved from http://www.statensnet.dk/pligtarkiv/fremvis.pl?vaerkid =12764&reprid=0&filid=22&iarkiv=1 [accessed 27 May 2016].

Sokou, K., and Schneider, H. 2013. 'U.S. suspends Bangladesh's trade privileges due to labor concerns.' *The Washington Post*, June 27. Retrieved from https://www.washingtonpost.com/business/economy/us-to-suspend -trade-privileges-with-bangladesh/2013/06/27/16171f08-df3d-11e2 -963a-72d740e88c12_story.html [accessed 7 January 2017].

Solidarity Center. 2016. 'Kerry backs unions for Bangladesh garment workers.' *Solidarity Center.* Retrieved from http://www.solidaritycenter.org/kerry -backs-bangladesh-workers-forming-unions/ [accessed 8 January 2017].

Sovacool, B. K., and Andrews, N. 2015. 'Does Transparency matter? Evaluating the governance impacts of the Extractive Industries Transparency Initiative in Azerbaijan and Liberia.' *Resources Policy*, 45: 183–192.

Spar, D. L., and La Mure, L.T. 2003. 'The Power of Activism: Assessing the Impact of NGOs on Global Business.' *California Management Review*, 45(3): 78–101.

Steurer, R. 2010. 'The Role of Governments in Corporate Social Responsibility: Characterising Public Policies on CSR in Europe.' *Policy Sciences*, 43(1): 49–72.

Steurer, R., Margula, S., and Berger, G., 2008. 'Public policies on CSR in EU Member States: Overview of government initiatives and selected cases on awareness raising for CSR, sustainable public procurement and socially responsible investment'. *ESDN Quarterly Report*, June. Retrieved from www.sd-network.eu/?k=quarterly%20reports&report_ id=9 [accessed 6 January 2017].

Stevens, P. 2005. 'The Resource Curse and How to Avoid It.' *Journal of Energy and Development*, 31(1): 1–20.

Stigler, G. J. 1971. 'The Theory of Economic Regulation.' *The Bell Journal of Economics and Management Science*, 2(1): 3–21.

Stiglitz, J. E. 2002. *Globalization and Its Discontents.* New York: W. W. Norton & Company.

Strigl, A. 2005. 'Austria: Concerted Action Towards Sustainable Development.' In A. Habisch, M. Wegner, R. Schmidpeter, and J. Jonker (eds) *Corporate Social Responsibility Across Europe.* Berlin: Springer.

Strike, V. M., Gao, J., and Bansal, P. 2006. 'Being good while being bad: Social Responsibility and the International Diversification of US Firms'. *Journal of International Business Studies* 37 (6), 850–862.

SustainAbility. 2006. 'Taxing Issues: Responsible Business and Tax'.

Sustainable Development Commission, 2011.

Teubner, G. 1983. 'Substantive and Reflexive Elements in Modern Law.' *Law and Society Review*, 17(2): 239–285.

Thaler, R. H., and Sunstein, C. R. 2008. *Nudge: Improving Decisions about Health, Wealth, and Happiness*. New Haven: Yale University Press.

Thelen, K. 2014. *Varieties of Liberalization and the New Politics of Social Solidarity*. Cambridge; New York: Cambridge University Press.

The Brookings Institution the National Press Club, n.d. *Transparency, Conflict Minerals and Natural Resources: What you don't know about Dodd-Frank*. Washington DC: The Brookings Institution the National Press Club,.

The Council of the European Communities, 1983. 'DIRECTIVE 83/349/ EEC' Retrieved from http://eur-lex.europa.eu/LexUriServ/LexUriServ .do?uri=CELEX:31983L0349:en:HTML [accessed 8 January 2017].

2013. 'DIRECTIVE 78/660/EEC' Retrieved from http://eur-lex.europa .eu/legal-content/en/ALL/?uri=CELEX%3A31978L0660 [accessed 8 January 2017].

The Economist, 2014. 'Corporate Transparency – The Openness Revolution'. *The Economist*. Retrieved from http://www.economist.com/news/ business/21636070-multinationals-are-forced-reveal-more-about -themselves-where-should-limits [accessed 17 June 2016].

2015. 'A Fight for Light: NGOs and Government Grapple Over Ownership of Mining and Energy Firms.' *The Economist*, October 24: 61.

Guardian, 2013. 'EU's new laws will oblige extractive industries to disclose payments.' Tran, M in the *Guardian*. Retrieved from https://www .theguardian.com/global-development/2013/jun/12/european-union -laws-extractive-industries-payments [accessed 12 December 2016].

The Hauser Institute for Civil Society, Kennedy School of Government and Harvard University, 2014. 'Initiative for Responsible Investment'. Retrieved from http://iri.hks.harvard.edu/ [accessed 31 May 2016].

The Huffington Post, 2012. 'Senate to SEC: Act on Cardin-Lugar Now!'. *The Huffington Post*. Retrieved from http://www.huffingtonpost.com/ sen-dick-lugar/senate-to-sec-act-on-card_b_1729306.html [accessed 11 June 2015].

The White House, 2010. 'Wall Street Reform: The Dodd-Frank Act.' *whitehouse.gov*. Retrieved from https://www.whitehouse.gov/embeds/footer [accessed 8 January 2017].

2016. 'FACT SHEET: National Action Plan on Responsible Business Conduct.' *whitehouse.gov*. Retrieved from https://www.whitehouse .gov/the-press-office/2016/12/16/fact-sheet-national-action-plan -responsible-business-conduct [accessed 8 January 2017].

Thelen, K. 2014. *Varieties of Liberalization and the New Politics of Social Solidarity*. New York: Cambridge University Press.

2015. 'Producer Coalitions in the Building of National Growth Strategies'. SciencesPo presentation, December, 2015 (unpublished).

Total, 2016. 'Extractive Industries Transparency International'. Retrieved from http://www.total.com/en/search/content/extractive%20industries%20%20transparency%20international [accessed 16 December 2016].

Trampusch, C. 2009. *Der erschöpfte Sozialstaat: Transformation eines Politikfeldes*. Frankfurt: Campus Verlag GmBH.

Transparency International. n.d. 'Transparency International.' Retrieved from www.transparency.org [accessed 16 December 2016].

2008. 'Promoting Revenue Transparency: 2008 Report on Revenue Transparency of Oil and Gas Companies.' *Transparency International*, April 26. Berlin, TI. Retrieved from http://www.transparency.org/what wedo/publication/promoting_revenue_transparency_2008_report_on_ revenue_transparency_of_oil_a [accessed 8 June 2016].

U.S. Securities and Exchange Commission (SEC), 2015. 'Enhancing the Transparency of Resource Extraction Revenue Payments'. Retrieved from https://www.sec.gov/news/statement/disclosure-of-payments-by -resource-extraction-issuers.html [accessed 26 june 2015].

Ueberbacher, F., Reuter, E. and Scherer, A. G. 2016. 'Fighting Off-shore Tax Evasion: United States' Hard Law Enforcement, Transnational Field Transformation, and the De-Institutionalization of Swiss Banking Security.' Paper presented at the EGOS Conference, Naples, 2016.

UK Parliament, 2012. 'Tax in Developing Countries: Increasing Resources for Development' 2nd March 2012.' Written evidence submitted by *Publish What You Pay*. Retrieved from http://www.publications.parliament.uk/ pa/cm201012/cmselect/cmintdev/writev/1821/tax17.htm. [accessed 1 June 2015].

United Nations Global Compact. n.d. 'The Ten Principles of the UN Global Compact.' Retrieved from www.unglobalcompact.org/what-is-gc/ mission/principles [accessed 26 June 2015].

2016. 'About the UN Global Compact. Frequently Asked Questions.' Retrieved from https://www.unglobalcompact.org/about/faq [accessed 8 June 2016].

United States Department of Labor (dol.gov). 2013a. 'ILAB News Release: Statement by the U.S. Government on Labor Rights and Factory Safety in Bangladesh.' July 19. Retrieved from https://www.dol.gov/opa/ media/press/ilab/ILAB20131494.htm [accessed 7 January 2017].

2013b. 'Labor Rights and Factory Safety in Bangladesh.' Retrieved from https://www.dol.gov/ilab/trade/preference-programs/bangladesh-gsp .htm [accessed 7 January 2017].

USAID, 2015. 'USAID Mobilizes Financing for Safety Improvements in Bangladesh Ready-Made Garment Industry.' Retrieved from https://www .usaid.gov/bangladesh/press-releases/sep-30-2015-usaid-mobilizes-financing-safety-improvements-bangladesh [accessed 6 August 2016].

USEITI. n.d. 'The United States Extractive Industries Transparency Initiative.' Retrieved from https://useiti.doi.gov/ [accessed 26 June 2015].

Utting, P. 2002. 'Regulating Business via Multistakeholder Initiatives: A Preliminary Assessment,' in P. Utting (ed.) *Voluntary Approaches to Corporate Responsibility: Readings and Resource Guide*, Geneva: NGLS.

Vallentin, S. 2013. 'Governmentalities of CSR: Danish Government Policy as a Reflection of Political Difference.' *Journal of Business Ethics*, 127(1): 1–15.

Van Wensen, K., Broer, W., Klein, J., and Knopf, J. 2011. 'The State of Play in Sustainability Reporting in the European Union.' *European Union*. Retrieved from ec.europa.eu/social/BlobServlet?docId=6727&langId= en [accessed 31 May 2016].

VandenDolder, T., 2013. 'These 9 Companies Have More Cash on Hand Than the United States Government.' *DCInno*. Retrieved from http:// dcinno.streetwise.co/2013/10/11/these-9-companies-have-more-cash -on-hand-than-the-united-states-government/ [accessed 12 December 2015].

Vogel, D. 2005. *The Market for Virtue: The Potential and Limits of Corporate Social Responsibility*. Washington DC: Brookings Institution Press.

2008. 'Private Global Business Regulation.' *Annual Review of Political Science*, 11(1): 261–82.

Voiculescu, A. 2006. 'The other European framework for corporate social responsibility: from the Green Paper to new uses of human rights instruments.' In D. McBarnet, A. Voiculescu, and T. Campbell (eds) *The New Accountability. Corporate Social Responsibility and the Law*. Cambridge: Cambridge University Press.

Waddock, S. 2008. 'Building a New Institutional Infrastructure for Corporate Responsibility.' *Academy of Management Perspectives*, 22(3): 87–108.

Weber, M. 1949. *The Methodology of the Social Science*. Glencoe: The Free Press.

Welzel, C., Peters, A., Höcker, U., and Scholz, V. 2007. 'The CSR navigator public policies in Africa, the Americas, Asia and Europe.' *Bertelsmann Stiftung and GTZ*.

Welzel, C. et al. 2007. 'The ... social responsibility in France: A mix of national traditions and international influences.' *Business and Society*, 9(4), 11–12.

Whitley, R. 1999. *Divergent capitalisms: the social structuring and change of business systems*. Oxford; New York: Oxford University Press.

Wolf, M. 2005. *Why Globalization Works*. New Haven: Yale University Press.

Wood, G. and Wright, M. 2015. 'Corporations and New Statism: Trends and Research Priorities.' *The Academy of Management Perspectives*, 29(2), 271–286.

Yaziji, M. and Doh, J. 2009. *NGOs and Corporations: Conflict and Collaboration*. Cambridge: Cambridge University Press.

Zadek, S. 2001. *The Civil Corporation: The New Economy Citizenship*. London: Earthscan.

Index

Lightning Source UK Ltd.
Milton Keynes UK
UKHW022228140719

346127UK00009B/68/P